SAVAGE DEMOCRACY

STEVEN T. WUHS

SAVAGE
DEMOCRACY

INSTITUTIONAL CHANGE AND PARTY DEVELOPMENT IN MEXICO

The Pennsylvania State University Press
University Park, Pennsylvania

Library of Congress Cataloging-in-Publication Data

Wuhs, Steven Todd.
Savage democracy: institutional change and party
development in Mexico/
Steven T. Wuhs.
p.   cm
Includes bibliographical references and index.
Summary: "Examines organization, leadership, and changes
within Mexico's historic pro-democratic opposition
parties, the Partido Acción Nacional and the Partido de
la Revolución Democrática. Explores the implications
for overall party organization and the future of Mexico's
democratic experiment"—Provided by publisher.
ISBN 978-0-271-03422-5 (pbk: alk. paper)
1. Political parties—Mexico.
2. Partido Acción Nacional (Mexico).
3. Partido de la Revolución Democrática (Mexico).
4. Democracy—Mexico.
I. Title.

JL1298.A1W84 2008
324.272—dc22
2008023706

The Pennsylvania State University Press is a member of the
Association of American University Presses.

It is the policy of The Pennsylvania State University Press
to use acid-free paper. This book is printed on stock
that meets the minimum
requirements of American National Standard for
Information Sciences—Permanence of Paper for Printed
Library Material, ANSIZ39.48–1992.

CONTENTS

TABLES AND FIGURES

Tables

Figures

PREFACE AND ACKNOWLEDGMENTS

I began the project that became *Savage Democracy* when the PRI still controlled Mexican politics. At the time, I was curious about how the PRI successfully retained power when other authoritarian regimes in Latin America had collapsed and been removed. Times change: Mexico is now governed by a democratically elected government and the PRI's poor showing in 2006 has the party on the defensive despite its strong base in state-level politics. The transformations I have seen in Mexico since starting this research both astound and alarm me. My hope is that this book captures some of the contradictions embedded in Mexico's new democratic regime and highlights where democracy builders need to focus their attentions.

Any project of this scope benefits from the contributions of many individuals and institutions. As a doctoral student at the University of North Carolina at Chapel Hill, I relied on my adviser, Evelyne Huber, for intellectual and practical guidance as I developed this project. I continue to even now. My other committee members, Jonathan Hartlyn, Dave Lowery, Lars Schoultz, and John Stephens, helped me frame my question in interesting theoretical ways and assisted me as I first waded through my data. I am also indebted to my friends the Gerton-Shrocks, the Copeland-Scotts, and the Kaiser-Potters for their support in Chapel Hill.

In September 1999, I moved to Mexico City and affiliated in the political studies section of Centro de Investigación y Docencia Económicas (CIDE). My colleagues there—especially Joy Langston, Yemile Mizrahi, and Benito Nacif—helped me refine my project and establish my initial contacts in the parties. My life in Mexico City was crazy and fantastic, and I'm so glad the Rosas family introduced me to Hernán Gómez and the Arredondos, friendships that I still value tremendously despite distance. Duke Knapp and Matt Wilhoit gave me somewhere to hang my hat at discounted rates, for which I'm still appreciative. In Mexico, I also made first contact with many of my Mexico colleagues: Jeff Staton, Matt Cleary, Ken Greene, David Shirk, Kate Bruhn, Allison Rowland, and Jacqueline Peschard.

At the end of fifteen months of fieldwork, I moved to the Center for U.S.-Mexican Studies at the University of California, San Diego, with the help of Kevin Middlebrook and Wayne Cornelius. Wayne, Graciela Platero, and the rest of the Center's staff helped make the experience a productive one, and my fellowship colleagues made it an enjoyable one. Through one of them, I had the good fortune of meeting Kimberley Coles at a barbecue. I'll always have many reasons to be thankful to San Diego.

I left the Center with a dissertation in hand and moved to Bucknell University, where I began revising, a process that continued when I moved to the Department of Government at the University of Redlands. At those institutions, I am particularly thankful to Scott Meinke and my Redlands departmental colleagues, especially Barbara Morris. I had the good fortune of being granted a year's leave from Redlands to move to Edinburgh, Scotland, in 2005, and it was there, in a state of relative underemployment, that I scrapped much of the dissertation and wrote the manuscript that would become *Savage Democracy*. The School of Social and Political Studies welcomed this Latin Americanist into their world, and despite their lack of familiarity with Mexico, my colleagues Charlie Jeffery, Luke March, Jan Webb, and David McCrone provided smart comments on my work as it evolved that year. Other friends and colleagues also offered their two cents on the manuscript and its development: Rod Camp, Heather Williams, Katrina Burgess, Todd Eisenstadt, Barry Levitt, Michelle Dion, and Sam Chambers all deserve thanks. Edinburgh would have been much less fun without my officemates Anne Jepson and Richard Whitecross, Sara and Bill Dorman, and the staff in Social Anthropology.

Just before leaving Edinburgh, I passed this manuscript on to Sandy Thatcher, who led it through the review and revision process. I am particularly thankful for his support and for that of Kristin Peterson, Kathryn Yahner, and Patricia Rosas, and for the very constructive comments I received from my two anonymous reviewers. I hope I have done them justice in the final iteration of this project, wrapped up in Redlands and with the help of my faithful research assistants Paulo Gusmão and Briana Cavion. Of course, the content of this manuscript and any errors within it are my responsibility alone.

I am indebted not just to the institutions with which I have been affiliated but also to the funding sources that allowed me to pursue this research. My doctoral research was supported by grants from the Tinker Foundation, the Institute for the Study of World Politics, and the National Science Foundation's Traineeship on Democracy and Democratization. Subsequent research in Mexico was funded through a Faculty Research Grant from the University of

Redlands. I am also grateful to Manuel Alcántara and Leticia Rodríguez at the Universidad de Salamanca for providing data included in this study. An earlier version of chapter 4 was published in *Estudios Mexicanos/Mexican Studies.*

Some people deserve particular mention here. I need to sincerely thank the leaders, activists, and members of the PAN and PRD who made time for my research in their busy schedules and shared with me the challenges they faced within their parties and within Mexico's developing democracy. Without their candid accounts of party life *Savage Democracy* could never have been written.

On graduating from Macalester College, I moved to Washington, D.C., to work as a research assistant for Seymour Martin Lipset, who passed away late in 2006. Without Marty's encouragement and guidance, I do not think I would have pursued my doctorate. Although my parents, my sister, brother, and Megan Manatt Lordos did not always know how I spent my days and nights in graduate school, in Mexico, or since then, they always kept me from getting too wrapped up in my "book learning." Lastly, I would like to acknowledge the unflagging support, insightful criticism, and restful breaks that Kimberley Coles provided while I wrote this book. I dedicate this book to two of those "breaks," Teo Frederick and Mara Brodie.

LIST OF ABBREVIATIONS

CD	Corriente Democrática/Democratic Current
CEN	Comité Ejecutivo Nacional/National Executive Committee
CNC	Confederación Nacional Campesina/National Campesino Confederation
COCEI	Coalición de Obreros, Campesinos y Estudiantes del Istmo/Coalition of Isthmus Workers, Campesinos, and Students
COFIPE	Código Federal de Instituciones y Procedimientos Electorales/Federal Electoral Institutions and Procedures Code
COPARMEX	Confederación Patronal de la República Mexicana/Mexican Employers' Confederation
CTM	Confederación de Trabajadores de México/Mexican Workers' Confederation
FDN	Frente Democrático Nacional/National Democratic Front
IFE	Instituto Federal Electoral/Federal Electoral Institute
ISI	Import-Substitution Industrialization
LOPPE	Ley de Organizaciones Políticas y Procesos Electorales/Law on Political Organizations and Electoral Processes
PAN	Partido Acción Nacional/National Action Party
PLANTAR	Programa de Acción Nacional en Acción Rural/Acción Nacional Rural Action Program
PMS	Partido Mexicano Socialista/Mexican Socialist Party
PNR	Partido Nacional Revolucionario/National Revolutionary Party
PPM	Promoción Política de la Mujer/Political Promotion of Women
PR	Proportional Representation
PRD	Partido de la Revolución Democrática/Party of the Democratic Revolution

PRI	Partido Revolucionario Institucional/Institutional Revolutionary Party
PRM	Partido Revolucionario Mexicano/Mexican Revolutionary Party
SIDEP	Sistema Integral de Desarrollo de Personal/Integrated System for Personnel Development
SMD	Single-Member District
SNTE	Sindicato Nacional de Trabajadores de la Educación/National Union of Educational Workers
TRIFE	Tribunal Federal Electoral/Federal Electoral Tribunal
UNAM	Universidad Nacional Autónoma de México/National Autonomous University of Mexico
UNT	Unión Nacional de Trabajadores/National Workers' Union

1

WHAT IS SAVAGE DEMOCRACY?

The democratic struggles of this party have created a savage democracy.
—PRD Deputy, 2000

The idea of democracy held Mexico's attention for decades, long prior to its democratic transition in 2000. Cries for democracy were heard from student protestors in Mexico City's Tlatelolco Square in 1968, when they publicly challenged the Partido Revolucionario Institucional's (Institutional Revolutionary Party, PRI) monopoly of power and encountered violent repression by the regime. Democracy was quietly whispered throughout the 1970s, as activists on the left and the right took up arms against the regime, quietly moved to fledgling opposition parties, or worked to reform the PRI from within. As Mexico entered financial crisis in the 1980s, demands for democracy were made openly, and they garnered widespread public support. The presidential election of 1988 saw the first serious challenge to the PRI's authoritarian rule. In that contest, PRI member and former governor Cuauhtémoc Cárdenas split from the party to head the broad left front that, despite losing the election, transformed into the Partido de la Revolución Democrática (Party of the Democratic Revolution, PRD) in 1989. Cárdenas was not alone in challenging the PRI that year: the Partido Acción Nacional (PAN), the PRI's longstanding "loyal opposition," mounted an aggressive campaign around charismatic businessman Manuel J. Clouthier. Although PRI candidate Carlos Salinas de Gortari assumed the presidency that year, the public calls for democratic change continued, and for the following twenty years, democracy would be the most divisive issue in Mexican politics.

Democracy permeated life inside the PAN and PRD, both of which sought to be the standard-bearers of democratic change in Mexico. The historical and contemporary leaders of these parties were ideologically committed to democracy, and their members and Mexico's activists and citizens hungered for what democracy promised. The strength of those commitments led the founders of the PAN and PRD to build their organizations on avowedly democratic foundations. Inside the parties, leaders were intent on the construction of vibrant party democracy. In the absence of competitive politics *between* parties, PAN and PRD founders aimed to maintain spaces where activists could participate and their interests could be represented *within* their organizations. PAN and PRD leaders also sought to democratize Mexico at the regime level by ousting the PRI regime from the presidency. Those two priorities and their organizational manifestations formed a powerful institutional "democratic imperative" that dramatically affected future party development. Although the goals of party democracy and regime democratization seem complementary, and this institutional "democratic imperative" appears virtuous, they held surprisingly vicious consequences for party life. Democracy was thought to promote stability, respect, tolerance, and equality, and to some extent, it did. However, it also unleashed savage forces within the parties, fostering intense intraparty factions, undermining the nomination of electable candidates, and interfering with the development of effective party organizations. This book demonstrates how the meanings that political actors attach to ideas like democracy can influence the developmental trajectories of institutions and can result in both fortuitous, expected consequences as well as problematic, unexpected ones. Specifically, in the case of Mexico's PAN and PRD, it explains how institutional commitments to democracy have resulted in counter-democratic practices. Phrased differently, it seeks to explain why savage democracy occurs.

Party Leaders and the Politics of Institutional Change

The key to explaining the origins of savage democracy lies with the historical and contemporary leaders of the PAN and PRD. Party leaders—including the elected heads of parties, their allies, and their rivals in party committees and councils—faced a series of difficult decisions as the Mexican political landscape was repeatedly shaken by changes in electoral law, in the behavior of the PRI regime, and in the structure and performance of the Mexican economy. In both the PAN and PRD, leaders faced a trade-off that crossed arenas of party life: they could work to build their organization into a competitive political force and advance their goal of regime democratization, or they could turn inward to preserve their internally democratic systems. Unfortunately for those leaders, the benefits of those options were largely mutually exclusive, and each entailed significant political costs. Building an electorally competitive party meant strengthening the central party office's administrative capacities, weakening its ties to activists and the rank and file, and nominating good candidates who might not be good partisans. But for both the PAN and the PRD, a weak party office, strong ties with activists, and the nomination of loyal *panistas* (PAN partisans) and *perredistas* (PRD partisans) were part and parcel of party democracy. Party leaders had unenviable choices to make, decisions that would privilege only one of the two sides of the democratic imperative.

Those leaders carefully weighed the potential benefits and costs of their decisions. Their choices were ultimately influenced not just by their assessment of the opportunities presented by their environments, but also by the decision-making autonomy they had from other party actors and the character of their parties' preexisting institutions.[1] These institutions figured especially prominently in leaders' decisions. The profound democratic imprints left on the PAN and PRD by their founders limited the possibilities for institutional development as institutional legacies were created that favored rules, practices, and customs perceived as "democratic," while delegitimizing other institutional forms. Because the founders of the PAN and PRD held diverging conceptions of what democracy meant, their paths of institutional development differed. Despite those differences, though, both parties evidence the pathologies of savage democracy.

Savage Democracy situates leaders' choices about party life *within* party life. Blaming the leaders of parties, trade unions, and social movement organizations for slouching toward oligarchy when they pursue their own interests over those of their rank-and-file members may be elegant, but it is too simplistic (Michels 1962). Leaders' choices are shaped by their social and political surroundings, both at moments of institutional design and during subsequent processes of institutional development. To best account for the decisions that leaders made when confronted with the trade-offs of the democratic imperative, I incorporate elements of both historical institutional and rational choice approaches.[2] Explaining leaders' decisions about institutional *design* demands

1. I adopt Douglass C. North's (1990) definition of institutions, whether formal rules or informal practices, as forces that structure human behavior by influencing the formation of actors' preferences and the decisions they make about how to pursue them.

2. These analytic approaches share a focus on institutions but disagree on how institutions, actors, and historical settings interact. Thelen and Steinmo (1992) identified the crucial difference between historical and rational choice institutionalism as the location of preference formation— exogenous in rational choice and endogenous to politics for historical institutionalists. Pierson and Skocpol (2002) highlight other distinctions: that rational choice theorists focus on "rules of the game" and the resolution of collective action problems while historical institutionalists consider the politics of resource distribution in institutional design, and that rational choice work

not just an assessment of their relative bargaining power and the position of veto players but also a consideration of how existing party institutions and other environmental influences shaped those factors and the preferences of the involved actors.[3] Likewise, the insights of both rational choice and historical institutionalisms are needed to elucidate downstream processes of institutional *development*. Although historical institutionalist work has shed considerable light on why institutional continuity occurs, without an actor-centered explanation, we cannot explain the advent of critical junctures that place institutions on long-term developmental paths. For example, crucial institutional changes in the PAN in 1989 (relating to professionalization) and the PRD in 1995 (concerning internal elections) occurred as a result of deliberate, strategic actions by party leaders. Still, to account for those leaders' decisions, we must also recognize that they were acting under the influence of particular institutional and political circumstances.

Bringing together those two schools of institutional work in this way mitigates against two limitations of institutional studies. The first is the assumption that leaders are strictly electoralist. In reality, plenty of parties and party leaders eschew vote-seeking. Leaders of green parties and protest parties, for example, often prefer staying loyal to members' goals to maximizing their number of parliamentary seats (see, for example, Kitschelt 1989), and for many years the PAN rejected vote-seeking in order to safeguard its democratic credentials (Loaeza 1999). Party leaders prioritize not just vote-getting but also representing their base, advancing party programmatic goals, and the like. As politicians, party leaders are indeed ambitious, but it is crucial to consider how the organization they lead, and the institutions structuring life within that organization, shape the ambitions they have and objectives they pursue. A related limitation is the assumption that organizational elites like party leaders are unconstrained in their actions. They clearly are not, and Robert Michels's oligarchs need to be embedded in the organization and amid the institutions where they allegedly reign. Party leaders come and go, but institutions tend to stick. If organizations are as oligarchic as they are often argued to be, that condition results not from individual leaders' preferences or from inevitable pathologies of organizations,

---

focuses narrowly on micro-level, discrete institutions, while historical institutions aim to make meso- or macro-level claims. Thelen (1999) and Clemens and Cook (1999) offer other comparative discussions of the approaches, as does Ostrom (1995). Schickler (2001) and Dion (n.d.) also bridge the supposed gaps between institutionalist approaches.

3. Pierson (2004, chapter 4) notes several limitations of simplified rational choice approaches to institutional design.

but more problematically, from institutions that facilitate the concentration of power and enable leaders to act with impunity against members' interests.

Although this book is devoted to explaining leaders' institutional choices, the particular institutions I examine are internal to political parties (candidate-selection rules, party bureaucracies, and party-society linking practices), and the individual institutional changes I explain are constitutive of broader processes of party development. For that reason, *Savage Democracy* straddles two related literatures (one on institutions, the other on parties) and draws from both. Kathleen Thelen (2003, 217) reminds us that drawing a distinction between organizations (like parties) and institutions is important, something that becomes clear through the questions asked here of the comparative literature on parties.[4] Often, this body of work divorces itself from leaders and other individual actors and instead relies on structural explanations for party change. Much of the recent literature on the subject, for example, has attempted to establish the environmental factors that underpin how and why parties change, highlighting the influence of new communications technology, opinion polls, independent funding for parties, reduced citizen interest in party organizations, economic crisis and reform, and more flexible patterns of party support.[5]

Those macro-level explanations are doubtless important to understanding contemporary party organization and democratic rule, but there are important missing links in many of these accounts. Parties are not organisms that respond isomorphically to changes in their habitat, nor do they undergo actorless

---

4. For example, she notes that within rational choice approaches institutions are the rules of the game whereas organizations are the players (citing North 1990, 5). Thus, if parties are the "players," then regimes, state structures, electoral systems, and party systems constitute pages in the rule book. Instead of focusing on the institutional environment in which parties organize, this study examines intra-party institutions, rules, and practices, similar to Panebianco's (1988, 33–36) "zones of uncertainty." Those zones include communications, rules development and enforcement, party finances, recruitment, and relations with external actors.

5. Because parties in the United States and Western Europe rarely introduced new cadres of voters into the larger political community in the late twentieth century, they failed to foster the strong ties with members and voters characteristic of, for example, the interwar period (Collier 1999; Luebbert 1991; Rueschemeyer et al. 1992). Reduced attachment to American parties was initially interpreted as a decline of parties, though Aldrich (1995, 273) instead characterizes the transformation in the Republican and Democratic parties as adaptations to a new, more candidate-centered political environment. Variations in institutional politics (like electoral systems) are also associated with changes in party organization (Schlesinger 1994, 47; Appleton and Ward 1997; Harmel and Janda 1982). Many of the macro-level changes in party organization in the advanced industrialized countries are summarized in Gunther et al. (2002) and Dalton and Wattenberg (2000). See also Dalton, Flanagan, and Beck (1984) and Mair (1990).

processes of institutionalization.[6] They are complex bureaucracies featuring individuals and institutions that weigh into how parties are adapted (rather than "adapt") to new environments. Although some authors examine the effect of mechanisms of accountability, like leadership-selection rules (see Kitschelt 1994; Levitsky 2003; and Samuels 2004), or the "punishing power" of rivals (Burgess 2004), work on parties too often pays inadequate attention to the logic of the actors who make discrete institutional choices about party development, and to the political forces that influence those actors. Leaders are clearly present, operating behind the scenes, but the influence, the complexity, and the contingent nature of their decision making is undersold. Furthermore, the transformations that party scholars examine rarely result from a singular shift at a particular moment. Instead, they reflect the cumulative effects of numerous actions by leaders over time.

Leaders' institutional choices are shaped not just by environmental shifts and "veto players" but also by the institutions that surround them. Herbert Kitschelt and others examine one set of party institutions—mechanisms of accountability. In reality, a wide array of party institutions constrains leaders' actions. Doctrines and ideologies shape the goals that leaders have for their parties; statutes and by-laws structure decision-making processes; and long-standing practices often favor certain types of decisions over others. Those institutions, many of which are implanted at a party's "birth," develop powerful reproductive tendencies and shape the logics of future institutional designers by favoring some institutional forms over others. This book explains those processes of design and development in the PAN and PRD and their implications for Mexican democracy.

The Logic of Savage Democracy

Many recent studies of both political parties and democratization in Mexico have attempted to account for major breakthroughs or the sudden appearance of new political actors. This book explains how over the course of decades, opposition party leaders and activists labored to build institutions that, in their

---

6. For example, Panebianco (1988, elaborating on Duverger 1954) sustains that as a party matures, it undergoes a process of institutionalization, in which elites gain an upper hand in organizational decision making and a dominant coalition forms to control "zones of uncertainty" in the party.

view, would hasten democratic development in Mexico. The changes considered here tend to be the result of specific, intentional action on the part of party leaders. For instance, PRD leaders in the early 1990s concluded that conventions were less effective mechanisms for candidate selection than a system of primaries would be, and so they pushed for a change in the party's formal selection rules. However, the collective effect of a series of smaller, intentional changes may be unexpected. Institutional change is a complicated process, and even the most carefully considered processes of institutional design may yield unintended outcomes.[7] The PRD's commitment to inclusive participation in candidate selection enabled the PRI to colonize local party offices and "steal" legislative seats from the party faithful. It is likely that the commitment to inclusive participation also undermined public confidence in the PRD. Its ideals of participatory democracy thus had unanticipated, backhanded antidemocratic outcomes—an example of savage democracy.

That PRD example highlights the connections suggested earlier between the micro level of institutional change and broader patterns of party development. After explaining discrete decisions made by party leaders about the stability and adaptation of existing party institutions, I pool those micro-level accounts, bearing in mind two goals: First, bringing those explanations together enables me to advance more compelling analyses of the conditions that facilitate institutional stability and change as well as identify broader patterns of institutional development. Second, I draw on those micro-level explanations to make more general statements about the development of the PAN and PRD as political parties and thus about the development of Mexican democracy in the early twenty-first century. Although some recent studies have focused on important transformations of party "type" occurring in Europe and Latin America, my interest lies in understanding the internal institutional world of party politics and its implications for party organizations, party systems, and democracy. As a result, my conclusions are geared toward suggesting how the institutional infrastructures of the two parties relate to the quality of representation in Mexico's new democracy.

I collected the bulk of the data during fifteen months of fieldwork in Mexico City from September 1999 to December 2000, including the campaign season for the 2000 federal elections (a blessing in many ways, but a curse in

7. Schickler's (2001) work on the U.S. Congress suggests that institutions often change through patterns of innovation, the sort of deliberate institutional changes examined here, and through responses, the often-unexpected outcomes of those innovations.

terms of setting up interviews). Follow-up research was conducted in 2004, 2005, and 2007. I elected qualitative research methods because they are particularly well suited for studying the organizational decision-making patterns and processes of longitudinal change that I examine (Kitschelt 1989, 302–3). This book includes a broad set of observations across three arenas of party institutional life (candidate selection, bureaucratic development, and linking with civil society), thus building greater reliability into the data and the conclusions I draw from them.

I conducted more than 150 open-ended interviews with a variety of Mexican party elites, selected in order to incorporate as broad an array of accounts of party development as possible. My interviewees included higher- and lower-level national party bureaucrats, senators and deputies elected by different formulas (both houses have seats elected through first-past-the-post, single-member districts and through proportional representation, multi-member districts), local party leaders in Mexico City, candidates and former candidates for office, and government employees who were party militants. I also worked to incorporate regional differences of opinion by seeking out legislators from all across Mexico and pushing for their local versions of national developments. Finally, I attempted to cover the different factions in each of the parties, a particular challenge in the PAN since many panistas deny such divisions. Besides the interviews—by far the most laborious part of my data collection—I pored over the PAN and PRD archives in Mexico City: the Fundación Preciado Hernández (for the PAN) and the Instituto para el Estudio de la Revolución Democrática (for the PRD). Both archives, but especially that of the PRD, contained many of the documents cited throughout this text. I also collected press accounts of institutional change from four Mexican national newspapers (*La Jornada, Reforma, El Universal,* and *El Norte*) and from the U.S. press.

My analysis of those data unfolds over the next six chapters. In chapter 2, I present the character of Mexico's authoritarian regime. This is a vital point of departure for this study, as both the PAN and the PRD were born in response to that regime, albeit fifty years apart. I argue that PRI authoritarianism had a powerful effect on the nature of PAN and PRD organization—indeed, the PRI is the source of the democratic imperative. The regime's institutional architecture shaped the logic of institutional design in both parties, since its control of the state allowed it to dictate the rules governing political competition over most of its seventy-one-year reign. Understanding the PRI is also crucial to understanding party leaders' efforts to adapt their institutions to best capitalize on changes in their political environment, since those changes were primarily wrought by the regime's diminishing capacity to contain the opposition and its gradual retreat from power. Chapter 3 then develops the "savage democracy" argument by re-examining the foundations of the PAN (1939) and the PRD (1989). From their respective establishments, those parties and their leaders adopted the democratic imperative—the twin desires to be internally democratic and to bring democracy to Mexico. Beyond re-interpreting the accounts of the two parties' foundations, this chapter uses party doctrine and other primary documents to identify the different meanings the parties attached to the idea of "democracy." The chapter also articulates how that idea shaped future processes of institutional development—the subject of my empirical chapters.

As noted earlier, I focus on multiple types of party institutions in this book. Each of the following three chapters focuses on how party leaders, weighing the maintenance of party democracy against the construction of a democratic regime, made decisions about institutional design and change. Chapter 4 documents how the democratic imperative conditioned formal institutional development inside the two parties through an examination of the selection rules parties used for legislative, presidential, and gubernatorial candidates. I continue my focus on formal institutions in chapter 5's study of the development of the "central party offices" of the parties in Mexico City and their state and municipal counterparts throughout the country. Chapter 6 demonstrates how the parties' linking institutions reflected leaders' efforts to forge ties with Mexican civil society while sidestepping allegations of corporatism, one of the cardinal sins of twentieth-century Mexican politics.

I begin the concluding chapter by examining processes of change across different types of party institutions and identifying patterns that emerged as party leaders chose to adapt those institutions. This chapter also explores the implications of those institutional changes for the development of Mexican political parties and for the future of democratic politics in Mexico. I raise particularly serious questions about the consequences of increasing party centralization and the de-linking of parties from their rank-and-file members. Lastly, I highlight the core intellectual insights of *Savage Democracy* for comparative politics—specifically, the centrality of ideas to institutional analysis and the importance of deeply embedding institutional design and change in time and space. The book closes with an epilogue that discusses the continuing influence of the democratic imperative on Mexican politics through an examination of the tumult that followed the July 2, 2006, presidential contest between PAN candidate Felipe Calderón Hinojosa and PRD leader Andrés Manuel López Obrador.

2

BEFORE SAVAGE DEMOCRACY: AUTHORITARIANISM IN MEXICO

"Mexico: The Perfect Dictatorship"
—Essay by Mario Vargas Llosa, 1991

The Partido Revolucionario Institucional (PRI) constructed the most durable authoritarian regime of the twentieth century around the dominance of that hegemonic party and its organizational predecessors, the Partido Nacional Revolucionario (National Revolutionary Party, PNR) and Partido Revolucionario Mexicano (Mexican Revolutionary Party, PRM). Unlike its South American counterparts, once consolidated, the PRI regime was led by a civilian, allowed some political pluralism, and even held regular elections. Those characteristics led both early comparativists, such as Dankwart Rustow (1967), and various students of Mexico (Scott 1965) to classify Mexico, alongside Costa Rica and Venezuela, as one of Latin America's few stable democracies. The political opposition in Mexico knew otherwise. Participation was not free, elections were manipulated, and power was centralized in the upper echelons of the PRI. Understanding the nature of PRI authoritarianism is crucial because of its profound and lasting effects on the development of Mexican political life (Magaloni 2006; Langston 2003, 2002; Garrido 1982; Greene 2007).[1]

This book examines one particular set of effects: the impact of PRI rule on the prodemocratic opposition. I argue that the PAN and PRD adopted and continue to abide by profoundly democratic ideals and practices that were crafted in response to PRI authoritarianism. The PAN and PRD were founded (in 1939 and 1989, respectively) as institutional mirror images of the PRI. Over the course of seventy-one years of PRI rule, authoritarianism in Mexico came to be equated with the PRI on ideological and institutional levels. Whatever the PRI

---

1. This chapter is not intended to be a full account of the organizational history of the PRI. For further information on the party's formation, see cited works by Langston and Garrido, as well as Hansen (1971), Middlebrook (1995), and Shirk (2005).

did was labeled authoritarian, and the opposite was defined as "democratic." This profoundly shaped how institutional design took place in the opposition parties.[2] Of course, capturing the PRI regime's inner workings and its impact on democratic development requires understanding it *as a regime*, a challenge given that scholars have tended either to regard it as an anomaly or to analyze it on the basis of its hegemonic party system rather than the authoritarian nature of its politics (Greene 2007; Mainwaring and Scully 1995; Craig and Cornelius 1995).[3]

This chapter outlines the foundation of the Partido Nacional Revolucionario, its transformation into the Partido Revolucionario Mexicano in the 1930s, and finally, its restructuring as the PRI in 1940s. These are not changes in name only—rather, they represent important developmental moments in PRI elites' construction of an authoritarian system built around a hegemonic party. After tracing the development of the PRI regime, this chapter chronicles how the party's grip on power weakened during the 1980s and 1990s. Understanding those transformations is crucial because just as the PRI, during its decades-long tenure in power, left indelible imprints on the organization of the PAN and

2. Recent scholarship, particularly on Eastern Europe, identifies prior regimes as key determinants of the development trajectories of newly democratized countries (Linz and Stepan 1996; Hartlyn 1998; Bratton and Van de Walle 1997; Ekiert and Hanson 2003a; Kitschelt et al. 1999; Grzymala-Busse 2002).

3. Mexico under the PRI awkwardly straddles the authoritarian and post-totalitarian regime types that Linz and Stepan (1996) detailed in their cross-regional comparative work. Like authoritarian regimes, it was somewhat tolerant of social and economic pluralism. However, like totalitarian regimes the regime propagated a guiding ideology: Though less encompassing that Marxism-Leninism, Mexican revolutionary nationalism did articulate very particular political values. The mobilization of subordinate sectors through Mexico's state corporatist system suggests affinities with the totalitarian and post-totalitarian cases. Lastly, in its leadership recruitment patterns, the PRI regime again resembled a totalitarian regime. It was party-driven elites in the PRI were recruited through the party's sectors or its territorial structure. However, as in authoritarian regimes individuals led within predictable norms. Mexico under the PRI was exceptional in its predictability: from the 1930s onward, the regime respected the Constitution's six-year presidential term and its prohibition on re-election. Middlebrook (1995, 9) classifies Mexico as an example of a post-revolutionary authoritarian regime, a group that also includes China, Cuba, and Nicaragua. He contends that such regimes are distinct because of the significance of mass actors in the governing coalition, the legitimating role of revolutionary ideals, and the dual importance of an interventionist state. Bruhn (1997) describes the Mexican regime as structured around three features: presidentialism, single-party rule, and state corporatism—all linked to the sole underlying political goal of centralizing authority. A handful of cross-regional comparativists have identified a set of structurally similar cases based on that same set of criteria: Senegal, Taiwan, and Korea (Wuhs 2007; Galvan 2001; Solinger 2001).

PRD, the regime's decay created new opportunities for opposition party leaders committed to democratic change.

The Construction of Authoritarianism

Mexico's authoritarian regime was built around the Partido Nacional Revolucionario, an organization with deep historical roots in the Mexican Revolution (1910–1917). The party's founders were generals who had participated in the revolutionary struggle. Former President Plutarco Elías Calles established the party in 1929 after witnessing the continued political instability that Mexico experienced in the 1920s. In the absence of the centralized order of the Porfirio Díaz regime (1880–1911) and in the wake of the revolutionary struggle, a multitude of militarized elite factions and regional and local political parties emerged across Mexico, while a counter-revolutionary social uprising, the Cristero Rebellion, flared in the Bajío region. Calles and others feared that continued political unrest might threaten Mexico's post-revolutionary order. Under his leadership, the PNR embraced the goal of incorporating national, regional, and local elite interests into a single political organization, thereby encapsulating conflict among them. The PNR was thus founded as an ideologically plural and politically pragmatic organization oriented toward attaining and retaining power, characteristics it would maintain beyond 2000.

The PNR's formation was the first step in the construction of Mexico's authoritarian regime. Between the mid-1930s and mid-1940s, Mexico's regime broadened its base beyond the elitist PNR. Following a series of short-term presidencies in the early 1930s, Revolutionary General Lázaro Cárdenas was named president of Mexico. During his six-year term (1934–1940), Cárdenas transformed Mexico's political economy and political institutions. He was responsible for nationalizing the Mexican railroad and oil industries, establishing the *ejido* system in rural areas following an ambitious agrarian reform, and laying the groundwork for Mexico's import-substitution industrialization (ISI) effort. He is also credited with incorporating non-elites into post-revolutionary politics, principally through the construction of sectoral organizations for workers, the Confederación de Trabajadores de México (Mexican Workers Confederation, CTM) and for ejido residents and peasants, the Confederación

Nacional Campesina (National Campesino Confederation, CNC).[4] A military sector was also established at the time but was phased out in the 1940s, and later, the urban popular sectors would be brought under the umbrella of the Confederación Nacional de Organizaciones Populares (National Confederation of Popular Organizations, CNOP). Each of those confederations was organically linked to the PRM, the successor to the PNR—making workers and peasant into party members through collective affiliation rules.

Although the confederations continued to give the organized sectors (and especially the sectoral leaders) influence in the formal political arena and to represent the interests of those classes, under the more conservative presidents who succeeded Cárdenas the confederations were transformed into mechanisms of control over subordinate classes, which amounted to a state corporatist system (Schmitter 1974; Collier and Collier 1991). The party-regime dominated the sectors through the selective distribution of payoffs delivered via the confederations. The regime counted on its mass membership for their votes at election time as well as public demonstrations of support between elections. It also depended on their political complacency or tacit support. In turn, agricultural and industrial laborers relied on those networks for the distribution of subsidies and other economic benefits. The corporatist sectors of the PRI also served as points of entry into the *camarilla* system that served as the primary means of political recruitment under PRI rule (Grindle 1977; Smith 1979). In that way, the corporatist system and its associated recruitment practices further reinforced the role of the Mexican president as the ultimate political patron.

The inclusionary practices of the party (which was renamed the Partido Revolucionario Institucional in 1946), reaching from the formal political arena deep into organized sectors of Mexican society, were one component of its hegemonic character. Electoral institutions also play a vital role for such parties (Sartori 1976). Regime leaders used electoral law to narrow the field of political opposition and to systematically disadvantage forces that chose to oppose the PRI. The Electoral Law of 1946 was passed by a PRI Congress and signed into law by a PRI president. It specified that all candidates needed the support of a registered "national political party," defined as organizations that had at least 30,000 members with 1,000 or more in at least two-thirds of Mexico's states and

---

4. On the rise of corporatism, see Collier and Collier (1991) and Spalding (1981). On corporatism and peasant politics, see Grindle (1977). For general overviews of the revolutionary transformations in Mexico and Mexican politics, see Levy and Bruhn (2006), Camp (2002), and Meyer and Beezley (2000).

territories. The regime increased the registration requirements for parties in 1954 and again in 1973, effectively shutting out regionalized opposition movements. In addition, the commission charged with ensuring the integrity of the electoral process was composed of a number of governmental delegates (effectively, PRI members) with only one representative from the political opposition. Although the electoral commission was eventually opened to allow for greater opposition voice, the PRI still ratified outcomes through the early 1990s.

The electoral system further complicated the political ambitions of the opposition. Prior to a 1963 reform, opposition politicians had to win a plurality in one of the single-member electoral districts of the Chamber of Deputies in order to gain any representation at the federal level. Even for parties like the PAN that managed to meet the demanding registration requirements, the chances of victory were slim. After a contentious presidential election in 1958 that was followed by public accusations of fraud, the regime introduced the Party Deputies system, a limited system of proportional representation in the lower house. Under the reform's rules, parties winning at least 2.5 percent of the national vote could gain between five and twenty seats in the Chamber. Because it offered a reasonable chance for representation, the Party Deputies system could be considered the PRI regime's first liberalizing reform. However, it also penalized opposition parties for political protest: if any of an opposition party's deputies did not assume their seats in the Chamber (for example, to challenge fraudulent electoral returns), the party faced the loss of its registration. Like the other election reforms promulgated by the PRI regime, this one both gave opposition actors a foothold in elected bodies and steered them away from the streets and toward institutional politics, where the PRI could more readily control them.

The construction of the PRI's corporatist system and the advantageous position it had vis-à-vis electoral law depended on the party's privileged access to the state during the 1930s and 1940s. After those crucial moments of institution-building, the party benefited from the reproductive forces of institutional resilience—vicious cycles or virtuous cycles, depending on one's vantage point.[5] Because it administered elections, the PRI regime could guarantee sufficient measures of support for the party while maintaining the illusion of democratic pluralism by recognizing limited opposition party achievements, a tactic that effectively managed much of the partisan opposition. Of course, those same resources

---

5. The next chapter develops the idea of institutional resilience and other core concepts of historical institutionalism.

discouraged the exit option from the PRI's own ranks, keeping most Mexican elites vested in prolonging the party's stay in power, at least for a time.[6]

The PRI gained support and legitimacy from Mexican citizens not just for its institutional work, but also—perhaps more so—for its management of a successful period of economic growth. The nationalist ideology of the Revolution dovetailed well with the global political-economic developments of the 1930s through the 1960s. Embodying the revolutionary goals of class restructuring and anti-imperialism, the regime was well-positioned to take credit for the nationalization of Mexico's oil reserves and the adoption of Mexico's ambitious state-led industrialization project. As in other Latin American countries, the Great Depression closed export markets in the north (and thus sources of foreign exchange), pressuring the Mexican government to undertake transformative projects to reduce dependence on exports to, and imports from, the developed world. To that end, successive Mexican governments pursued import-substitution industrialization in the 1940s, 1950s, and 1960s, fueling impressive growth rates throughout a period often called the Mexican Miracle. The strong economy had important spillover effects on the legitimacy of the regime as long as the growth continued. Standards of living improved (especially in urban areas), worker salaries increased, and there was a limited expansion of the middle class. These changes, regime actors argued, reflected the PRI's commitment to its revolutionary goals. Less idealistically, sustained economic growth also substantially increased revenue flows to the central government, some of which could then be funneled through the regime's corporatist network and the state's bureaucracies to bolster support for the PRI on the ground.[7]

Opposition leaders, as did scholars of Mexican politics, tended to base their analyses of the PRI on the regime's structure at its zenith in the 1960s, after the consolidation of corporatism, the launch of ISI, and the creation of privilege through electoral law, but prior to significant political or economic liberalization (fig. 1). The PAN, founded more than twenty years earlier, began incorporating explicit condemnations of PRI rule into its core documents during this period, while PRD leaders looked back at this era as one in which the PRI began to stray from its commitment to revolutionary nationalism.

---

6. See Langston (2002) on how the PRI managed to prevent significant schisms throughout most of its hegemonic period.

7. Fox (1994) argues that a number of government programs were important clientelistic mechanisms.

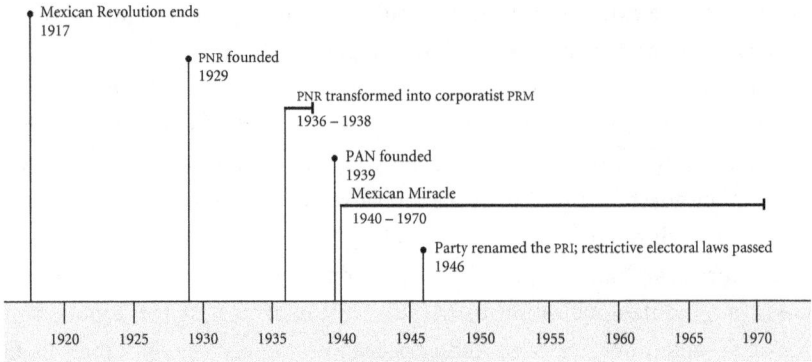

Fig. 1   Key moments in the PRI regime's consolidation.

Opposition party elites shared a set of criticisms of PRI rule. They denounced its extremely centralized nature, especially the *dedazo,* the informal practice of presidential-candidate selection, in which outgoing presidents named their successors (Langston 2006b), and the predominant role played by patronage politics. Opposition leaders also resented the layered institutional and political obstacles the PRI placed in the way of party-builders. The PRI never enacted a de jure one-party state, but it made building the opposition a tremendously costly venture. Finally, although the party gave ostensible voice to organized peasants and workers through its corporatist structures, those same structures subjugated those classes to the state. For both the PAN and PRD, *this* was the PRI that opposition leaders so consciously rejected in the ideologies they propagated and the institutions they built during the transition to democracy.

Undoing the Perfect Dictatorship

The PRI regime with which the democratic opposition competed from the late 1980s on featured a different set of internal institutions and practices. Its golden age was the period of the postwar Mexican Miracle, when the ISI-based economy sustained some of the highest growth rates in Latin America. By the late 1970s, though, the economic and institutional foundations of PRI rule were showing some wear. Troubling signs first appeared in the 1960s: domestic demand for substituted goods crested, the state began accumulating debt and running a trade deficit, and underinvestment in agriculture forced the importation of basic staples. President Luis Echeverría (1970–1976) responded to those economic challenges and the political instability epitomized by the 1968 protests in Mexico City with populist policies that further stretched the fiscal and administrative capacities of the state.

"Elected" in a climate of austerity, President José López Portillo (1976–1982) benefited from the discovery of substantial oil deposits a few months into his term in office. In the context of high oil prices (resulting from two OPEC price hikes in the 1970s), López Portillo used the expectation of future oil rents to contract massive loans from overseas lenders in order to placate the elite and mass interests of the PRI and to postpone abandoning the ISI model. During his *sexenio,* Mexico's external debt grew from US$19 billion to $53 billion (Bruhn 1997, 64). Then, in 1981, oil prices fell as interest rates rose, sending the Mexican economy and state into a downward tailspin and kicking off Mexico's "lost decade."[8] In 1982, the PRI government defaulted on payments on its overseas loans and sought assistance from the international financial institutions. A second crisis in 1985–1986 brought deep structural reforms, including broad-based trade liberalization, deregulation, and privatization of state-owned enterprises. As the PRI governments of Presidents Miguel de la Madrid (1982–1988) and Carlos Salinas de Gortari (1988–1994) strategized to manage the economy, Mexican citizens simply "muddled through" as they watched their standards of living plummet. There were signs of successful adjustment by the late 1980s—evidenced by the negotiations surrounding the North American Free Trade Agreement—but the economy again fell into crisis in December 1994 as *priísta* Ernesto Zedillo assumed the presidency. The crisis capped fifteen years of negative growth for Mexicans, whose per capita GDP in 1995 was 10 percent lower than it had been in 1980.

The economic challenges the PRI regime confronted between the late 1970s and the mid-1990s triggered important transformations in authoritarian rule in Mexico. Prolonged fiscal crisis undercut the capacity of PRI governments to maintain the allegiance of the sectoral organizations and their members through direct payoffs, subsidies, and other social benefits, an obstacle turned into an opportunity by regime elites bent on restructuring the party. Although rural-sector interests had been neglected during ISI, under Salinas, the structural underpinnings of the CNC and the ejido system were transformed through a constitutional reform that enabled individual *ejidatarios* to rent or sell their portion of previously communal landholding (De Janvry et al. 1997). Organized labor's influence had been reduced by structural adjustment

---

8. See Lustig (1998) on the Mexican economic crisis of the 1980s.

policies, but labor's voice in the PRI was muted as well, as was evidenced by its reduced presence in the PRI's legislative delegation (Langston 2006a). The state also changed its relationships with urban popular movements in the 1980s—co-opting some and dividing others, and undermining their potential coalescence as a single potential challenger (Haber 1994). In place of the inclusive and structural ties the regime once maintained with its organized constituents, Salinas and Zedillo (1994–2000) relied on targeted clientelistic mechanisms, through social programs like the Programa Nacional de Solidaridad (National Solidarity Program, PRONASOL) and the Programa de Educación, Salud y Alimentación (Education, Health, and Nutrition Program, PROGRESA) (Dion 2000; Cornelius, Craig, and Fox 1994), and they fortified the territorial structure of the party (Langston 2003).

Those transformations were part of a more generalized centralization of power that occurred during the 1980s and 1990s. Presidential power in Mexico was always exaggerated by PRI rule—although the president was constitutionally weak, as leader of the hegemonic party he gained "meta-constitutional" powers that included, among others, naming candidates for public office and the ability to replace the governors of Mexico's states (Mainwaring and Shugart 1997; Weldon 1997). Under de la Madrid and Salinas, regime decision making became even more exclusive, leaving out some PRI factions, most importantly, the revolutionary-nationalist wing associated with Cuauhtémoc Cárdenas. In addition, a rising group of technocrats (especially neoliberal economists) gained substantial influence over macroeconomic policy and other policy areas (Centeno 1994).

During the same period, the regime adapted its approach to the political opposition, increasingly directing it toward formal politics and away from the streets. Repression at the hands of the regime had stymied popular uprisings in 1968 (most notably in Mexico City's Tlatelolco Square) and driven left activists underground in the 1970s. But from the López Portillo administration on, the regime instead sought to channel social discontent into electoral politics. The 1977 Ley de Organizaciones Políticas y Procesos Electorales (Law on Political Organizations and Electoral Processes, LOPPE) legalized the electoral left, created additional proportional-representation seats in the lower chamber of the legislature, and gradually reduced the PRI's role in electoral administration, among other important changes.[9] The institutional strategy, paired with more frequent recognition of opposition victories, brought relative political stability

9. Appendix 1 chronicles the major electoral reforms passed during the transition.

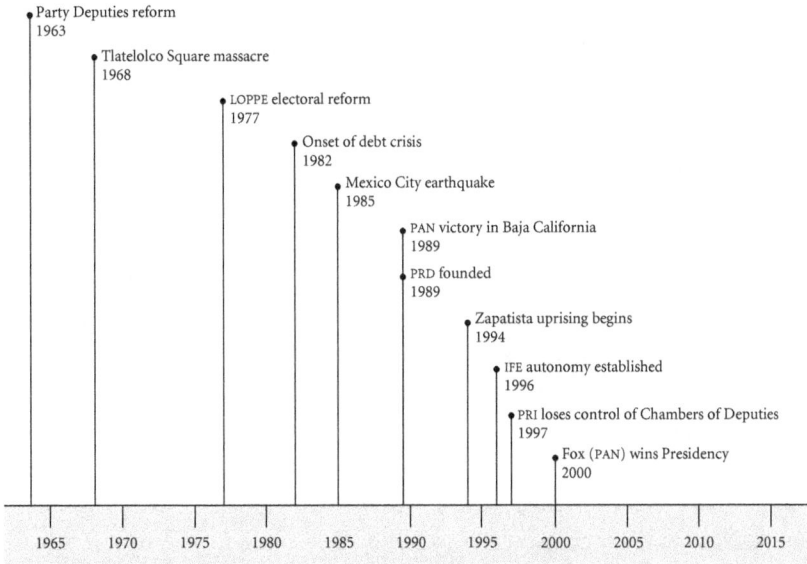

```
• Party Deputies reform
  1963
    • Tlatelolco Square massacre
      1968
          • LOPPE electoral reform
            1977
                • Onset of debt crisis
                  1982
                    • Mexico City earthquake
                      1985
                        • PAN victory in Baja California
                          1989
                        • PRD founded
                          1989
                            • Zapatista uprising begins
                              1994
                                • IFE autonomy established
                                  1996
                                  • PRI loses control of Chambers of Deputies
                                    1997
                                    • Fox (PAN) wins Presidency
                                      2000
```

Fig. 2   Key moments in the PRI regime's deconsolidation.

but also gradually undermined the PRI's lock on power. Although institutional reforms were the more common response of the PRI to liberalizing pressures, there were also notable violent episodes associated with political opening: the 1994 assassinations of the PRI's reformist presidential candidate Luis Donaldo Colosio and its secretary general José Francisco Ruíz Massieu, and the PRI's violent response to the uprising by the Ejército Zapatista de Liberación Nacional (Zapatista National Liberation Army, EZLN, or Zapatistas) that began on January 1, 1994 in the southern state of Chiapas, on the day the North American Free Trade Agreement (NAFTA) took effect.[10]

The PRI's decomposition invited increased mobilization from its opposition, further challenging the PRI's hold on power (fig. 2). Four opposition surges signaled the weakening of the PRI's grasp on power. The PAN wrested the governorship of Baja California from the PRI in 1989, breaking the PRI's decades-long hold on state governments and opening up a subnational dimension to the country's democratization process. The 1997 federal elections produced two important results. For the first time, the PRI lost its majority in

10. The Zapatistas continue to struggle for greater recognition of indigenous rights and municipal autonomy, among other issues. For an analysis of the Chiapas rebellion, see Harvey (1998).

the Chamber of Deputies, and thus faced an unavoidable institutional check, or veto point, in its efforts to retain power. Until 1997 the party-regime had been able to pass legislation without opposition support, but after 1997, the PRI was forced to negotiate with one of the opposition parties in order to advance any bill in Congress (Lawson 1997). The same election featured the first-ever competitive election for the Head of Government (or mayor) of Mexico City, home to about one-quarter of Mexico's resident population. Cuauhtémoc Cárdenas, the highest-profile figure among the founders of the PRD, defeated his PAN and PRI rivals, ushering in a period of as-yet uninterrupted PRD control of Mexico City. The final opposition advance of the late 1990s was the campaign and election of 2000, producing modern Mexico's first non-PRI president, panista Vicente Fox.[11]

The union of an inclusive party and state corporatism endowed PRI leaders with the political and economic tools to establish the party as a hegemonic political actor. Opponents of the PRI labored in parties, civic organizations, and social movements to challenge the party-regime, but until the late 1980s, they had few visible successes. As PRI rule decayed, the opportunities for its two primary competitors, the Partido Acción Nacional and the Partido de la Revolución Democrática, steadily improved. The following chapters analyze the development of those two parties between the late 1980s and 2006. Despite shifting the focus to the opposition during the PRI's decline, PRI rule itself remains omnipresent. The party's character and its infrastructure indelibly marked the opposition parties, shaping their political goals and institutional practices and setting the stage for savage democracy.

11. See Greene (2007) and Dominguez and Lawson (2005) on the election. Mizrahi (2003) and Shirk (2005) both explain Fox's victory from a PAN-focused perspective.

3

ORIGINS OF THE DEMOCRATIC IMPERATIVE

[The PRD] understands democracy to be not only a political system
but also a way of life.
—PRD Declaration of Principles, article 6, 1991/2001

Because democracy as a way of life and government is based upon the essential
equality of all human beings, it is the best form of legitimation of political power and
the optimal system to respect human dignity.
—PAN Principles of Doctrine, article 5, 1939/1965

Until 2000, two characteristics defined the PAN and the PRD: they were opposition parties and they were prodemocratic. The former resulted from the foundation of both parties in opposition to the hegemonic PRI: the PAN in 1939, in
opposition to the left-leaning reforms of President Lázaro Cárdenas, and the
PRD in 1989, in opposition to a neoliberal PRI led by technocrats like Carlos
Salinas.[1] The prodemocratic posture reflected the primary objective of both
organizations: the end of PRI hegemony. In practice, though, these two characteristics meant one and the same thing. The PRI's authoritarian monopoly
of power transformed the reference point for "opposition" from government
to regime. "Opposition" did not simply imply the "out-of-government party"
or connote minority-party status, as it might in a parliamentary system or a
multiparty congress. It carried with it the objective of fundamentally transforming the rules that governed access to power in Mexico.

---

1. For lengthier discussions of the foundation of the PAN, see Loaeza (1999), Mizrahi (2003),
Mabry (1973), Reveles Vázquez (1993), and Shirk (2005). For more detailed accounts of the PRI
schism and the formation of the PRD, see Bruhn's (1997) definitive account as well as Garrido's
(1993) analysis of the Corriente Democrática and Borjas Benavides (2005) on the PRD's experiences
until 2003.

The institutional arrangements of the PRI regime strongly conditioned the foundations of Mexico's opposition parties. PRI rule created dissenting groups that sought alternative modes of political representation, but the structures of PRI rule also shaped how those actors perceived their interests and influenced the goals they embraced and the organizations they built. The result was the adoption by the PAN and PRD of the democratic imperative, a fervently prodemocratic set of ideals and institutional structures shaped by panista and perredista conceptions of democracy and by the parties' respective experiences under authoritarianism.

Partido Acción Nacional: From Democratic Dissidents to Activists

In 1934, Revolutionary General Lázaro Cárdenas was elected president of Mexico. Although he was a member of the elitist PNR, Cárdenas represented a faction of the party that advocated a left-leaning agenda. He transformed the PNR from a narrow circle of elites to a mass party, the PRM, that guaranteed representation for peasants, workers, and the military through sectoral organizations tied to the party. For many, it appeared that Cárdenas was intent on realizing the goals of the Revolution.

Cárdenas had widespread support, but it was far from unanimous. The PAN was founded in September 1939 by a conglomeration of political interests left behind by the president's reforms. The driving force behind the party's development was Manuel Gómez Morin, a lawyer and academic from northern Mexico who had been active in the Mexican Revolution and the post-revolutionary governments of the 1920s and who later became a rector at the Universidad Nacional Autónoma Mexicana (National Autonomous University of Mexico, UNAM). Gómez Morin, convinced that the regime was unlikely to tolerate political opposition, began distancing himself from the government in the late 1920s as the PNR took shape under the revolutionary generals. After a short period of voluntary exile in the United States, he returned to Mexico, and in the shadow of Cárdenas, he began the process of party building.

Three constituencies came together under his leadership. First, he attracted conservative intellectuals from UNAM and middle-class professionals who objected to Cárdenas's statist economic policies and the strengthening of the presidency through the creation of the PRM's corporatist sectors. Second, the movement appealed to Catholic activists angered by the Revolution's restrictions on the political role of the Catholic Church. Members of Catholic organizations, such as the Acción Católica Mexicana and the Asociación Católica de la Juventud Mexicana, objected in particular to the infusion of the educational system with "socialist values."[2] Third, Gómez Morin and the PAN initially counted on the support of entrepreneurs and landholders, whose interests were threatened by the Cárdenas reforms, although many shifted their loyalties from the PAN to the PRI following the selection of Cárdenas's pro-business successor, Manuel Ávila Camacho.

The PAN is a center-right party, similar to Christian Democratic parties in its aim of achieving the *bien común* (common good) through a *tercera vía* (third way) that lies between free-market capitalism and communism. Panista doctrine is firmly committed to the idea of private property, and views the state as responsible for the "realization of the common good, which implies at one and the same time attaining justice and safety, defending the interests of the collectivity, and respecting and protecting the individual."[3] Balancing the principles of subsidiarity and solidarity, the party's principles specify: "As much society as possible, as much government as necessary" (PAN 1993). Accordingly, government should only intervene when private sectors (especially the family) are insufficient, and should always respect and protect private enterprise (as private property "dignifies" the individual).

In its early years, the party sought not to win elected office but rather to moralize politics and engage Mexico's citizens, which Gómez Morin believed was unlikely to occur under the party-regime. During the party's early years, the goal of winning office did not even appear in the PAN's official documents. Politics was about public service and the idea of political ambition was anathema to PAN members. Many panistas discussed these aims in terms of developing Mexicans' democratic consciences—principles to help them make ethical political decisions. Because electoral victory was next to impossible given the PRI's hold on power, party activists were "political missionaries," who

2. In many ways, the political activism of this group was a continuation of the Cristero Rebellion in the Bajío region during the 1920s. Efraín González Luna, who would become the leader of the doctrinaire faction of the party from the 1940s through the 1960s, was the most prominent member of this group. Others included Luis Calderón Vega, who is the father of Felipe Calderón Hinojosa, the current Mexican president.

3. These ideas are codified in two papal encyclicals that form the basis of much of Christian Democratic thought, the Rerum Novarum (1891) and the Quadregesimo Anno (1931). Quotes and translations by Mizrahi (2003 passim). See Mizrahi and Loaeza (1999) for more extensive discussions of the evolution of panista thought.

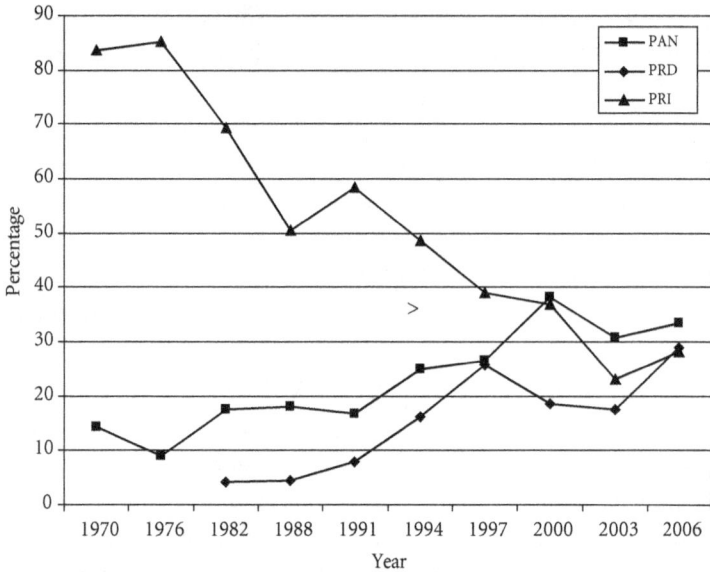

Fig. 3   Chamber of Deputies vote shares, 1970–2006. For 1982, the PRD line represents the vote totals of the main left parties, while in 1988 it represents the FDN's vote share. Data provided by the Instituto Federal Electoral.

gave their time with no tangible reward (Mabry 1973, 187). Indeed, at various moments in PAN history, party elites debated fiercely whether participation in an unjust political system was even worthwhile. Those in favor of participation, led by Gómez Morin himself, believed that the party would gradually become a national political force, whereas many of the Catholic activists, including ideologue Efraín González Luna, contended that the party should abstain from elections and focus on spreading the party's doctrine and program. Thus, when the Catholics gained more power in the party, with the exit of the entrepreneurial sector upon Ávila Camacho's election (1940) and the retirement of Gómez Morin from the party presidency (1949), the party grew more marginalized.

The PAN existed in relative isolation until the early 1960s.[4] Over the course of that decade, conflicts between pragmatic and doctrinaire elements of the

4. Analysts of the PAN often discuss this period of PAN history using the biblical metaphor of "crossing the desert" (Mizrahi 2003; Loaeza 1999). This period is especially important because during this time, the PAN represented the only real opposition to the regime, and yet it was truly marginal in terms of elected representation. Its continued participation in a nondemocratic political system earned the party the reputation of a "loyal opposition." Until the 1970s, public

party grew more intense, with the pragmatists gaining the upper hand once representation in the lower house of Congress was effectively guaranteed through the Party Deputies reform in 1963. The pragmatists' influence rose further throughout the 1960s and into the early 1970s, evident in the adoption in 1973 of the partisan goal of winning elections. They consolidated their dominance after a second electoral reform (LOPPE) created one hundred proportional-representation seats in the lower house. As Yemile Mizrahi (2003) documents, during the 1980s and 1990s, as the PAN moved progressively farther from its sectarian roots, it had ever-greater electoral success (fig. 3).

Partido de la Revolución Democrática: Democratizing the Revolution

Like the PAN, the PRD formed at a crucial moment in the history of the PRI regime. Whereas the PAN emerged while the PRI was building its hegemonic party system, the PRD was founded while the PRI transformed dramatically under the leadership of the neoliberal technocrats. As the regime's import-substitution-led economic model faced declining returns in the late 1970s and then crashed in the early 1980s, the PRI regime closed ranks and sought to stem the economy's downward slide through neoliberal reforms. President de la Madrid (1982–1988) headed the PRI during the initial years of the crisis, and despite multiple reform attempts, was unable to bring the economy out of crisis.

The failure of the government's neoliberal reforms aggravated existing tensions between the traditional *Cardenista* (named for Lázaro Cárdenas) wing of the PRI and the rising neoliberal technocrats over questions of policy and the distribution of candidacies and governmental posts (Bruhn 1997; Garrido 1993). In 1986, the Cardenistas formed a pressure group within the PRI, the Corriente Democrática (Democratic Current, CD), to voice their concerns about both the regime's deviation from its revolutionary goals and the PRI's very centralized internal selection processes. Three PRI elites spearheaded the development of the CD: Cuauhtémoc Cárdenas (governor of Michoacán and son of Lázaro Cárdenas), Porfirio Muñoz Ledo (former secretary general of

---

protests by PAN elites were rare. The most evident exception to this rule involved 1958 PAN presidential candidate Luis H. Álvarez, who led protests against alleged electoral fraud. Interview with former PAN president and Sen. Luis H. Álvarez, March 10, 2000, and Loaeza (1999).

the PRI), and Rodolfo González Guevara (a prominent intellectual). Through their personal and political networks, the CD's support base spread through the Cardenista wing of the PRI.[5] Paired with the increasing insulation of the de la Madrid administration's economic policy making, the CD's organization destabilized the power-sharing arrangements that had ensured political elites' allegiance to the PRI over its decades of hegemonic rule.

Though the CD began as merely an internal faction in the PRI, its activities quickly alienated its leaders from the rest of the PRI's leadership. Throughout 1986 and early 1987, the CD encountered increased hostility: individuals faced marginalization within the party and the group received harsh treatment from the regime-sympathetic press. However, as the economic crisis continued, the movement also found growing support among Mexicans enduring its shocking effects. At the PRI's Thirteenth National Assembly in March 1987, the conflict between the regime and the CD peaked. In their speeches, CD leaders advocated internal party democracy and championed the working classes, implicitly (or explicitly) condemning the regime's practices over its then-six decades of rule. In the assembly's closing ceremonies, the neoliberal dominant coalition of the party sharply criticized the CD and attacked its proposals. This public offensive provoked some CD members to immediately exit the party, while many remaining CD militants left following the formal designation of Carlos Salinas as the PRI's 1988 presidential candidate.

By October 1987, one of the parastatal parties, the Partido Auténtico de la Revolución Mexicana (Authentic Party of the Mexican Revolution, PARM), completed negotiations with Cárdenas to be its 1988 presidential candidate.[6] Other opposition forces, including the other parastatal parties, autonomous left parties, and organizations from civil society came together in January 1988 to form a broad electoral coalition, the Frente Democrático Nacional (National Democratic Front, FDN). Although important tensions existed between the FDN and the independent electoral left, the Partido Mexicano Socialista (Mexican Socialist Party, PMS) candidate Heberto Castillo renounced his candidacy in June 1988 when it became clear that Cárdenas had captured the electoral base of his party—students and urban popular movements.[7] Although the PMS

5. See Bruhn (1997, 78–79) for a map of the social network behind the CD's growth.

6. The Partido Auténtico Revolucionario Mexicano is one of a cluster of marginal parties (the so-called "parastatals") that regularly supported the PRI in federal elections during the transition period.

7. The independent electoral left was obviously strongly opposed to the PRI during its period of hegemony. The PMS, which itself resulted from a process of unification of smaller left parties

refused to join the FDN, its leadership did sign cooperative pacts with both the CD and Cárdenas. Ultimately, Cárdenas's campaign effort failed: a mysterious "computer malfunction" occurred that tilted the vote count to Salinas. The allegations of fraud that followed Salinas's installation carried the popular mobilizations of the 1988 campaign through to the 1989 foundation of the PRD. The PMS offered its electoral registry to the FDN coalition, around which a new party, with new principles and statutes, was constructed from a base in the CD, the PMS, and various civic organizations.[8] This party, the PRD, was legally registered on May 14, 1989.

The PRD is a self-proclaimed left party. The party was founded on the promise of achieving the goals of the Mexican Revolution (especially economic and social justice) that had once been espoused by the PRI but, in the view of perredistas, had been abandoned with the regime's turn to neoliberalism in the 1980s. The party's official documents outline nine principles that guide the party: democracy, justice, equality, work, liberty, dignity, sustainable development, sovereignty, and political ethics (PRD 1991). Many of the party's principles dovetailed in its frequent strong criticism of the neoliberal policies of the "official party" of Mexico. Therein were the party's two foremost political objectives: a turn away from the neoliberal orthodoxy of PRI presidents since the 1980s and the removal of the PRI from the presidency.[9]

Adopting Democratic Ideals

The elites that spearheaded the construction of the PAN and PRD challenged authoritarian orders: Gómez Morin rejected the presidentialism that followed Lázaro Cárdenas's revolutionary government, whereas Cuauhtémoc Cárdenas and his *compañeros* indicted the PRI's neoliberal authoritarianism. Their initial party documents and later revisions are imbued with enduring core

---

during the 1980s (detailed in Carr 1992), found it challenging to build political support for a former member of the PRI.

8. The parastatals returned to the PRI's fold after the 1988 election results, thus ensuring their continued legal registrations.

9. In an interesting 1997 forum in the newsmagazine Proceso, prominent leaders of the Mexican left analyzed the PRD and its politics, and many touched on the two sides of the democratic imperative (Jáquez 1997). Rosalbina Garavitos, for example, resisted boxing the PRD into a political geometry, and she argued that what unified the PRD's varied elements was its identity as a democratic party. For Gilberto Rincón Gallardo, the PRD's identity was centered on its oppositional politics.

democratic values, many shared between the parties and some that distinguish the PAN and PRD from one another.[10] Leaders were conscious of the parties' shared commitment to democracy as well as the distinctions between their conceptions of it: One PRD leader, for example, recognized that both parties were historically prodemocratic, but argued that his party favored democracy "for the plebeians," and the PAN advocated a Roman democracy.[11]

The PAN's democratic commitments run deep and wide. Although the party's early documents do not specifically articulate a panista concept of democracy, the values that underpin are apparent in them. Justice and the rule of law were primary components of contemporary conceptualizations of democracy evident in its doctrine at the party's foundation. The party's *Principios* document states that injustice can only be avoided through the *recto ejercicio* (just exercise) of authority by the state (PAN 1939, article 3). In fact, the realization of justice is the primary responsibility assigned to the state by those principles (PAN 1939, article 13). The party's vision of social justice is equally order-based: it is *not* to be achieved through class struggle, but rather through reasoned intervention by the state to confront "all types of disorder and injustice in society" and to protect the fundamental rights of individuals (PAN 1939, article 3).[12]

The PAN amended its principles of doctrine for the first time in 1965. In addition to further detailing the conditions under which justice and the rule of law could be achieved (including through the separation of powers and municipal autonomy), a new article specifically discussed the party's understanding of democracy. The conceptualization of democracy specified in article 5 structured party thinking until after Fox's 2000 election (when the party's principles were next revisited). According to it, democracy "requires the effective participation of individuals in the collective activity that shapes their own personal destinies . . . It is the best form of legitimation of political power and the optimal system to respect human dignity" (PAN 1939, article 5). The article further specifies some of the characteristics of democratic regimes from a panista perspective:

10. All translations in this section are by author unless otherwise noted.

11. Interview with PRD Secretary of Planning and Institutional Development Agustín Guerrero Castillo. Interestingly, the PRD in Mexico City had a training program that included reading Howard Fast's novel *Spartacus*.

12. Dion (2005, 31) suggests that Christian Democratic approaches to welfare-state development adopt similar ideological positions, eschewing class struggle in favor of the paz social (social peace).

All democratic regimes should respect, promote, and guarantee
not only the theoretical recognition but also the real exercise of the
fundamental rights of individuals, that is, those that are due to all
members of the political community. (PAN 1939, article 5)

And:

All democratic regimes should respect, promote, and guarantee,
through objective and impartial electoral processes, the expression
and representation of minorities, the rights of citizens to participate
in the process of formation of the government to which they are
subject and to form part of that same government, and [all democratic regimes] should ensure that freedom of information and
freedom to criticize those in power is guaranteed to all citizens.
(PAN 1939, article 5)

When the party reconsidered its guiding principles after the 2000 presidential
election, the new 2002 document again did not include a specific "Democracy"
article, but a new article titled "Politics and Social Responsibility" stated that
"the good functioning of democracy requires institutions and citizens con-
science of their obligations in an organized society" (PAN 1939, article 2).

PAN documents emphasize the centrality of institutions to democratic
rule, and they place particular emphasis on elections while simultaneously
disdaining social struggle and extra-institutional mobilization. Democracy,
for the PAN, is a product of the voluntary will of engaged, individual citizens,
and as such, a democratic regime depends tremendously on the protection of
the rights of those individuals to participate in institutional politics. Panista
thought argues that Mexico will be democratized when the proper institutional framework is in place and Mexicans act according to their democratic
consciences. Seen through the lens of comparative democratic theory, the
PAN's understanding of democracy and democratic regimes amounts to an
endorsement of procedural or "formal democracy."[13] The party advocates
strong institutions to guide individual behavior and preserve order, but it
also questions strong parties, out of a fear that they could trample on the

---

13. Huber et al. (1997, 323) identify formal democracy as a procedural minimum, characterized
by "regular free and fair elections, universal suffrage, accountability of the state's administrative
organs to the elected representatives, and guarantees for freedom of expression and association."

expression of an individual's will. The PAN's "democratic" institutional life, then, is characterized by a focus on the elaboration of effective rules to facilitate those individually driven outcomes.

The PRD Declaration of Principles "understands democracy to be not only a political system but also a way of life" (PRD 1991 article 6). Like the PAN, the PRD acknowledges the institutional bases of democracy. Article 1 of the PRD's founding document emphasizes the centrality of "the constitutional principles of the democratic rule of law" as well as the protection of the rights and liberties of citizens and their organizations (PRD 1991). However, the PRD attaches significant social and economic dimensions to those institutional preconditions. Democracy in PRD documents often refers to the sort of society that perredistas envision: one "where everyone can organize themselves freely to defend their interests; where citizens have access to information and to culture, and these are produced and diffused freely" (PRD 1991, article 6). In the same article, the party details the society it hopes to construct. The PRD "aims to build a democratic society in which solidarity and brotherhood among all prevail; in which the rights of minorities, of diversity, and of difference are respected; and which guards individual, social, and collective rights; that is, a representative, participatory, inclusive, and plural democracy, so that all citizens may be free to express their opinions and choose their way of life." The party's principles envision a democratic society where workers are free to organize, where public policies are redistributive, government is transparent and efficient, and corruption and authoritarianism have been eradicated (PRD 1991, article 6, sections 3–4). The state is conceived of as an organization serving society, one that, like Mexico, should be "democratic and federal, representative and participatory, [and] pluriethnic and pluricultural" and ought to work toward "the general and individual welfare of Mexicans" (PRD 1991, article 6, section 6).[14]

Although the PRD accepts the constitutional and institutional foundations of democratic rule, its conceptualization of democracy also places additional

---

14. Bruhn (1997, 172–73) encountered similarly maximalist conceptualizations of democracy in her fieldwork among PRD activists in the first years after the party's establishment. However, she noted that those militants did not agree about what precisely democracy meant. Some saw democracy in institutional terms, but others emphasized the importance of social and economic participation, social equality, and transparent government.

conditions on formal democracy.[15] The statutes and doctrine of the party repeatedly acknowledge the centrality of mass participation and the freedom of citizens and, notably, workers to organize to protect their rights and advance their interests. Furthermore, PRD documents demand that the state protect both collective and individual rights and pursue the general welfare of all Mexicans. Given that the PRD's understanding of democracy is significantly broader than the PAN's, it is unsurprising that its institutional manifestations are more complicated. The party's "democratic" institutional life favors participation (orderly or not) by broad sectors of the elite and rank and file through inclusive institutions like low thresholds for membership and the incorporation of minority voice into debate. PRD institutions display a concern not just for democratic process (as do the PAN's institutions) but also for democratic outcomes. As an added complication, the different *corrientes* (or factions) of the party espouse their own visions of democracy and interpretations of the democratic imperative, with some favoring *democracia hacia abajo* (that is, a party democracy inclusive of interests from below) over democracy at the regime level.[16]

The parties' respective "positive" conceptions of democracy complemented "negative" associations with the PRI's brand of authoritarianism. Interestingly, straightforward condemnations of PRI rule rarely appeared in party principles and doctrine. In one notable exception, the PAN's 1965 statutes include a specific condemnation of PRI rule in the form of a statement on political parties. Article 6 states that one-party political systems are antidemocratic instruments of autocratic rule, and it further adds that in a democratic setting neither the state nor the government should identify with a particular political party. Despite the scant explicit mention of PRI rule, though, disdain for two particular elements of the party regime had particularly demonstrable effects on the ideas and institutions adopted by the PAN and PRD. First, opposition elites criticized the bureaucratic and authoritarian nature of PRI politics (and by extension, Mexican politics).[17] The president of Mexico sat at the apex of an

15. The PRD's democracy resembles both participatory democracy, in that there are no systematic and significant variations in participation across social groups, and social democracy, in which the government pursues (or, in this case, the party should pursue) higher levels of socioeconomic equality. See Huber et al. (1997, 324).

16. Interview with Dep. Felix Salgado Macedonio (PRD), November 9, 2000.

17. This is not to be confused with the Bureaucratic Authoritarian (BA) regimes of the southern cone analyzed by O'Donnell (1973). Important distinctions between the PRI regime and the BA regimes include the PRI's civilian leadership (as opposed to the military leadership of the BA regimes) and its corporatist mobilization (in lieu of violent suppression) of labor. Still, since the

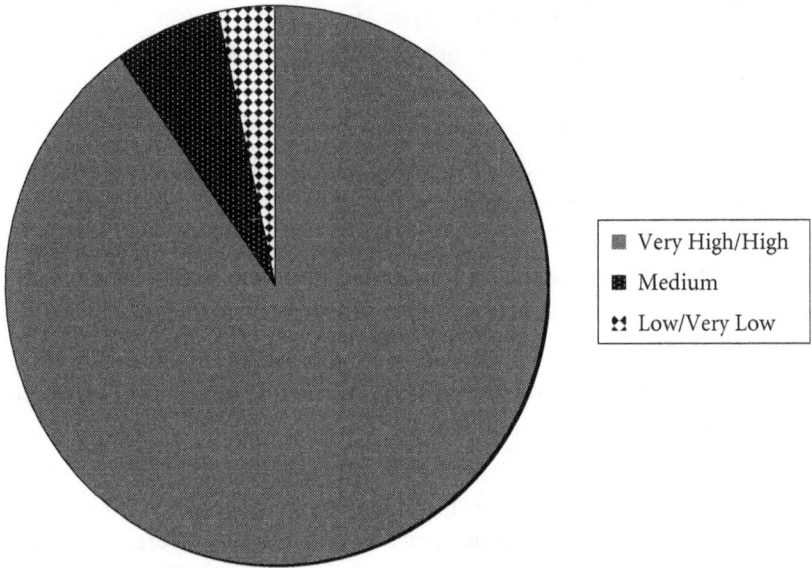

Fig. 4   Perceptions of democracy among PAN legislators, 1997–2000. Data presented are the proportion of total survey sample for each response (n = 31). Data provided by Manuel Alcántara, director of the Proyecto de Élites Latinoamericanas (Latin American Elites Project, PELA), Universidad de Salamanca (1994–2005).

immense bureaucratic structure that encompassed both the party and the state and blurred the distinctions between the two. As a result, both PAN and PRD leaders favored weak central offices, activist-driven organizations, and decentralized power. Second, PAN and PRD leaders considered the relationships that the PRI maintained with its affiliated trade unions, peasant associations, and popular movements to be antidemocratic and contrary to the interests of those organizations' members. Those party leaders extrapolated from the particularities of the PRI's corporatist practices to judge the term itself (*corporativismo*) and the very idea of parties having institutionalized relationships with organized sectors of civil society as authoritarian.

The parties grafted these indictments of PRI rule on to their respective conceptions of democracy to form comprehensive partisan articulations of what "democracy" meant. Although there were clearly common elements, the parties differed in how they understood the place of individuals, institutions, and

election of Vicente Fox in 2000, it has come to light that the PRI governments of the late 1960s and early 1970s engaged in counterinsurgent tactics against left activists (similar to the tactics followed by the BA regimes).

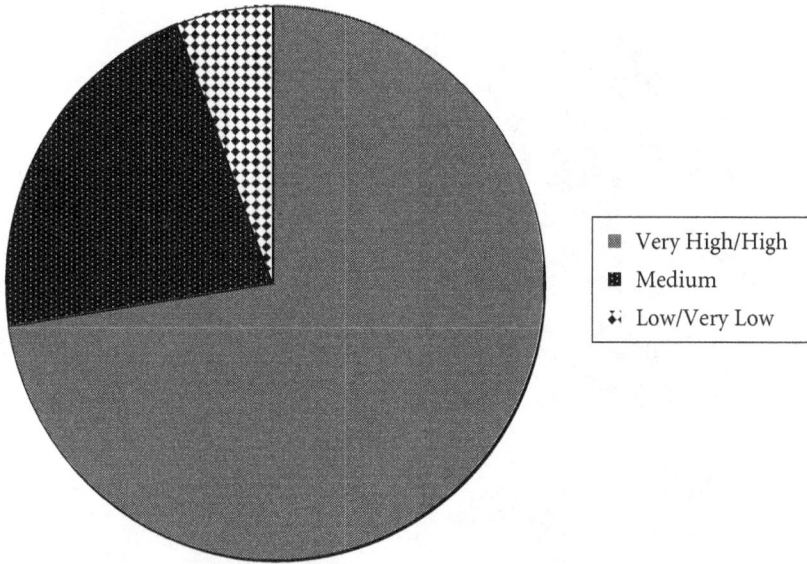

Fig. 5   Perceptions of democracy among PAN legislators, 2000–2003. Data presented are the proportion of total survey sample for each response (n = 51). Data provided by Manuel Alcántara, director of the Proyecto de Élites Latinoamericanas (Latin American Elites Project, PELA), Universidad de Salamanca (1994–2005).

social struggle in democratic change, and they had fundamental disagreements about the "depth" of democracy. Those distinct visions, though products of particular historical moments, contributed to institutional commitments that framed party program, strategy, and organizational development through 2006, both in relation to their understandings of party democracy and their imaginings of a democratic Mexico.

The emphasis on democracy in the PAN and PRD extends even beyond their founding documents. Contemporary members of the parties identified their organizations as strongly democratic across two waves of a comparative survey on parliamentary elites in Latin America. In that survey, members of the Mexican Chamber of Deputies were asked to rate the level of democracy in their parties. The data reveal that PAN deputies rated their democracy stronger than their PRD colleagues did, and in both cases, perceptions of democracy in the parties declined from the first to the second legislative session (figs. 4–7). Still, only a small proportion of legislators felt their parties were only weakly democratic, which suggests that party members have internalized their parties' democratic character. By way of comparison, in the second wave of the survey *no* PRI deputies rated their party as very highly or highly democratic,

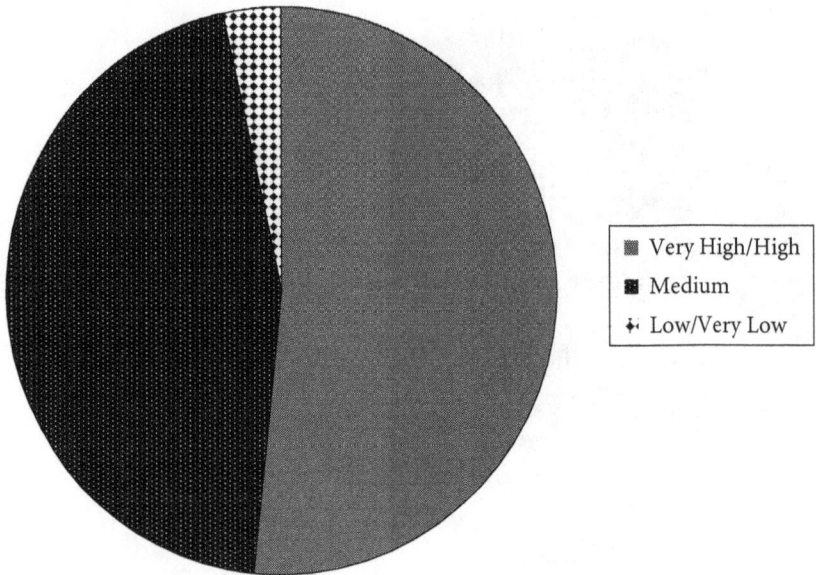

Legend:
- Very High/High
- Medium
- Low/Very Low

Fig. 6   Perceptions of democracy among PRD legislators, 1997–2000. Data presented are the proportion of total survey sample for each response (n = 31). Data provided by Manuel Alcántara, director of the Proyecto de Élites Latinoamericanas (Latin American Elites Project, PELA), Universidad de Salamanca (1994–2005).

three-quarters of the respondents rated its democracy as "medium," and more than a quarter judged the PRI's democracy as low or very low. How can we explain this continued emphasis on democracy in the PAN and PRD, seventy and twenty years, respectively, after each was founded?

Democratic Paths and Institutional Change

Understanding the power of the democratic imperative demands theorizing the prodemocratic origins of the PAN and PRD in response to PRI authoritarianism as well as explaining the perpetuation of democratic ideals and institutions in the decades following their establishment. One possible explanation for the endur-ing nature of the democratic imperative is that foundation in opposition to PRI rule locked in a certain set of institutional attributes. According to that logic, leaders' rejections of PRI rule and conceptions of democracy would be one of a series of characteristics of party emergence (alongside the presence of external sponsoring organizations, party formation within or outside parliament, and the mode of territorial expansion of the party) that could be linked to long-term

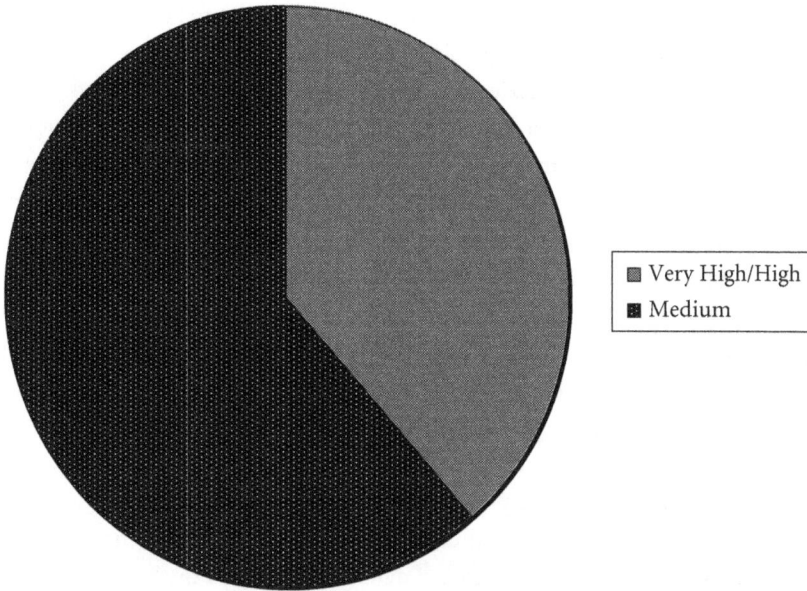

Fig. 7   Perceptions of democracy among PRD legislators, 2000–2003. Data presented are the proportion of total survey sample for each response (n = 13). Data provided by Manuel Alcántara, director of the Proyecto de Élites Latinoamericanas (Latin American Elites Project, PELA), Universidad de Salamanca (1994–2005).

party institutionalization and party system structure (Panebianco 1988; Duverger 1954).[18] "Lock-in" arguments have two inherent problems, though. The first is that they have difficulty accounting for the "unlocking" of institutional characteristics. The fact is, although the ideals of democracy espoused by PAN and PRD leaders have been relatively consistent, the institutional manifestations of those ideals changed substantially over time. A second problem is that lock-in arguments too often bracket environmental factors from founding processes. In Mexico, where an authoritarian party-state controlled the mechanisms for

18. Duverger (1954, XXXV) believed that "It is the whole life of the party which bears the mark of its origin." In his case, the formation of parties, within parliament or outside it, paired with their initial basic elements (caucus, branch, cell, or militia) set parties on particular developmental trajectories as organizations. Panebianco (1988, esp. 50–53) attempts to advance the genetic argument by offering three characteristics that explain within-group variation that Duverger's framework fails to account for. Specifically, Panebianco argues that how parties expanded over territory (via penetration, diffusion, or a mix of the two), the presence or absence of external sponsors, and the presence of charismatic leaders critically condition the way parties are initially built and their long-term prospects for institutionalization.

party registry and the legal structures that governed electoral competition, the influence of the parties' "place of birth" cannot be undersold.

Some examples from Mexico and elsewhere attest to the centrality of heavily weighing environmental factors in leaders' institutional choices at founding moments. By Maurice Duverger's criteria, the PAN is clearly an "external organization," formed as it was outside the legislature. But extra-parliamentary emergence was the only available option for any party at the time, given the near-monopoly of state power the regime maintained at the time. PRI rule dictated the choices Gómez Morin made. PRI rule also precluded nascent party alliances with organized labor or peasant groups, making "external sponsorship" or "indirect structures" impossible. Likewise, Gómez Morin and Cárdenas steered their parties' early lives from Mexico City, suggesting territorial "penetration" instead of "diffusion," but they did so because electoral laws effectively banned regional parties and made diffusion nearly impossible.[19] Again, the political-institutional environmental had preponderant influence over party leaders' decisions. Similar dynamics unfolded in the countries of the former Eastern Bloc during their transitions in the 1990s, as the common configuration of institutions and structures associated with totalitarian rule and state socialism produced identifiable cross-national similarities in party development (Grzymala-Busse 2002), constitutional engineering (Stanger 2003), and social policy evolution (Inglot 2003). There, the legacy of Soviet domination created a common "institutional time" in which environmental factors structured processes of institutional design and rendered common institutional outcomes (Ekiert and Hanson 2003b, 20).

The choices made at moments of institutional design are crucial points of departure for institutional development, but to understand how those choices are made requires looking beyond the behavior of strategic actors (Pierson 2004, 109–22). Instead of extracting decision-makers from their political surroundings and focusing solely on their efforts to broker solutions to collective problems, the analysis of those interactions must actively incorporate the temporal and spatial moments in which institutional design occurs ("institutional

---

19. Regarding basic elements of the parties, the PAN is normally treated as a caucus organization because of the fairly elite character of its supporters, its reputation as a "pavement" party with an urban middle-class base. The PRD is imagined as a mass party, with branches or cells as the basic unit. In truth, while the PRD is a left party, it is not a mass party—its membership is insignificant compared to that of the PRI. Duverger's categories may not capture the realities of party life for late-emerging parties in developing countries, where the class cleavage does not clearly serve as the primary axis of competition.

time" and "institutional space"). Context is not just a setting for institutional design, but it is instead an essential contributor to it, influencing how actors perceive and pursue their individual and collective interests.

Once initial institutions are crafted, they are placed on trajectories along which future development takes place through repeated interactions between actors, existing institutions, and the environment. Institutions are often resistant to efforts to alter them (that is, they "stick"), but that stability does not mean that institutions are static or that actors have reached consensus about those them. Instead, obstacles get in the way of actors who are intent on institutional change.[20] Actors may be unable to build or change institutions because they fail to find common objectives (coordination problems) or their efforts might be stymied by opposing forces (veto points). Often, actors adapt their goals and strategies to institutional settings (as is suggested by Levi 1997; North 1990; Pierson 2000), and as a result the potential population of institutional reformers dwindles (asset specificity).[21] Institutions also stick due to a self-reinforcing institutional momentum, termed "increasing returns," that reduces the likelihood of institutional change (path dependency).

Possibilities for institutional adaptation always exist, but as an institution proceeds along a given path, the likelihood of adaptation decreases while that of institutional lock-in increases. In truth, though, institutions are rarely completely locked.[22] Institutional change can and does occur, either through the adaptation of existing rules and practices (that is, when reformers are able to overcome the mechanisms of reproduction discussed above) or by means of alternative paths. Through processes like layering, when actors build new institutions without eliminating old ones, and conversion, when actors redirect existing institutions to new ends, actors sidestep resilient institutions and craft innovative means of achieving their goals (Pierson 2004; Thelen 2003).

The PAN and PRD were born into similar institutional times despite emerging in different historical eras. The institutional infrastructure of the PRI (just forming in 1939 and weakening in 1989) shaped the political mobilization of

20. For detailed discussions of patterns of institutional reproduction, see Ekiert and Hanson (2003a), Pierson (2004; 2000), Mahoney and Rueschemeyer (2003), Thelen (2003), and Steinmo et al. (1992). These particular obstacles are elaborated upon by Pierson (2004, 142).

21. Though Schickler (2001) and others would note that there are usually "losers" (those who are not granted power through existing institutional arrangements) who remain advocates of future adaptation.

22. Pierson (2004, 157–60) offers a handful of examples of "deep equilibria" cases in which the lock may indeed by closed because of the scant chances for adaptation.

opposition forces, influenced their preferences and goals, and conditioned party founders' logic of institutional design. The PRI excluded some actors from the Revolutionary Family of the 1930s and ejected particular factions from the PRI's leadership in the 1980s. Those actors, the founders of the PAN and PRD, built institutions like programs, rules, and bureaucracies to direct and manage party life. Organizing in opposition to an inclusive authoritarian regime, leaders of the parties opted for institutions that were "democratic," on one hand, and that rejected the "antidemocratic" way the PRI did its work, on the other.

Those profoundly democratic ideological and institutional imprints conditioned future development in the parties through two avenues. First, the democratic character of the parties was reinforced through the mechanisms associated with institutional resilience. Actors inside the parties, including elites and activists, adjusted their strategies in order to fit those democratic institutions, resulting in long-term institutional stability and, often, legitimacy. When actors were unable to pursue their interests through existing institutions, they worked to adapt those institutions or created new institutions alongside the old ones. In either case, they still faced strong expectations of democratic character, or at least could not impinge on parties' democratic commitments. The parties' democratic institutions and commitments thus should not be seen as static but as dynamic and subject to powerful reproductive forces.

An additional significant way that the democratic imperative conditioned party development was through its externalization to the broader political-institutional environment. Beginning in the early 1970s, the PAN campaigned on an explicitly prodemocratic platform, and with the arrival of the neopanistas in the early 1980s, it publicly and virulently indicted the character of PRI rule.[23] The PRD's foundation in 1989 introduced a second voice condemning PRI rule and mobilizing voters around the idea of democratization. Meanwhile, the Mexican electorate was growing increasingly weary of the PRI regime. The debt crisis and the government's neoliberal turn undermined the historic bases of PRI legitimacy and weakened the party's corporatist network, while the government's underwhelming response to a

23. The term *neopanista* refers to a "group encompassing politically nonconformist groups and members of the business class who embraced the PAN in the 1980s, particularly after the 1982 bank nationalization and the onset of Mexico's debt crisis" (Wuhs 2001, 136). The neopanistas were responsible for many of the gains the PAN made at the subnational level during the 1980s and early 1990s. See also Mizrahi (1994).

devastating 1985 earthquake alienated Mexico City residents from the party (see Klesner 2005; Greene 2007; Moreno 1998; Magaloni 2006, 1997; and Dominguez and McCann 1996). An increasingly receptive electorate latched on to the democratic proclamations of the opposition parties, triggering a tremendous political realignment.[24] By the late 1980s the traditional left/right axis of competition in Mexico was complemented by a cross-cutting pro-regime/anti-regime axis (Molinar Horcasitas 1991). The opposition parties' efforts lent ever-greater salience to that axis, which by the late 1990s dominated Mexican politics.

The presence of the pro-regime/anti-regime axis raised the costs for reversing political course for the PAN and PRD (that is, for abandoning their prodemocratic commitments), and those costs only increased over time. PAN leaders could campaign as Christian Democrats and Catholic activists, but their programmatic centerpiece was their crusade to democratize Mexico. Likewise, elites in the PRD sought to revive the egalitarian ideals of the Mexican Revolution but could only do so through removal of the PRI from power. By identifying themselves as "democratic" opposition parties, the PAN and PRD limited the appeals they could effectively make to the electorate and constrained their strategic and institutional options. They helped create, and then were "locked into," a competitive space where democracy reigned supreme. And the legacy of PRI rule did not dissipate—the relative stability of the regime and its institutions, particularly through the late 1980s, further reinforced the institutional structures of the opposition.

Foundational Democratic Imprints

Paired with their common indictment of PRI centralism, bureaucracy, and corporatism, the parties' respective understandings of democracy conditioned how leaders initially constructed the institutions that governed party life. Those influences can be seen in how leaders developed their candidate-selection rules (chapter 4), how they built their central party offices (chapter 5), and how they chose to relate to organizations in civil society (chapter 6).

The PAN sought to develop institutions that guaranteed order and provided spaces through which committed individuals could act on their consciences.

---

24. Bruhn (1997, 69–70 and passim) discusses the process of detachment of both selected elites and voters from the PRI during the second half of the 1980s.

For its candidate-selection processes, the party built elaborate representative institutions that were by and large moot: prior to the 1980s, the PAN rarely won elections and their candidates were typically sacrificed to the PAN's mission of building a democratic citizenry. PAN leaders managed a set of conventions from the municipal level up to the federal for all selection processes, with supermajorities required for gubernatorial and presidential candidacies. Implicit in the PAN's emphasis on internal democracy, of course, was a rejection of the dedazo. But the PAN's democracy, although strong on representation, was only narrowly participatory: the party's rigorous membership requirements dramatically limited participation in its nominating conventions. Having a strong membership filter helped assure that membership was meaningful and not instrumental, and also helped to preserve order in the party.

The commitment of party leaders to individuals and their consciences contributed to a strong anti-bureaucratic bias the party held through the 1980s. PAN leaders proudly recalled how their national office's paid staff included only a secretary and a security guard until the 1970s, while the president of the party and the members of the Comité Ejecutivo Nacional (National Executive Committee, CEN) worked without pay.[25] For much of its first fifty years, the PAN operated as a network of regionalized activists, and even when the party began to consolidate a national political presence in the 1980s, its leaders were reticent to invest party resources in the development of a bureaucratic apparatus. Not only was such an apparatus only debatably necessary, it was also distasteful, as it suggested a desire for power in a way that contravened panista notions of what politics was (a devotion, not an ambition).

The panista conception of democracy, particularly its strongly liberal elements, also shaped how the party conceived of its relations with Mexican civil society. The absence of a specific treatment of the corporatist system in its 1939 principles and statutes suggests that Gómez Morin and the other PAN founders, although concerned about the Cardenista reforms, did not anticipate the power that the CTM and the other official confederations would come to hold (PAN 1939). By 1965, when the PAN revised its principles, it was clearer. Article 10 of the 1965 version of the *Principios de doctrina* reaffirmed the right of workers to organize and the right of unions to participate in public life, but it implored them to "abstain from directly participating in political matters, particularly in elections, and to respect the political freedoms and rights of their members" (PAN 1939). Likewise,

25. Interview with former PAN president and Sen. Luis H. Álvarez, March 10, 2000.

agrarian associations (that is, the ejido-based units of the CNC) were advised to "function democratically and be respected in their free decision making, without the State imposing its leaders and without being used as instruments to pressure the rural population and secure its affiliation to political parties" (PAN 1939). The party advanced a model of party-civil society articulation that saw links between them as antidemocratic, per se, and that urged civic organizations to distance themselves from the realm of formal politics. Party leaders believed (and many still believe) that the party had no business working with civic organizations but should invite individual members of those organizations to consider membership in the party.[26] Through the 2000 elections, it regularly employed allegations of corporatism in political attacks against both the PRI and the PRD.

The PRD was exceptional in its fierce statutory articulation of internal democracy. Its documents (especially the 1991 *Declaración de principios y estatutos*, chapter 1, article 2) specify more than fifteen conditions that guide the pursuit and maintenance of party democracy, including (among others) equal rights and responsibilities for all members, decisions by majority rule, recognition and respect for minority rights, proportional representation in the formation of governing bodies of the party, and provisions for the representation of women, youth, indigenous Mexicans, and foreign migrants (PRD 1991). Despite the clarity of its specification of democracy, the PRD's foundation as a fusion of ex-PRI members, militants from the electoral left, and activists from the social left has consistently complicated the party's approach to its maintenance. This is evident in party debates about selection processes and especially the development of its bureaucracy and its linkages with civil society.

In contrast to the PAN, the PRD was born into relative success, given the FDN's performance in the 1988 election, and it adopted selection rules that were participatory (with low requirements for membership) and public (taking the form of conventions—but ones that invited the *pueblo* (the people) to participate, in contrast to the PAN). In its case, the deep commitment to participatory democracy reflected, in addition to elite preferences, a strong desire to distinguish the PRD (and its ex-PRI leaders) from the PRI's authoritarian selection rules and its sectoral quotas.

Many of the PRD's founders shared with PAN elites a deep suspicion of bureaucracy, and with good reason. Some, despite their own bureaucratic experiences, had recently encountered alienation from bureaucratic structures

---

26. Interview with Sen. María Elena Álvarez de Vicencio (PAN), March 2, 2000.

(like Cárdenas, Muñoz Ledo, and the other CD members).[27] The social movement activists who joined the party after 1989 found bureaucracy thoroughly objectionable, and they favored a party-movement structure in lieu of a bureaucratized party. The party leaders who originated in the electoral left, however, had few qualms about strong parties, as they had operated under the principles of democratic centralism in the communist and socialist parties, which thus set the stage for prolonged disagreement in the party about bureaucratic development.

Again like the PAN, the PRD strongly condemned the PRI's corporatist system. In its first statutes, the party included an explicit provision on workers' rights in its elaboration of what democracy meant. In chapter 13 (PRD 1991, articles 81 and 82) of that document, the party pledged to respect the "independence and autonomy" of the social movements and civic organizations that were so crucial to the FDN's 1988 electoral success. Furthermore, "the affiliates of the party and its base committees will reject all forms of corporatist or other political control that impedes, coerces, or limits the freedom of the members of movements and organizations to freely and democratically decide on matters that affect them" (PRD 1991, article 82). However, because of the strong presence of social movements in the FDN and at the party's foundation, and the subsequent formation of a faction representing their interests in the party's leading institutions, the PRD's relationship with civil society was always considerably less clear than its programmatic stance, opening the party to damning critiques of corporatist behavior.

Those founding institutions, shaped by their respective democratic commitments, left crucial imprints on the parties. In selection processes, the PAN was characterized by an emphasis on voluntary individual participation through representative institutions, whereas the PRD sought broad participation. They shared public commitments to the relative autonomy of parties and civic organizations and they were suspicious of strong party central offices, but in the PRD's case, these stances masked more complicated political realities.

Despite forces to the contrary, institutional change occurred in the parties. They adapted their candidate-selection rules, transformed their central party bureaucracies, and reconsidered their stark anticorporatist positions. But party

---

27. Despite their aversion to the PRI's bureaucratic centralism, as late as 2006, former PRI members in the PRD were regularly accused of acting like priístas due to their tendency to build the party's organizational strength.

leaders felt the constraints of the democratic imperative and the weight of pre-existing institutions as they did so, especially as their electoral opportunities improved. Debates about candidate-selection procedures in the PAN centered on the importance of representing of activists' views versus picking nominees with popular appeal, whereas PRD leaders who favored participatory processes faced unruly primaries and colonization by outside interests. In both cases, their abilities to win elections from the PRI hung in the balance. When the parties considered investing their resources in professionalizing their central offices, arguments about the evils of bureaucracy confronted pragmatic goals of effective electioneering. And finally, whereas until 2000, being a "democratic" political party meant divorcing oneself from an organized base in civil society, after 2000, the PAN and PRD began reconsidering the value of stable bases in civil society for party organizations. Each of these highly politicized debates required party leaders to weigh one part of the democratic imperative (party democracy) against the other (regime democracy). The following chapters explain how they made their decisions, and how leaders worked to craft new institutions and adapt existing ones in light of those competing demands.

4

SELECTING LOYALISTS VERSUS PICKING WINNERS

> The PAN practiced democracy internally for fifty years, but never externally. Yes, it
> was possible to live democratically, inside the party.
> —Carlos Castillo Peraza, former PAN president, 2000

PAN and PRD leaders often observed that candidate-selection rules were among the primary battlegrounds in party politics, given their centrality to recruitment, representation, and accountability. Party debates about candidate selection were also key sites for discussing democracy and actualizing the democratic imperative, since leaders regarded these rules as being the basic building blocks of party democracy and evidence of their prodemocratic positions at election time.[1] The PAN always prided itself on the democratic character of its selection processes. Until the 1990s, they were orderly events that incorporated the party faithful and produced candidates who, if elected, would loyally represent panista ideals. Of course, they rarely were elected. In contrast, the PRD from its founding gave priority to inviting the Mexican pueblo into the party in order to determine its nominees for public office. Both sets of opposition party leaders found themselves in a difficult position between 1991 and 2006 as they encountered new opportunities for winning office. They could push for further "opening" of the selection processes, drawing in new members and nominating more electable candidates, or they could maintain "closed" rules that would ensure better representation of party program and would build strong parties. Either option had clear benefits and costs for the leaders themselves, their parties, and their respective democratic commitments.

---

1. This chapter is an adaptation of Wuhs 2006. There are relatively few theoretical analyses of how candidate-selection rules are chosen that endogenize rule adoption in the manner accomplished here. See Meinke et al. (2006) for an exception. Many prior studies of the outcomes of candidate-selection rules (including Gallagher and Marsh 1988 and Lundell 2004) draw associations between patterns of historical development or institutional arrangements and rule outcomes, without inserting rules into the logic of party politics.

The PAN and the PRD both evidence a trend toward more inclusive, open rules, suggesting a concerted effort by party leaders to prioritize vote-getting. However, they have never been freed from the other demands of the democratic imperative. This chapter explains the adaptations that were made to the PAN and PRD selection rules for legislative and executive posts between 1991 and 2006, a period of substantial upheaval in Mexican politics. Mexico's mixed-member electoral system, bicameral Congress, and federal structure offer an array of institutions for consideration; here, I examine how the parties named their candidates for the single-member-district (SMD) seats for the Chamber of Deputies and the Senate, as well as for their gubernatorial and presidential nominees.[2] Party leaders, especially from the PAN, took advantage of Mexico's evolving mixed electoral system to mitigate some of the costs and benefits of opening, enabling them to both loyally represent activists' preferences and win office through popular but "less partisan" candidates.

Leaders' Strategic Choices About Candidate Selection

The PRI's dedazo occupies one end of a continuum of "closed" to "open" candidate-selection rules that also includes the smoke-filled backroom negotiations of the nineteenth-century United States, caucuses, conventions, and closed and open direct primaries. The opening of a selection process normally occurs when the size of the "selectorate" (the set of actors incorporated into selection decisions) is increased, for example, shifting from a closed primary (where only party members can participate) to an open primary (where all voters may participate).[3] Rules can also be opened through a change in the

2. Later in this chapter, I also discuss the party's rules for naming their PR candidates to the legislature. They are not discussed at length due to their stability during the 1990s and through 2006.

3. For some scholars, the move toward more inclusive rules is considered the "democratization" of candidate selection (Pennings and Hazan 2001, 268; Bille 2001). In assessing the level of democracy in candidate-selection processes, Rahat and Hazan (2001) incorporate inclusivity and also a measure for the level of rule decentralization—that is, the extent of functional organizations' (like trade unions) influence over selection outcomes, and which territorial level of a party (national, state, or local) has a voice in selection processes. Although they frame candidate-selection rule changes as "democratizing" or not, I use the terms "opening" and "closing" here for two reasons. The first is analytical: ever-greater inclusivity certainly makes candidate selection more participatory, but as Katz (2001) demonstrates, there may be important negative antidemocratic effects as well—including empowering those who donate to primary campaigns. Second, further use of the term "democratizing" may obscure more than it clarifies in a study

mode of selection itself (for example, shifting from a convention to primary voting, holding participation rules equal). This sort of change can remove effective barriers to participation in the candidate-selection process, including, for example, the costs associated with traveling to conventions. Other party regulations have important mediating effects on how inclusive or open selection processes actually are. Restrictive delegate-selection rules, for example, can transform conventions into plebiscitary rubber-stamping meetings, while certain membership rules can make one closed primary much "more closed" than another.

The particular rules that parties use reflect how party leaders weigh their goals of maximizing the performance of their party on election day, of building the party in the electorate, of representing party doctrine, and of preserving their own power bases. Selection rules can be used to advance these varied goals, but leaders cannot simultaneously maximize their pursuit of *all* goals through any particular rule. Indeed, rules typically present parties with a choice about which goals they should seek to advance. Deciding to open candidate-selection rules to greater popular participation offers party leaders a series of potential benefits, most of which lead to improved election day performance. Although more open selection rules obviously increase the scope of participation in the process itself, they have also been shown to increase voter participation in the general election (Kanthak and Morton 2003; Mayer 1996, 124–27). As selection processes grow more inclusive, the selectorate also begins to resemble the voting public and their preferences begin to approximate those of the median voter. All things being equal, more open selection processes should result in the nomination of more "electable" candidates. They also can have benefits where transparency is concerned: By moving the naming of candidates from smoke-filled backrooms to public ballot boxes, party leaders can gain the confidence of the voting public by demonstrating the democratic character of the selection process.[4]

Although the potential benefits of opening candidate-selection processes seem propitious, there are also substantial potential costs. For party leaders, opening candidate-selection rules threatens their control over one of the most important responsibilities of parties in electoral regimes. Forfeiting

---

such as this one, in which a political environment galvanized by democratic ideals constrains opposition parties.

4. This final set of benefits was a principal motivation behind the adoption of state-administered direct primaries in the United States during the Progressive Era. See Wuhs (2004).

their influence over candidate selection weakens both individual party leaders and the power of the party bureaucracy responsible for in-house nomination decisions. Opening selection processes thus requires party leaders to undermine their own power. The same decision may also alienate party activists, the group typically both empowered by caucuses and conventions and most sympathetic to the preferences of party leaders (Mayer 1996; McCann 1996). Finally, more open selection rules may also have longer-term consequences for parties in government. The flip side of the benefit of electability is the cost of having public officials who are only weakly partisan in their politics and weakly accountable to the party central office. Thus, open selection rules may also threaten parties' and leaders' abilities to structure government and formulate policy.

Leaders of the PAN and PRD weighed those benefits and costs alongside other complications, including weak party loyalties and the often-inferior administration of primary contests.[5] The PRD's most visible leader, Cuauhtémoc Cárdenas, split from the PRI in anticipation of defeat in selection processes, and he was merely the trendsetter; Mexican politicians frequently jumped between parties as new opportunities arose for winning office. Although well-administered primaries can add transparency to the political process, poorly run ones (which was more often the case in Mexico, particularly in the PRD) have deleterious effects on public confidence in political parties and political institutions more generally. Party leaders also expressed concerns about open rules creating a climate of plebiscitarianism, chaotic patterns of participation, and brazen electoralism.[6]

The question of whether or not to open internal party processes to greater popular participation was debated by Mexico's opposition parties throughout the 1990s and continued after Fox's election in 2000. Those discussions revolved around how to select winning candidates without sacrificing the party's identity, an issue so weighty that it often became the most divisive one in the parties. It was particularly important in the PAN, where conflict among

---

5. Interviews with PAN Secretary of Relations Jorge Ocejo, April 6, 2000; PAN Secretary of Electoral Affairs Arturo García Portillo, June 7 2005; PAN Secretary of Organizational Development Alfredo Rivadeneyra Hernández, September 1, 2000; PAN Secretary of Research Salvador Beltrán del Río, February 14, 2000; PRD Director of the Commission for the Refoundation of the Party Jesús Martín del Campo, November 14, 2000; and PRD President of the National Committee of the Electoral Service Mauricio del Valle Morales, July 1, 2004.

6. Interviews with PRD President Amalia García, December 14, 2000; Dep. Petra Santos (PRD), November 27, 2000; Sen. José Fernando Herrero Arandia (PAN), March 13, 2000; and Sen. Luisa María Calderón Hinojosa (PAN), June 15, 2004.

pragmatist and doctrinaire teams within the party had structured internal politics for the better part of its history.

Selecting the Rules in the Democratic Opposition

The PAN's founding selection institutions lasted through the 1970s with minimal revisions. They were tightly controlled, orderly, and relied on closed rules that enabled the party faithful to nominate candidates for office who would dutifully represent the panista program.[7] To pick its nominees for the SMD legislative seats in both chambers, the PAN relied on national-level conventions of party delegates. As the party grew in the late 1980s and 1990s and the likelihood of PAN candidates actually taking office improved, those conventions grew increasingly unwieldy. The March 1997 national electoral convention was particularly chaotic, competitive, and divisive, generating negative publicity for a party that promoted itself as programmatically coherent and politically and ethically sacrosanct. That experience led the party to shift from a national convention to state-level conventions for the SMD Chamber and Senate candidates, although in 2000 it shifted to closed primaries for its Senate candidates.

As was the case for the PAN's legislative nominations, the party historically used a convention closed to nonmembers to select its presidential and gubernatorial candidates. Until the late 1970s, a potential presidential candidate needed 80 percent support at the party's national electoral convention to gain the nomination. After 1976, when no candidate achieved that vote share in repeated rounds and the party failed to nominate a candidate, PAN leaders reduced the required proportion of the convention vote, to two-thirds in 1986 and three-fifths in 1992. However, the process remained closed and included costs (such as traveling to the convention) that prevented all but the most ardent of PAN supporters from participating. In 1999, as the pragmatic faction of the party consolidated its control, the PAN abandoned the national convention for selecting its presidential candidate and adopted a closed primary conducted at the district level. After a contentious debate, party leaders

---

7. The rules for the selection of candidates in the PAN are specified in two party documents, its statutes and its body of regulations (or reglamentos), and executed by the party's National Executive Committee and National Council. Party statutes are debated at the triennial National Assemblies of the party, while the regulations result from the work of the National Council and its subcommittees. See PAN 2002, 1999, 2000, and 2002.

agreed to allow second-tier party members (called *adherentes*) to participate in the contest alongside the full party members (the *activos*).[8] As it happened, Vicente Fox was the only candidate to register, so the primary amounted to a plebiscite on Fox's popularity among PAN militants and supporters.[9]

In 2005, the PAN experimented with a new rule for presidential candidate selection, a regionalized, three-stage primary open to activos and pre-registered adherentes, with a potential fourth-stage runoff. This rule, which leaders of the PAN felt demonstrated the strength of the party's institutions, also enabled PAN candidates to generate momentum similar to that normally associated with the U.S. primary season. As that process unfolded in September and October 2005, Felipe Calderón surprised pundits and his top rival, Interior Minister Santiago Creel, by besting Creel in all three rounds. Calderón's strong performance is owed to his and his family's strong party network throughout the country and his courting of party stalwarts during the primary competition. Creel, in contrast, ran his primary campaign as a prelude to the general election, and he failed to gain adequate support from the activos who composed 80 percent of primary voters.[10]

The party historically selected its gubernatorial candidates in state-level conventions that, like the presidential selection processes, initially required successful candidates to win supermajorities, though statutes later mandated a simple majority (PAN 1999, article 40). In 2001, the PAN shifted to closed primaries, a change of selection rule but not of selectorate, since the process still included only activo members. Since 2000, the PAN has also occasionally experimented with the rules for gubernatorial candidate selection by using, at

8. Notably, this is not a presidential preference primary (that is, to select delegates to a national convention, as in the U.S. case), but a direct primary to select the presidential candidate. The second-tier membership of the adherentes was created in 1997 by then-party president Felipe Calderón Hinojosa to capitalize on the bubble of support the party received after its 1994 campaign. Closed primaries prior to 2000 usually excluded the adherentes, and since 2000, the CEN has alternately included and excluded the adherente members, who greatly outnumber the activos.

9. Fox had mobilized such a strong extra-party campaign organization, Amigos de Fox, that he effectively sidelined any potential opponents from throwing their hats in the ring.

10. Consistent with prior rules, the 2005 presidential candidate-selection process faced high expectations of a democratic character. The PAN was the only party with an effectively competitive selection process, which lent additional credence to the party's democratic claims. See Kiavelo (2005) and Omaña del Castillo (2005). Interview with PAN Secretary of Elections Arturo García Portillo, April 23, 2007.

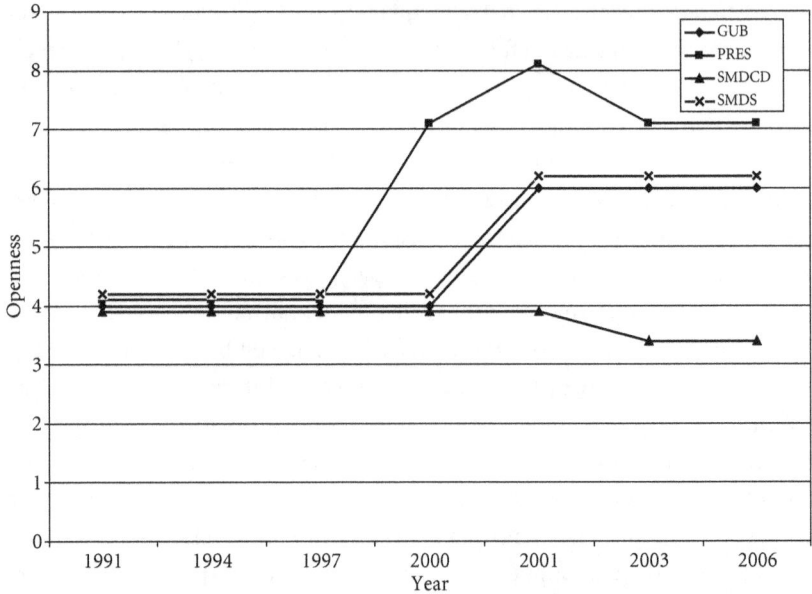

Fig. 8   Selection rules in the PAN. Rules are ranked on an eight-point scale: (1) individual imposition, (2) national elite decision making, (3) local elite decision making, (4) closed convention with high membership threshold, (5) closed convention with low membership threshold, (6) closed primary with high membership threshold, (7) closed primary with low membership threshold, and (8) open primary. Some values have been slightly adjusted to make all trends visible. PRES and GUB refer to presidential and gubernatorial selection rules; SMDS and SMDCD refer to the single-member district seats in the Senate and the Chamber of Deputies. I include 2001 data, an off-election year, because both parties made important changes to their rules that year. Those rules were subsequently altered for the 2003 contest. Data are drawn from party documents, elite interviews with party members, secondary sources, and expert interviews.

the CEN's discretion, open primaries, closed primaries, and diagnostic public opinion surveys to gauge pre-candidates' respective electabilities.[11]

A demonstrable trend toward opening has been evident in the PAN, particularly in executive positions (fig. 8). At the same time, PAN leaders continued to employ state-level conventions for their nominations for the three hundred

11. In the CEN after 2000, additional efforts were made to add flexibility to the PAN's selection rules, including a failed attempt to offer the party leadership three options for nominating senators, governors, and mayors: open primaries, closed primaries that included the adherentes, and primaries open to only activos. Interview with PAN Adjunct Secretary General Arturo García Portillo, June 9, 2004.

SMD seats in the Chamber of Deputies. In a sense, those conventions actually grew more selective. Until the 1990s, PAN conventions were open to any panista who could travel to the convention, but by 2003, delegate selection in the PAN had become increasingly complicated and bureaucratized, requiring delegates to demonstrate municipal party support and gain the approval of their municipal party committees. This drove down the number of delegates attending conventions, but it may well have had an additional political effect of strengthening the presence of doctrinaire voices at these conventions (PAN 2000).

In its short history, PRD leaders have significantly altered most of the party's selection rules, so that these increasingly emphasize the participatory nature of the institutions and the party itself.[12] The party's legislative candidates for the 1991 midterm elections were selected at a national convention of party members, but following the party's poor showing, party leaders under Cuauhtémoc Cárdenas chose to open processes of candidate selection. Opening in this case did not change who participated, but how they participated, since the PRD maintained very lax membership rules throughout its first decade. For the rest of the 1990s, the PRD deployed rules structured around direct, universal, and secret voting by members (that is, closed primaries) for the SMD seats in both chambers of the Congress. Likewise, in anticipation of the 1994 presidential race, the party opted for a closed primary to select its candidate, a rule it employed again for the 2000 election and for its gubernatorial candidates (PRD 2002, articles 47–55).[13]

Since the election of Fox, the party has taken new steps to remove the few remaining barriers to participation in its selection contests. In the 1990s, the PRD allowed only registered members of the party to participate in selection processes, but at a 2001 national congress, the PRD adopted a rule that empowered the party's National Executive Committee to choose between a closed or an open primary for *all* posts except the PR candidacies (discussed below). That rule was further revised in 2004, when selection processes for all SMD legislative posts as well as gubernatorial and presidential selection contests were opened to anyone with a voter credential (then termed the *voto abierto a la*

---

12. In the PRD, the National Council, the party's more than two-hundred-member deliberative body, is responsible for elaborating the specific regulations that govern candidate-selection processes. The party's statutes, which articulate the general framework for candidate selection, are revised in triennial meetings of the National Congress. See PRD (1991, 2002).

13. In both 1994 and 2000, Cárdenas was the foregone conclusion of whatever selection process was utilized for picking the PRD's presidential candidate. Clearly, the gubernatorial candidates were selected in statewide primaries.

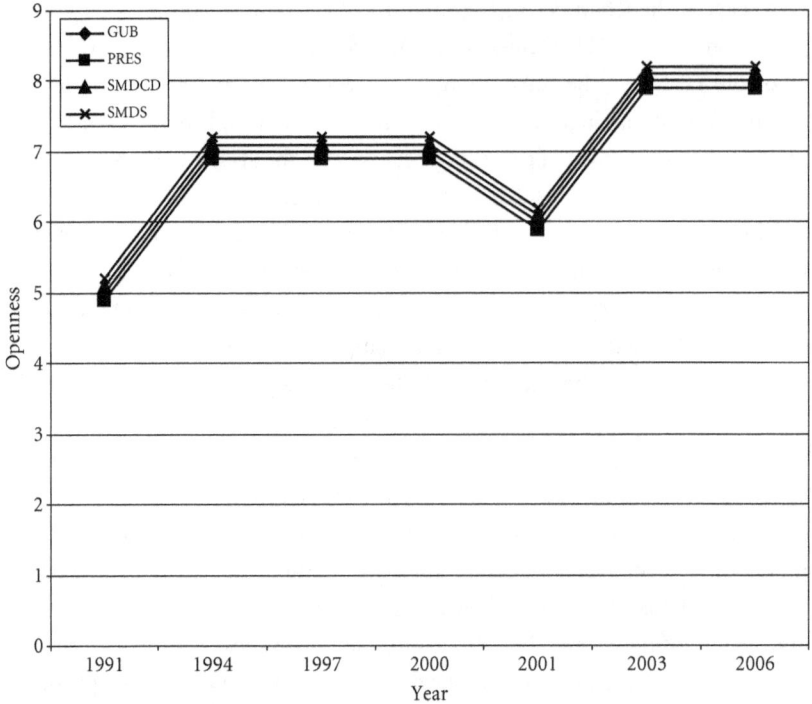

Fig. 9   Selection rules in the PRD. Rules are ranked on the following eight-point scale: (1) individual imposition, (2) national elite decision making, (3) local elite decision making, (4) closed convention with high membership threshold, (5) closed convention with low membership threshold, (6) closed primary with high membership threshold, (7) closed primary with low membership threshold, and (8) open primary. Some values have been slightly adjusted to make all trends visible. PRES and GUB refer to presidential and guber-natorial selection rules; SMDS and SMDCD refer to the single-member district seats in the Senate and the Chamber of Deputies. I include 2001 data despite its not having been an election year because of important changes in both parties' rules during 2001 that were changed by the 2003 contest. Data are drawn from party documents, elite interviews with party members, secondary sources, and expert interviews.

ciudadanía). Like the PAN, the PRD also increasingly turned to alternative modes of candidate selection in the interest of picking "electable" candidates. Under party president Rosario Robles (2000–2003), party leaders made frequent use of public opinion polls to measure the popular support of its pre-candidates. Although selection decisions were not based on those polls, party leaders used them to encourage some pre-candidates to seek the party's nomination (and to discourage others).[14]

14. Interview with PRD leader Silvia Gómez Tagle, June 24, 2004.

The PRD's process of opening has been much more dramatic than the PAN's (fig. 9). The openness of PRD processes is particularly noteworthy given its membership rules. Unlike the PAN, the PRD allowed same-day registration of members and participation in internal decision making (including candidate selection). Consequently, closed primaries in the PRD were not very closed. The open nature of PRD membership also created spaces for opportunistic politicians to mobilize their supporters to gain nominations, especially in the district-level primaries, sometimes resulting in the colonization of PRD local offices by outsiders (usually priístas). After 2000, the PRD amended its membership rules and required a six-month waiting period for participation in internal elections.[15] However, that reform was quickly followed by the decision to open most party selection processes to any Mexican voter (undermining any effect that the higher membership requirements might have had).[16] The PRD retained its open rules through the 2006 process, though there was no competitive contest for its 2006 presidential candidacy because of the tremendous popularity of Andrés Manuel López Obrador.

Explaining Selection Rule Changes

A new structure of political opportunities in the 1990s triggered transformations in selection rules by party leaders. As electoral administration became more impartial and the electoral system was modified to dramatically increase the representation of minority parties (with 40 percent of Chamber seats and 50 percent of Senate seats determined by some form of proportional or minority representation), leaders saw new chances to improve their parties' representation in government. They often turned to more open selection rules to capitalize on the benefits they often offered. However, leaders' decisions were complicated, since they had to bear in mind the potential costs of open rules as well as pursue other party goals. Furthermore, leaders were not usually free to impose the rules of their choosing on the party: rank-and-file members, rival leaders, and other veto players also influenced the selection rules the parties adopted.

---

15. This regulation is similar to the PAN's membership requirement. See PRD 2002, chapter 2, article 5.

16. Because of the significance of the 2001 revision to PRD selection processes discussed above, it has been incorporated into figure 9.

There was a period of stability in the PAN's selection rules between 1991 and 1999, a period of greater dynamism between 1999 and 2003, and stability after 2003 (fig. 8). In the first period, there are important changes in selection processes but no substantial changes in opening or closing the rules. If party leaders had favored more open selection rules, they could have made that change without fear of sacrificing their positions of power, since the party's indirect leadership-selection rules protected leaders from quick punishment by angry activists. Yet they did not. In part, this stability reflects the ideological position of the PAN's leadership bodies during much of the 1990s. The party's new leaders, including its president from 1989 to 1996, Luis H. Álvarez, were entrepreneurial pragmatists, but the CEN and National Council were still in the hands of the founding families of the PAN (Wuhs 2001). Those bodies were quite wary of allowing individuals who were not "good panistas" to run on the party ticket, and they also sought to reward individuals from their own ranks who had served the party during its decades as the "loyal opposition."[17] PAN leaders and legislators frequently commented on longtime panistas' *"ya me toca"* ("it's my turn") mentality that surrounded candidate-selection processes in the 1990s.

Toward the end of that decade, the pragmatic forces had increased their representation in the CEN and National Council of the party while retaining the party presidency. The year 1999 marked a transition from the more conservative leadership of Felipe Calderón Hinojosa to that of Luis Felipe Bravo Mena, the PAN's president through 2005. Although the formal mechanisms for selecting party leaders remained stable, the preferences of elected leaders shifted in the late 1990s from the right toward the political center. Given their stable position in the leadership, party pragmatists were anxious to reap the electoral benefits of open rules. They focused on the presidential and gubernatorial rules, a reflection of two strategic goals of the party leaders during the 1990s. First, they hoped to "own" Mexico's democratic transition by defeating the PRI presidential candidate in 2000.[18] Second, they continued to follow the "federalist" strategy of centripetal organizational growth, which the party had developed after its success in the 1989 gubernatorial election in Baja California, by nominating electable candidates for those posts after 2000 (Lujambio 2001). Still, party leaders did not ignore more doctrinaire

17. Interview with Sen. José Fernando Herrero Arandia (PAN), March 13, 2000.
18. The strong showing of PAN candidate Diego Fernández de Cevallos in the 1994 presidential election (in part based on his performance in Mexico's first-ever televised presidential debate) let PAN leaders grasp the possibility that even a conservative panista had the potential to oust the PRI from the presidential palace.

members of the National Council as well as PAN activists: they took care to preserve the SMD Chamber candidacies for them and forestalled the opening of the SMD Senate slots until after 2000.

After that year, and particularly after the disappointing midterm elections of 2003, its leaders reevaluated the costs and benefits of opening, recognizing the potential of selection processes to draw new constituents into the party and pro-duce better candidates.[19] Realizing that PAN militants might be resistant to losing their privileged input, leaders who supported a political opening attempted to broker an exchange with its activist base at the party's National Assembly in 2001. In return for more open *candidate*-selection processes, militants were offered continued privilege in *leadership*-selection decisions. The assembly members soundly rejected the proposal—effectively reiterating their prioritization of party democracy and programmatic representation over electoral gain. As a result, since 2003 the PAN's rules have not changed in the selectorate, though its three-stage presidential primary in 2005 was an important adaptation in the rule itself.

The PRD's rules can be broken into three periods: one of increasing openness in the early 1990s, a second period of stability throughout much of the 1990s, and a third of radical opening after the 2000 election (fig. 9). The first shift, from using a national electoral convention to a system of closed primaries for SMD leg-islative and executive posts, came on the heels of the 1991 midterm elections, in which the PRI managed to hem in the expansion of Cárdenas's party. Cárdenas effectively controlled the party's development during this early period—not yet counterbalanced in party politics by the factions that emerged in the mid-1990s (Bruhn 1997; Greene 2002; Wuhs 2002). He recognized that the PRI's locally heavy repression of PRD militants closed the local arena off for his party in many parts of the country in the early 1990s. Using his charismatic authority and power as the party's president, he pushed through a set of rule changes despite protests from his main rival at the time, Porfirio Muñoz Ledo, who feared that the shift to closed primaries would undermine institutional life in the party. Despite his support among perredistas from the electoral left, Muñoz Ledo could not muster a veto of Cárdenas's reforms.[20] Supporters of the shift to primaries believed that moving from conventions to ballot boxes would broaden the party's support

19. Interviews with PAN Secretary of Organizational Development Alfredo Rivadeneyra Hernández, September 1, 2000, and PAN Adjunct Secretary General Arturo García Portillo, June 9, 2004.

20. Interview with PRD President Amalia García, December 14, 2000. At the time of that reform, 1993, no faction or rival leader was able to counterbalance Cárdenas in party politics, particularly when the voting behavior of PRD activists was concerned.

base by attracting prodemocratic voters who indicted the PRI's authoritarian tactics. Such a step would thus take better advantage of a perceived ideological convergence between the party and Mexican voters.[21]

From that initial opening through the 2000 election, the PRD's rules were stable, and because of lax membership requirements, its closed primaries for executive and SMD legislative posts were fairly open. That stability held despite the 1995 introduction of the *planilla* system, a new institutional mechanism for selecting the party's national leadership based on a list-based vote of party members resembling proportional representation.[22] The introduction of the planilla system created new veto players by making leaders directly accountable to party members, and so it had the potential to change the behavior of those elected party officials. That no significant changes occurred or were even proposed attests to the adaptation of both leaders and members to the primary system and the stickiness of those institutions.

Events following the party's disappointing performance in 2000 did trigger revisions, though. The first years of the Fox Administration were marked by repeated corruption scandals in the PRD, incidents that increased PRD leaders' concerns about the party's public image. Although the party initially ratcheted up its membership requirements after 2000 in the hopes of fortifying its base, party leaders quickly proceeded to open all candidate-selection processes (save the PR legislative seats) to all Mexican voters. This move aimed to build the electorate's confidence in the party and position it as the voice of the pueblo, something that was increasingly important since under Fox, the party was forced to defend its center-left territory from the PRI. That radical opening was likely to exact costs on the party, but the electoral demands necessitated that decision, according to party leaders. One party elite acknowledged, for example, that open selection rules could weaken party identity, but that in areas of the country where the party was a marginal presence, they were willing to take that chance.[23]

Although trends in the *individual* party data are interesting, greater insight into the forces behind changes in the candidate-selection rules can be gained

<hr/>

21. It is not clear whether such a convergence existed, especially as 2000 approached. Most studies of partisan and citizen ideological positions suggest that the PRD may share common ground with the Mexican electorate regarding privatization (in 2000, energy sector privatization), but not on many of the other issues that divide the electorate. See Dominguez and Lawson (2005) and Dominguez and McCann (1996).

22. The planilla system also created an institutional anchor for the corrientes of the PRD. Its influence is elaborated upon in subsequent chapters.

23. Interview with Del Valle Morales, July 1, 2004.

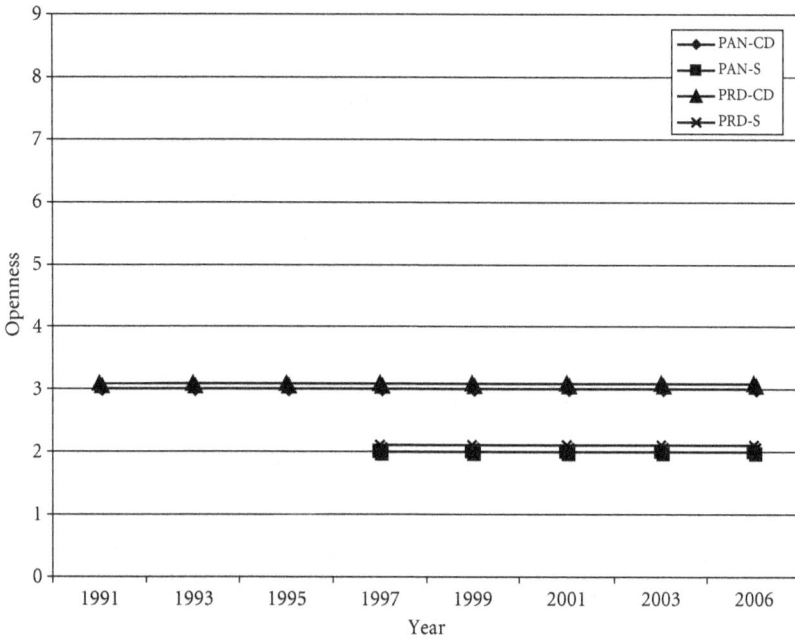

Fig. 10   PR legislative selection rules in the PAN and PRD. Rules are ranked on the following eight-point scale: (1) individual imposition, (2) national elite decision making, (3) local elite decision making, (4) closed convention with high membership threshold, (5) closed convention with low membership threshold, (6) closed primary with high membership threshold, (7) closed primary with low membership threshold, and (8) open primary. Some values have been slightly adjusted to make all trends visible. The rules for PR seats in the Senate are marked "–s," while those in the Chamber of Deputies are marked "–cd." I include 2001 data despite its not having been an election year because of important changes in both parties' rules during 2001 that were changed by the 2003 contest. Data are drawn from party documents, elite interviews with party members, secondary sources, and expert interviews.

by pooling the experiences of the two parties across the different rules. First, a very clear tendency is for party leaders to retain their control over the selection rules for the proportional-representation seats in both chambers (two hundred in the Chamber of Deputies, in the Senate) (fig. 10). Given the nature of proportional representation systems (particularly the closed lists of Mexican PR), this is not surprising. These were mechanisms through which party leaders installed allies in the legislature and rewarded good partisans for their loyalty. Because these candidates were not subject to a candidate-centered popular vote, party leaders did not confront the same sort of trade-off as in the case of the other legislative and executive rules.

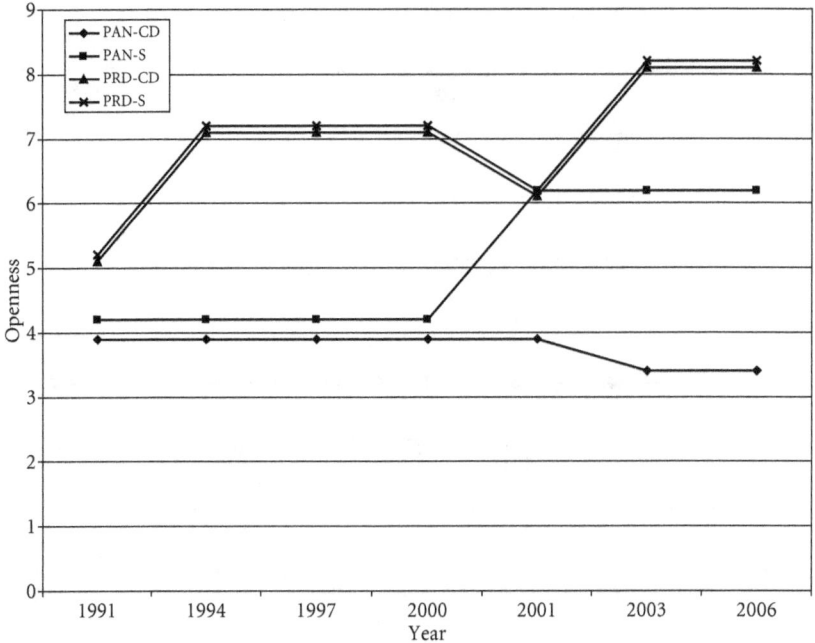

Fig. 11   SMD Legislative selection rules in the PAN and PRD. Rules are ranked on the following eight-point scale: (1) individual imposition, (2) national elite decision making,
(3) local elite decision making, (4) closed convention with high membership threshold,
(5) closed convention with low membership threshold, (6) closed primary with high
membership threshold, (7) closed primary with low membership threshold, and (8)
open primary. Some values have been slightly adjusted to make all trends visible. Senate
rules are marked "–s," while Chamber of Deputies rules are marked "–CD." I include
2001 data despite its not having been an election year because of important changes in
both parties' rules during 2001 that were changed by the 2003 contest. Data are drawn
from party documents, elite interviews with party members, secondary sources, and
expert interviews.

Leaders did face trade-offs where the SMD legislative posts were concerned
(fig. 11). Overall, the trend was toward more open selection rules. The only
counterevidence was offered by the PAN's Chamber of Deputies candidacies,
which were subject to the same rule in 2006 that they were in the late 1970s but
now followed more stringent delegate-selection processes. The trend suggests
that indeed party leaders were increasingly electoralist, seeking those payoffs
and willing to risk the negative side effects of opening. The outlier, the PAN's
SMD deputies rule, on the other hand, reflected some party leaders' desires to
retain spaces for loyal activists as well as activists' unwillingness to cede their
power to the voting public. In one sense, the costs of keeping that rule closed

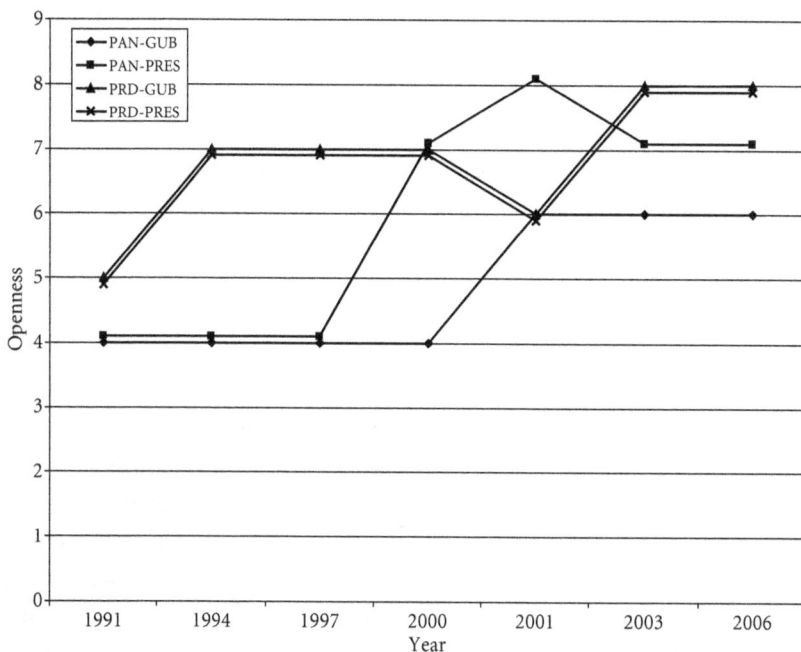

Fig. 12   Executive selection rules in the PAN and PRD. Rules are ranked on the following eight-point scale: (1) individual imposition, (2) national elite decision making, (3) local elite decision making, (4) closed convention with high membership threshold, (5) closed convention with low membership threshold, (6) closed primary with high membership threshold, (7) closed primary with low membership threshold, and (8) open primary. Some values have been slightly adjusted to make all trends visible. PRES and GUB refer to presidential and gubernatorial selection rules. I include 2001 data despite its not having been an election year because of important changes in both parties' rules during 2001 that were changed by the 2003 contest. Data are drawn from party documents, elite interviews with party members, secondary sources, and expert interviews.

were limited for party leaders since the opposition parties had scant chances of winning one of the majority seats. In 1991, only ten of the PAN's eighty-nine Chamber seats were in the majority districts, whereas none of the PRD's forty-one seats were. By 1994, the overall seat counts for both parties had increased (119 for the PAN and seventy-one for the PRD), but the PAN won only eighteen of those in single-member districts and the PRD only five. Legislative representation for the PAN and PRD depends on the PR seats, which were at the behest of national party leaders.

The parties' executive-selection rules shifted the most dramatically and showed the strongest overall trend (fig. 12). Leaders targeted these positions as mechanisms for party growth. The consistency of those reforms suggests that as party leaders assessed competing goals, they came to believe that winning gubernatorial posts and the Mexican presidency would be crucial to building the party's presence in the electorate, but running popular candidates for those posts did not directly threaten organizational goals or their own power base. Whether that calculation held true was another question. Fox may have poked a hole in that logic, given that tension between him and the party bureaucracy ran high during his administration.

Democratic Selection and the Logic of Institutional Change

In an increasingly open electoral environment, Mexican party leaders rede-signed the rules that their parties employed to select candidates. As they con-templated the decision to open or to close those selection rules, they weighed their desire to increase their share of seats in government and strengthen the party in the electorate against their inclination to protect their own influence and the potential backlash of activists deprived of their voice in selection processes. Party leaders favored opening the rules for executive candidacies, maintaining very tight control over PR nominations, and cautiously opening the SMD legislative candidacies. In the PAN, leaders juggled a complicated and evolving set of internal interests. As the party leadership grew more pragmatic and centrist over the 1990s, party leaders had less to fear from opening. Still, they were tentative in their approach. They maintained their own influence over PR nominations and simultaneously placated conservative activists by allowing them to retain their legislative-nomination powers, all the while advocating broader opening in executive contests where they could grow the party without serious risk. Although those PAN leaders were fairly insulated from rank-and-file members of the party, decisions in the PAN were subject to inter-elite negotiation. The leaders of the PRD were more vulnerable to punish-ment from rank-and-file members after 1995, but that new accountability did little to affect the party's selection rules. That party's rules were altered after particular electoral outcomes, specifically after a poor performance in 1991 and a third defeat for Cárdenas and the party in 2000. PRD leaders shaped and reshaped their selection rules because of changes in the competitive space the party occupied in the Mexican party system.

Party leaders were proponents of candidate-selection rule changes, but they were often constrained in their actions by other actors in the party. Rank-and-file members were indeed influential: they stymied one effort at opening in the PAN. But they were not the only actors checking leaders' influence. Rival leaders, elected officials from the parties, and opposing factions were also involved in efforts at institutional change, sometimes pushing rule reforms through (as in the PAN's late 1990s opening) but sometimes failing in their efforts to block them (in the PRD's early 1990s shift to primaries). One risk of opening was that it would produce candidates party leaders might object to, and it appeared party leaders considered that possibility. In the PAN, doctrinaire actors forestalled the opening of candidate-selection rules; it was not until pragmatists gained greater representation in the National Council and the CEN *and* controlled the party presidency that the rules were opened. But the clearest finding is that a party's competitive environment shapes how party leaders weigh the various costs and benefits of opening selection processes to greater popular participation, confirming Joy Langston's (2001) analysis of the PRI.

The comparative nature of this analysis highlighted another crucial factor in explaining how party leaders make their decisions about candidate selection. The trade-off used to frame this analysis presumes that those leaders are confronted with the choice of giving priority to some party goals and not to others. Mexico's mixed electoral system allowed party leaders to achieve opposing goals simultaneously by adopting heterogeneous selection mechanisms for different candidate posts. To serve party electoral goals (and achieve "democratic" ends), they could open the field for executive contests and benefit from statewide and nationwide primary competition. They could also preserve the unity of partisan elites, and help build cohesive parties that might aid democratic consolidation, through the distribution of PR seats among key party leaders and factions. Preserving control of those candidacies also buttressed the power of the party leaders themselves. And, most evident in the PAN, party leaders placated activists, who otherwise might oppose open rules and elite decision making, by using processes that were closed to the party rank and file (reinforcing the party's traditional understanding of democracy).

5

PARTISAN MYSTICS VERSUS POLITICAL PROFESSIONALS

> In reality, we need a well-structured party . . . that isn't subject to comings and
> goings, is effective, and is modern. This leadership is making an effort toward
> institutionalization.
> —PRD President Amalia García, 2000

The democratic imperative required the PAN and the PRD to simultaneously maintain democratic systems within their organizations *and* effectively campaign and win elections in the broader political arena. But as Mexican politics grew increasingly competitive and media- and technology-centered, party leaders recognized that the desire to win elections placed certain demands on their parties and institutions. Their central party offices, based in Mexico City, needed to prepare for and participate in campaigns, devise policies and strategies for elected officials, and build the party organization itself—both in Mexico City and throughout the country. Performing those tasks mandated the development of stronger, more professionalized party institutions. But the notion of such a party organization, strongly associated with the bureaucratically mammoth PRI, was anathema to opposition party leaders. Many (but, importantly, not all) PAN and PRD leaders openly disdained the ideas and practices associated with the bureaucratization of party life.

Yet, over the 1990s and since 2000, leaders of both the PAN and PRD focused on professionalizing the work of the central party offices and strengthening their parties' bureaucratic structures. In this chapter, I detail how party leaders negotiated the tensions surrounding party building through examinations of transformations in the central party office and the construction of regional party structures. Across those arenas, party leaders cautiously considered and fiercely debated the electoral gains that organizational development promised and the losses to activist participation and party democracy it was thought to entail. In the end, leaders of both parties opted to bureaucratize and professionalize their parties, though the timing and extent of those processes was powerfully conditioned by internal party politics. As becomes clear, some of the debates about organizational and institutional change are more profound in the PRD than in the PAN, confirming the opinions of many PAN leaders that their party is characterized by greater internal unity than the PRD. Still, PAN leaders were far from unanimous about many of the changes examined here, a fact that led to disaffection, alienation, and even a formal split in the party.

Party Leaders and the Politics of Bureaucratic Development

Party leaders face complicated calculations as they contemplate building their parties' bureaucratic structures. They must first weigh the relative importance of the varied tasks their organization performs, since different roles can mandate different types of organization. A party that favors representing organized interests from civil society will be structurally dissimilar from a protest party, and both would differ from an elitist electoral vehicle.[1] Leaders must also respond to the demands of their political environments as they consider the organization of their parties. For example, European and North American party leaders encountered important societal transformations over the course of the twentieth century that encouraged them to build more professionalized organizations and develop campaigning expertise and that discouraged mass mobilization and perhaps even constituent service (Aldrich 1995; Kirchheimer 1966; Scarrow 1996; Ware 1996, 11).[2] In order to ensure that their parties'

---

1. Downs (1957) and Schlesinger (1994) treat parties as teams of office-seeking individuals, as does Aldrich (1995), though he acknowledges an important role for party leaders who control resources. Kay Lawson (1980, 3) describes parties as "agencies for forging links between citizens and policymakers." Sartori (1976) also focuses on elections but adds more emphasis on the representation of citizen interests and parties' role in "channeling the public will" after assuming office. "Bureaucracy," a term often used in this chapter, is most associated with discussions of mass parties, which typically featured more developed bureaucratic structures than cadre-based conservative parties, charismatic parties, or green parties. However, even charismatic parties, for example, need administrators to manage leaders' relations with their followers (Kitschelt 1999, 47; Panebianco 1988).

2. Whether a result of broad-based value shifts, the "unfreezing" of affiliations based on cleavage structures, or the rise of television, in Western Europe and North America, the era from the 1960s to the present has been associated with de- and re-alignment of voters and transitions from mass parties and toward "catch-all" parties or even "candidate-service" organizations. See Inglehart (1977), Lipset and Rokkan (1967), Flanagan and Dalton (1990), Dalton, Flanagan, and Beck (1984), Mair (1990), Crotty (1968), and Wattenberg (1986). Adaptations in campaigning, and particularly the role of parties in campaigning, mirrored these broader transformations in

electoral fortunes improved, leaders were charged with fitting their parties' operations to the increasingly media- and technology-driven environment of modern electioneering, often at the cost of tasks their organizations once also performed.

Mexican opposition leaders confronted those same societal and political challenges, but they had substantially less time to adapt their organizations. Technology access and media savvy arrived late to Mexico, only penetrating Mexican politics in the 1990s. For example, the country experienced its first-ever televised presidential debate during the 1994 campaign. Although their counterparts in the advanced industrialized countries restructured their parties over the course of the postwar era, PAN and PRD leaders faced compressed timeframes—a decade or less. They also encountered other complications. The PRI's political hegemony had stunted the early organizational development of the opposition by making opposition politics unappealing for candidates (who were unlikely to win), for activists (who might attract unwanted negative attention from the PRI regime) and even for voters (whose support of the opposition was potentially punished by a reduction in public subsidies). As a result, even fifty years after its foundation, the PAN maintained a loosely organized national committee, had a sparse regional presence, and ran ineffective campaigns, whereas the left was underground (prior to its legalization in 1977), highly factionalized (in the 1980s), or tasked with building a new party from scratch in an incredibly hostile environment (after 1989). To make things even trickier, Mexico's weak independent media and the PRI's historic reliance on patronage and clientelism rather than policy and program, further undercut the opposition's party-building efforts.[3]

Building the Central Party Office

As the political arena opened to increased levels of competition after the 1988 election, many PAN and PRD leaders recognized that their central offices were ill-equipped to attract new members and voters and to coordinate efforts to

---

party organization. See Farrell and Webb (2000, esp. 103–8) for an overview of the trajectory of campaign techniques and styles in western democracies.

3. See Chappell Lawson (2002, 2000) on the media's development and independence during the transition.

oust the PRI from power.[4] Other leaders were wary of the development of professional party bureaucracies. Having read the works of Robert Michels (1962)
and Max Weber (1978) and drawing on their own observations of the PRI, they
concluded that bureaucratic parties were antidemocratic. The trade-off for
leaders was clear: they could bureaucratize and professionalize in the hopes
of gaining power, while risking being likened to the PRI and thus alienating
activists and members, or they could remain an activist- or volunteer-driven
organization and likely disappoint on election day. These issues entailed very
difficult decisions for party leaders, including having to choose between inviting
professionals to direct party affairs or continuing to rely on activists and party
"mystique."[5] Turning away from activists meant that the PAN might abandon its
famoso voluntariado (celebrated volunteers) and the PRD might alienate its mass
base, actions that would strike at each party's democratic conception of self.[6]
But professionalization carried with it tremendous potential electoral benefits,
on one hand, and gains in administrative efficiency, on the other.[7]

4. Appendix 3 details the internal structure of both parties. At first glance, the PAN and
PRD appear to be strikingly similar organizations. They even seem quite similar to the PRI.
A constellation of institutions dictated by Mexican electoral law govern all three: a National
Executive Committee, headed by the party president and based in Mexico City, that manages day-
to-day party life; a National Council of approximately two hundred members who meet regularly
to discuss party strategy, weigh in on candidate-selection processes, and other matters; and a
National Convention or Assembly, meeting at least triennially, which is charged with revising basic
party documents, constructing the party platform, and nominating certain kinds of candidates.
The superficial uniformity in bureaucratic structures masks not only crucial and profound
differences in party organization but also the structures of decision-making in the parties as they
evolved over time.

5. In both parties (but especially the PAN), the term *misticismo* (mystique) is employed in
conversations about party foundation and party history, particularly in reference to periods of
political marginalization. Interview with Sub-Coordinator of the PRD National Council Gabriel
Santos Villareal, July 17, 2000, and Sen. José Fernando Herrero Arandia (PAN), March 13, 2000.

6. Volunteers were seen as crucial in the PAN not just as campaign soldiers but also as integral
participants in local party building. Interview with Sen. María Elena Álvarez de Vicencio (PAN),
March 2, 2000.

7. As Panebianco (1988, chapter 12) notes, "bureaucracy" and "professional" are conceptually
messy terms deployed with minimal care by both scholars and practitioners. Unsurprisingly,
Mexican party leaders had varied conceptions of what professionalization meant. However, many
agreed that it involved, at a minimum, systematization of information, foundation of archival
and investigative units, creation of a permanent and skilled party staff, and the parties' increased
use of consultants or similar professionals. Interview with PRD Secretary of Human Rights María
Rosa Márquez Cabrera, July 18, 2000. One member of the PAN associated professionalization with
increasing reliance on incentive structures, systematic processing, administration, and hierarchy.
Interview with PAN General Director of Administration and Finance Eduardo Seldner Ávila, June
8, 2004.

The PAN began with a narrow social base in the 1930s and remained essentially a cadre party through the 1980s. Its leaders remembered the party, even up through the 1988 election, as a network of committed volunteers and activists who rarely received salaries and often paid party expenses out of their own pockets. Many members of the national leadership recalled experiences similar to this one, described by PAN Dep. Gustavo Vicencio: "Between 1985 and 1988, when I was the budget officer of the party, we were just three paid staff in the CEN: myself, the executive secretary, and the director of Political Promotion of Women. Without public financing, the presidents of the party [at the national and state levels] kept their day jobs and dedicated their free time to the party."[8] After the watershed election of 1988, though, the opportunity structure of the PAN was transformed: party leaders had increased access to subnational office, a larger legislative voting bloc, and relatively hopeful prospects for the 1994 presidential contest. The PAN also gained access to public financing for the first time (discussed in detail below), a crucial development for the impoverished local party offices.[9] Party leaders responded to those opportunities with administrative reforms designed to enable the party to take advantage of the public groundswell of panista support. In the federal elections of 1994, the PAN's vote share was about ten million, up from four million in the 1991 midterm elections. "Imagine you have a four-liter vase, ten liters of water is poured. . . . You have to change the vase," remarked former PAN President Carlos Castillo Peraza.[10]

The first reform was the *Redimensionamiento* (redesigning) program led by Castillo Peraza in the mid-1990s. The motivation was to facilitate communication and coordination among related subunits of the PAN to increase organizational effectiveness and efficiency. The primary means to those ends was the introduction of a new set of principal-agent relationships that transferred oversight authority from the party president and secretary general to the next administrative tier down (the secretariats for relations, for elections, and their peers).[11] Castillo Peraza, the self-proclaimed "idea man" behind the reform

---

8. Interview with Dep. Gustavo Arturo Vicencio Acevedo (PAN), March 24, 2000.

9. Most local party offices were funded through the party members' dues, but the party had very few members during this period, even in its strongest states. Some of the public funds were directed to supporting state and local party organizations for one year, while they sought out additional resources. Interview with Sen. Luis Mejía Guzmán (PAN), March 8, 2000.

10. Interview with former PAN President Carlos Castillo Peraza, March 1, 2000.

11. New bureaucracies were also established as part of the effort. Those included the Secretary of Government Activity, the Department of Electoral Affairs, the Department of Membership Registry, and the National Coordinator of Local Deputies.

process, believed these reforms could rebuild the party into an organization that would draw in new interests, incorporating them into the fabric of the party and facilitating synergy across arenas of party life. This would enable the PAN to develop a more powerful and enduring political presence.[12] Under Castillo Peraza's leadership, the PAN encountered great success: by the end of his term (1996), the party claimed to govern 30 percent of Mexico's population. The Redimensionamiento program, according to many party leaders, can be credited for achieving some of that. His successor in the PAN presidency, Felipe Calderón Hinojosa (1996–99), carried the reform process to the state level with some success, though Calderón's attention was distracted by the pressing matters of the 1997 federal elections and the first direct election of Mexico City's mayor. Related reforms were also extended to the legislative arena, where the party's delegation received further training, more extensive research support, and improved access to technology.

Alongside the organizational reforms of Redimensionamiento, party leaders undertook an ambitious, multifaceted professionalization effort. Although its origin can be found in key events of the late 1980s (discussed below), the professionalization of the PAN's central party office began in force in 1996 through the CEN's Committee for Personnel Development. Its goal was to promote a "culture of quality" in the CEN. Among its first steps was the construction of a civil service in the party (*servicio civil de carrera*). The party's administration was separated into two levels: short-term appointments (*puestos de término*) and career appointments (*puestos de carrera*).[13] The first category included political appointees to the party's administrative apparatus (such as the party president and CEN members). The remaining PAN administrative staffers (from the directorate level down the hierarchy) were to be permanent employees, effectively civil servants to the party. The goal of this aspect of party professionalization, according to National Director of Administration Dora Luz Molina, was to "build an efficient bureaucracy, not necessarily a *party* bureaucracy," one that would perform with high levels of professionalism and sophistication the tasks associated with party organization and campaigning.[14]

12. Interview with Sen. Ricardo García Cervantes (PAN), April 4, 2000.
13. Interview with PAN Adjunct Secretary General Cecilia Romero Castillo, March 15, 2000.
14. Interview with PAN National Director of Administration Dora Luz Molina, July 31, 2000. One potential debate around this professionalization is whether is relates to a Weberian transformation or one more ideologically consistent with managerial economics. In either case, though, the emphasis was on increasing the administrative capacity of the party apparatus. A more helpful distinction might be drawn between this bureaucratization effort and the pejorative notion

For civil service posts, the PAN asked that the employees be party sympathizers but not necessarily members. Thus, in 2000, only about 60 percent of the civil servants in the PAN were party members. In her own case, Molina believed she was chosen for her position as director of administration over a number of other candidates based on her private industry qualifications, not her panista credentials.

Professionalization brought increased regimentation in the party across four processes that were grouped together in the Sistema Integral de Desarrollo de Personal (Integrated System for Personnel Development, SIDEP): selection of personnel, evaluation of personnel, salary administration, and personnel training. SIDEP documents proposed bureaucratic mechanisms to regulate the selection of party personnel, including the clear definition of the responsibilities of a given position; an ideal candidate's characteristics; the appropriate selection tools for a given position (such as admission exams); technical interviews; and final decisions about hiring a candidate. SIDEP documents also specified which current party administrator was responsible for each step in the selection process. Regulations for evaluating personnel performance by supervisors were similarly specified. This was a tremendous transformation, since "about ten years ago . . . the people who came to the party [as employees] didn't pass through any filter at all."[15]

Salaries were also regularized across the party. Prior to the reform, CEN members negotiated their salaries individually, often in reference to what they knew other members of the CEN earned. "Now, there are tables for everything," including salaries. Further, Molina commented that this sort of regimentation led to professional accountability: "Now, it's clear that the responsibility that you have relates to the pesos you earn."[16] A reform established a base salary for CEN members (using a formula pegged to the pay of federal deputies), with prior experience determining where an employee would fall on the pay scale.[17] Specific criteria for salary raises were also laid out. Finally, the SIDEP program specified means to improve the performance of party administrators through training programs (*capacitación*). Party administrators, both CEN members

---

of bureaucracy associated with the PRI's extreme centralism and heavy reliance on patronage politics.

15. Interview with Molina, July 31, 2000.

16. Interview with Molina, July 31, 2000.

17. Some longtime members of the PAN raised concerns about the "corrupting elements" of having personnel that were so handsomely rewarded. Interview with PAN Secretary of Formation and Training María Esperanza Morelos Borja, April 3, 2000.

and civil servants, were newly subjected to qualifying exams and training programs to assure improved performance in their duties. The PAN adopted a similar set of initiatives for its legislative delegation in the 1990s hoping to improve their knowledge and skill base.

The party's professionalization efforts continued after 2000, spurred on by the increase in public funds based on its strong electoral performance that year. For example, some of those funds were used to bring the salaries of the CEN secretaries into line with those of federal deputies. But the program stalled after 2003 as a result of two unanticipated developments. First, in response to the party's poor electoral performance that year, the IFE cut public funding, and second, it fined the party for electoral law violations during the 2000 campaign by Fox's organization, *Amigos de Fox.* According to the PAN's finance officer, the combination of those two factors created a cash flow problem in the PAN that led to salary reductions in the CEN of up to 30 percent and a downsizing of its employees from 260 to 200.[18]

Related changes during the late 1990s and early 2000s complemented the very deliberate professionalization of the party's administrative apparatus. First, the PAN grew increasingly reliant on external and even international consultants in the areas of marketing, human resources, and campaigning. As one panista remarked, "The party is still in diapers" in these areas.[19] Although PAN leaders were often reticent to speak concretely about the use of external consultants, one confirmed that in the 2003 midterm elections, the party turned to more consultants than ever before in public relations, survey research, and campaigning. Second, the SIDEP-related reforms also involved more regular use of personnel and policy manuals and increased monitoring of employees by area supervisors. Finally, the PAN built a new national party headquarters in Mexico City in 2001—a large, imposing building in the Colonia del Valle that centralized the CEN secretariats and administrative offices that had previously been scattered across the Federal District. Complete with a formal pressroom, high-tech security passes, and a large courtyard for public events, it would consolidate the institutional life of the party. According to Molina, it was bound to trigger a cultural shift in the PAN:

18. Interview with PAN General Director of Administration and Finance Eduardo Seldner Ávila, June 8, 2004.
19. Interview with Sen. Candidate (from the Federal District) Jesús Galván Muñoz (PAN), April 5, 2000.

Now [before the new headquarters had opened], since the offices of the PAN are all over the place, in spite of a fixed work day (9 A.M. to 6 P.M., with a lunch hour), there isn't any strict discipline [among employees]. Meeting one's own goals is what matters most. [The move] will facilitate communication and create a clearer mentality. It may be tough for old-timers accustomed to the *"asunto familiar"* [family way of doing business] in the PAN.

The "family way" was inconsistent with party goals, and that discipline and a common mindset would contribute to the party's further growth—signaling a clear transition to professional party politics.

The PRD began as a fusion party, drawing together former PRI members (including Cárdenas), leaders and activists from Mexican civil society, and militants from Mexico's left parties. (Those organizations had been marked historically by stark divisions, but by the 1988 election cycle, they had coalesced into the Mexican Socialist Party.) The PRD's origin as the confluence of these three tendencies left a tremendous imprint on the structure of the national party office by embedding different preferences for party organizational type in the structure of its factions, or corrientes. As a result, party leaders never settled on a *línea organizativa* (or organizational order), remaining instead committed to different visions of the party.

One debate among PRD leaders centered on whether or not the PRD should strive for institutionalization or maintain a looser organization styled on the "party-front" or "party-movement" model (similar to 1988's FDN, the Mexican left's great national achievement).[20] Evident since the party's founding, party leaders regularly clashed over this fundamental issue of party life even after the 2003 midterm election. Advocates of an institutionalized party organization argued that such a party would bring electoral success as well as enable the party to develop a stronger and more enduring presence in the electorate.[21]

20. Mexican left leaders suggest that the difficulty of defining what it means to be a left party (both programmatically and organizationally) is not unique to Mexico. Other leaders conceptualize the two visions or perspectives in different ways. For example, one CEN member linked with the partido-frente camp identified the options as either an electoralist party or a party which views itself as a delegate of society, with meaningful links to civil society (his camp). Interview with PRD Secretary of Electoral Affairs José Antonio Rueda Márquez, July 6, 2004.

21. The corrientes associated with this position are the groups that formed around Amalia García and Jesús Ortega in the 1990s. The first group is referred to as the Amalios or as Foro Nuevo Sol, while Ortega's group is called either the Chuchos (for his nickname, shared with fellow faction

Amalia García, former PRD president and governor of Zacatecas, argued that institutionalization was necessary in order to ensure that the party was "effective and modern," rather than being subjected to the influence of caudillo figures, particularly Cárdenas. Citing her own experience as a militant in the Communist Party, she suggested that more "structured parties" minimized confusion both within the organization and about the organization in the electorate.[22] Following Angelo Panebianco (1988), García also rejected the pejorative use of the term *burocracia* by opposing camps in the party, arguing that the term was being deployed as a scare tactic that deliberately raised the specter of PRI centralism and authoritarianism among PRD members. As an example of that use, one of García's rivals for the party presidency, Raúl Alvarez Garín, argued that the party had an "excessive bureaucracy" despite its weak administrative capacities and underdeveloped organic identity (Pérez and Saldierna 1999). The party leaders who favored fluid party structures and the party-movement model contended that institutionalizing or bureaucratizing party structures empowered party leaders and closed the party off from its base.[23] By 2004, one of those leaders strongly stated, "We realized that in order to win elections, we need a party of the citizenry. . . . That's why we returned to the FDN logic."[24]

A second and related point of contention among leaders in the PRD posited a choice between party institutionalization, on one hand, and charismatic leadership and *caudillismo* (in which prominent figures have preponderant influence in party affairs), on the other hand. Like the debate about organizational form, positions were tied into factional politics—in fact, the positions of the corrientes on this point mirrored their positions on the prior one. Advocates of the institutionalized party model tended to favor an end to caudillismo, arguing that the party needed "solid institutions, independent of any leader"[25] and that "no individual should be above the party."[26] The historic focus on this debate was clearly Cárdenas, who wielded tremendous influence in the first half of the 1990s and even after the corrientes emerged to counterbalance his power in the mid-1990s. By the late 1990s, however, a second generation

---

leader Jesús Zambrano) or Nueva Izquierda. These factions have historically controlled most of the formal apparatus of the party. For a fuller, though somewhat dated, discussion of the evolution of PRD corrientes through 2000, see Wuhs (2002).

22. Interview with PRD President Amalia García, December 14, 2000.

23. Interview with former PRD President and presidential candidate Cuauhtémoc Cárdenas, December 12, 2000.

24. Interview with Sen. Demetrio Sodi de la Tijera (PRD), July 5, 2004.

25. Interview with Sen. Antonio Soto Sánchez (PRD), November 15, 2000.

26. Interview with PRD President Amalia García, December 14, 2000.

of leaders was emerging as potential new charismatic leaders: former PRD president, Mexico City mayor, and 2006 presidential candidate Andrés Manuel López Obrador; former Zacatecas governor Ricardo Monrreal; and former party president and Mexico City mayor Rosario Robles.[27]

Party leaders favoring stronger institutions argued that the weight of these major figures could be contained through greater bureaucratization. Few party leaders openly spoke in favor of caudillismo—unsurprisingly, given that it is associated with Mexico's history of strongman rule in the nineteenth century and of the hegemonic power of the Mexican president under the PRI regime. However, both Cárdenas and the PRD leaders who originated in the social left spoke less critically about the role of prominent leaders in party life, suggesting that even the party's relatively weak institutions before 2000 limited their influence, which was less notorious than often perceived. Cárdenas, for example, maintained he had "never interfered, at any moment, in any . . . decision of the party," nor could he, given the party's internal checks and balances.[28] As López Obrador's influence over the party grew in the run-up to the 2006 contest, CEN members repeatedly voiced concerns about the party's capacity to influence his campaign and his actions, even while remarking positively on the growing sense of institutional identity in the party.[29] Those comments belie the complexity caused by the presence of caudillos in the PRD's life. Although López Obrador was a unifying force among the party's corrientes (if largely based on anticipated coattails effects), rival leaders were, at the same time, doubtful of the party's ability to influence his choices during the campaign.

Whereas the PAN's periodic bureaucratic reshuffling occurred following extensive planning and consultation, the PRD's National Executive Committee demonstrated relative stability and, when it did change, rarely did so as a result of concerted, deliberate self-study. Instead, changes in the CEN reflected the distinct preferences and priorities of successive party leaders. For example, under party presidents Rosario Robles and Leonel Godoy (2000–2003), the party contracted five secretaries of Organization, a dramatic increase from the typical single secretary, signaling the perceived centrality of organizational work to party success—even under presidents associated with party-movement corrientes. Although there were visible efforts to build up the institutional presence of the party, they were always

27. Robles was involved in a tremendous corruption scandal that appeared to end her political career, at least in the PRD.

28. Interview with Cuauhtémoc Cárdenas, December 12, 2000.

29. Interviews with PRD Secretary of Electoral Affairs Trinidad Morales, June 13, 2005, and PRD Secretary of Political Relations and Alliances Hortensia Aragón Castillo, June 8, 2005.

counterbalanced by CEN offices dedicated to catering to the party's perceived social base (peasants, workers, indigenous Mexicans, and social movement activists), with substantial swings in funding between party presidents of different stripes.[30]

Given the PRD's inconsistent commitment to institutionalization, it is perhaps unsurprising that the party leadership was also ambivalent about party professionalization through the 1990s. As with other dimensions of party growth, differences of opinion about the costs and benefits of professionalization became embedded in the core debate about what being a left party meant, organizationally speaking. Thus, the rhetoric surrounding the idea of professionalization in the PRD has rarely been positive. In practice, though, the PRD's experience with professionalism can be broken into two periods. From the party's foundation until after 2000, many leaders were hesitant about building a strong central party office with professionalized staff—an opinion felt especially strongly by the corrientes favoring a stronger role for social movements in the life of the party. In fact, prior to 2000, the party's meager resource base and the anti-bureaucratic bent of Cárdenas, its most powerful leader, sidelined most discussions about professionalization. An important exception followed the 1997 federal elections (when Cárdenas was elected the mayor of Mexico City and the PRI lost control of the Chamber of Deputies). The PRD, then led by Andrés Manuel López Obrador, directed its IFE-provided public funds to staff training in key areas of party life (especially electoral administration and campaigns and elections) and to ensure that the national leadership (all the secretaries and perhaps subsecretaries) and six employees in each state would work full time for the party.[31]

The challenges the party faced after its disappointing performance in 2000 prompted action by party leaders, which led, first, to perverse, negative outcomes and then to more promising ones for the party. Former Mexico City Mayor Rosario Robles succeeded Amalia García as the PRD's president, and she guided the party through a tremendous bureaucratic expansion marked by patronage and clientelism rather than improvements in the administrative capacity of the office. Subject to few checks, Robles left the party nearly bankrupt following a corruption scandal in the summer of 2003. Her successor, Leonel Godoy Rangel, consequently had to reduce the CEN staff by two-thirds;

30. Interview with PRD Secretary of Labor Issues Armando Tiburcio Robles, November 29, 2000.

31. Interview with PRD Secretary of Communication and Press Carlos Navarrete Ruíz, August 14, 2000. Navarrete also suggested that the influx of funds after 1997 may have led to clientelistic practices, including scholarships for widows and orphans, schoolbooks in PRD-governed municipalities, and along the U.S. border, offices to serve migrants.

to cite one example, Godoy reduced the monthly salary roll in the CEN's financial administration office from $1.3 million pesos to $450,000 pesos.[32]

Despite the setbacks created by Robles's tenure as party leader, the PRD after 2003 displayed a renewed commitment to professionalizing the central party office based on its encouraging midterm performance, the PAN's poor showing, and the emergence of Mexico City Mayor Andrés Manuel López Obrador as the 2006 front-runner. Especially following an effort by the PAN and PRI to impeach López Obrador and remove him from the Mexico City mayor's office, the party brass unified around propelling the mayor to the presidency in 2006. By 2004, party bureaucrats held ambitious plans for party development, including the creation of a civil service-like staff and the performance of detailed "X-rays" of the party throughout Mexico in order to assess its institutional strengths and weaknesses, a survey of its organizational presence throughout Mexico, and systematization of information about the national and subnational structure of corrientes in the party.[33] Leaders also aimed to improve the quality of training and staffing in party bureaucracies, taking the party's Comité General de Servicio Electoral y Membresía (the semi-autonomous electoral authority of the party) as a model.[34]

By 2004 and 2005, party leaders recognized the PRD had become increasingly professionalized—some of the PRD's leaders even denied any trade-off existed between being a professionalized electoral apparatus and being a party-movement, whitewashing one of the primary zones of conflict in party affairs.[35] In the run-up to the 2006 federal elections, the PRD also elected a new president, former Baja California Sur Governor Leonel Cota Montaño, who was credited (or perhaps blamed) for deepening the bureaucratization of party life. Prior to being named the PRD's gubernatorial candidate in Baja California Sur, Cota was a PRI militant and regional leader. Members of his CEN contended that he had managed the life of the central party office like a priísta—"He comes from a PRI tradition, where secretaries are executives, with defined responsibilities"—as opposed to the less-formalized work groups that

---

32. Interview with PRD Secretary of Organization Guadalupe Acosta, June 22, 2004.

33. These are all components of a partisan database envisioned by Acosta. Interview with Acosta, June 22, 2004.

34. In the late 1990s, the PRD's National Council debated dissolving the party's electoral service. Advocates of its dissolution felt that either internal election supervision should be decentralized to the state party organizations or that the office lacked the resources to effectively perform its primary tasks.

35. Interview with PRD Secretary of Electoral Affairs Trinidad Morales, June 13, 2005.

characterized prior PRD administrations.[36] Cota's bureaucratizing leadership, paired with greater consensus about the need to professionalize in advance of the 2006 contest, drew the attention of the party's competitors: one PAN leader acknowledged that the PRD had changed its modus operandi, in apparent recognition that its past approaches did not work. In addition to moderating its discourse, PAN Secretary of Political Campaigns Arturo García Portillo noted the increasingly professional campaigns and marketing of the PRD.[37] Finally, following the PAN's lead, in 2005 the PRD consolidated its offices in a single building in Mexico City, in Colonia Escandón (a working-class neighborhood, in contrast to the location of the PAN's central office).

Building the Regional Parties

Despite deliberate efforts by the Mexican government to decentralize, Mexico City remains the epicenter of Mexican political life.[38] Regardless of this apparent centralization, peripheral areas (be they regions, states, or even municipalities) have figured centrally in the life of the parties. As leaders of the PAN and PRD organized and mobilized to remove the PRI from the presidency over the 1990s, they also worked to wrest governorships and major municipalities from PRI control in order to grow their parties in the electorate, to demonstrate their capacity to govern effectively, and to use them as platforms for further critiques of the PRI.[39]

Their organizational and electoral rationales were clear: the PRI had had decades to develop a strong organizational presence throughout the Republic, and neither the PAN nor the PRD had anything similar, even by 2006, despite their status as "national political parties." Mexico appeared to have a three-party system at the national level, but in truth, it was better characterized as a conglomeration of two-party systems centered on regions or states, in which the PRI competed with one of the two opposition parties, while the other ran a clear and distant third (Klesner 2005, 1997). The parties could legitimately

---

36. Interview with PRD Secretary of Organization Hector Bautista, June 8, 2005.
37. Interview with PAN Secretary of Political Campaigns Arturo García Portillo, June 7, 2005.
38. See Grindle (2007) and Rodríguez (1997) for accounts of decentralizing efforts and their outcomes in Mexico.
39. A number of important works have explored democratization at the state level in Mexico, including Rodríguez and Ward (1995), Solt (2003), and Cleary (2007). Mizrahi's (2003) and Shirk's (2005) works also have substantial attention directed to the state level. Bruhn's (1997) analysis of the PRD's founding years also featured state-level case studies.

claim some sort of institutional presence in all of Mexico's states, but achieving that had been a bumpy ride and the level of development varied widely, despite the consensus in both parties about the imperative of regional party building.

During the 1990s, PAN leaders heavily emphasized expanding the party struc-
ture at the state and municipal levels throughout Mexico, in keeping with their federalist electoral strategy and building on the party's early successes in guber-
natorial races in Baja California and Chihuahua. Ironically, the party's growing popularity often complicated its state-level party-building efforts. On one hand, it created unequal state party organizations. States governed by the PAN, con-
taining large municipalities controlled by the PAN, with a comparably large PAN membership, or from which powerful PAN elites hailed (like Baja California, Chihuahua, Guanajuato, Jalisco, and Yucatán) developed "strong parties," while others remained quite weak.[40] On the other hand, the party's growth prior to and following the 2000 election transformed state party organizations into valuable resources that PAN members, old and new, battled to control.

When struggles among activists and politicians for control of local resources undermined the capacity of the state party committees to perform their statutory functions, the PAN's National Executive Committee (CEN) retained the right to abolish the sitting state party committee and impose a team (called a "state delegation") charged with cleaning up the party's local operations. The CEN made fre-
quent use of state delegations throughout the 1990s and into the 2000s (table 1).

State delegations were meant to be temporary, lasting about one year. However, overcoming internal divisions and other organizational problems often took substantially longer. A wide range of circumstances could prompt the CEN to impose a state delegation, including cases of infiltration (as in Sonora), stagnating member-
ship growth, irregularities or fraud in internal party elections, abuses by state party leaders, or irreconcilable differences among competing groups in the party. The case of Tlaxcala was illustrative of this final circumstance, where a historic conflict between three groups interfered with candidate-selection processes, left talented people out of the directive organs of the organization, and stalled party growth

40. Strong party organizations at the state level had many clear benefits for the party: improved electoral performance, recruitment of electable candidates, and growing memberships. However, strong parties also engendered conflict (discussed below), and in some cases, led to the formation of ideologically distinct state party organizations. The party in Jalisco (home of Guadalajara, Mexico's second largest city) was known to be very conservative, with strong ties to the Catholic Church, and it made pronouncements that embarrassed the national leadership, such as undertaking a now-infamous effort to ban miniskirts.

Table 1 PAN state delegations, 1986–2005

State	Delegation appointed	Delegation withdrawn
Aguascalientes	1982	—
Baja California Sur	1997	—
Campeche	1986	—
Chiapas	2001	—
Guerrero	1998	—
Hidalgo	ca. 1987	—
México	2005	—
Nayarit	2005	—
Oaxaca	1989	2000
Quintana Roo	1997	1999
Sonora	1997	1999
Tabasco	1998	—
Tamaulipas	1997	2000
Tlaxcala	2000	—
Veracruz	1993	1998

Source: Secretariat of Organization, Partido Acción Nacional.

(as members' energies were focused on internal power struggles). Following numerous attempts at resolving the conflict, the CEN imposed a state delegation.[41] The explicit goals of the state delegations appeared reasonable, but some party dissidents argued they were also vehicles for intervention by the national leadership, and that party leaders even fomented state-level conflicts in order to then impose the delegation, install allies, and redirect the party's development.[42]

In their desire to deepen the PAN's penetration in Mexican society, party leaders also devoted considerable attention to strengthening the party at the

41. From the internal document "Delegaciones Estatales," obtained from the PAN Secretariat of Organization, 2000.

42. In the case of Baja California Sur, a former PAN senator, now no longer affiliated with the party, argued that a group of ambitious politicians in that state, who had little concern for the party, joined the organization with the hope of gaining power. According to this account, PAN president Felipe Calderón, supported by various high-level party bureaucrats, dissolved the state directive committee and imposed a delegation to facilitate the political ascent of these ambitious individuals.

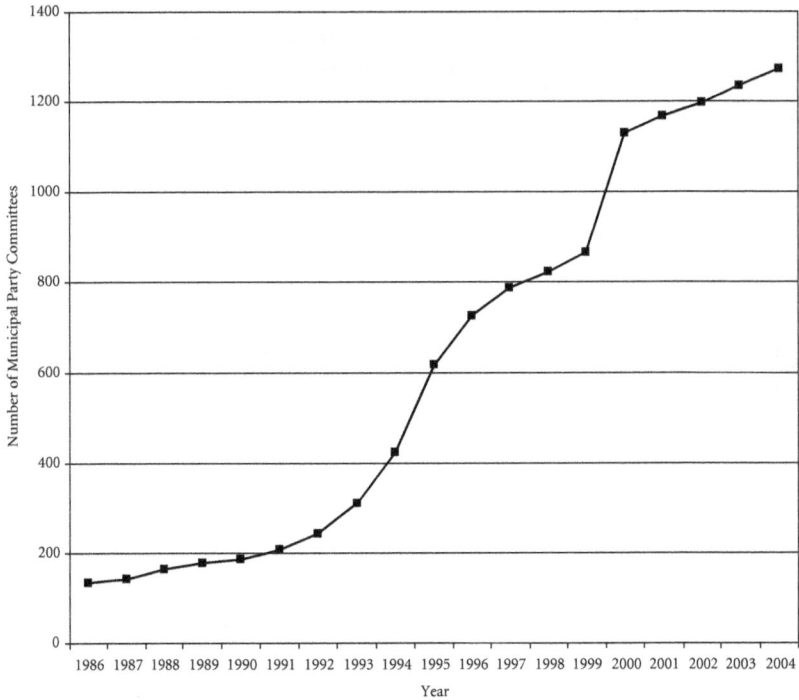

Fig. 13   PAN municipal committees since 1986. In 2000, Mexico had 2,432 municipalities, and the PAN had structures in 1,671 of them, but the Secretariat of Organization lacked data on 801. Because it is not known if these 801 are accredited committees, they are not included here. Data for 2000 and after reflect the total number of party committees and delegations in municipalities for which the PAN has data. These data may not be strictly comparable to prior years' data. No data were available for 2001 and 2003, so those values are estimates based on overall trends. Data provided by the Secretariat of Organization, Partido Acción Nacional.

municipal level. Until 1986, the PAN's lowest level of effective organization was the legislative district, where it had regional committees. With broad support from the party's National Council, a statutory reform created local committees with partisan responsibilities, which, it was reasoned, would lend permanence to the party between elections while also avoiding the dislocating effects of legislative redistricting (fig. 13).[43]

43. Interviews with PAN Secretary General Federico Ling Altamirano, July 21, 2000, and PAN Adjunct Secretary General Cecilia Romero Castillo, March 15, 2000.

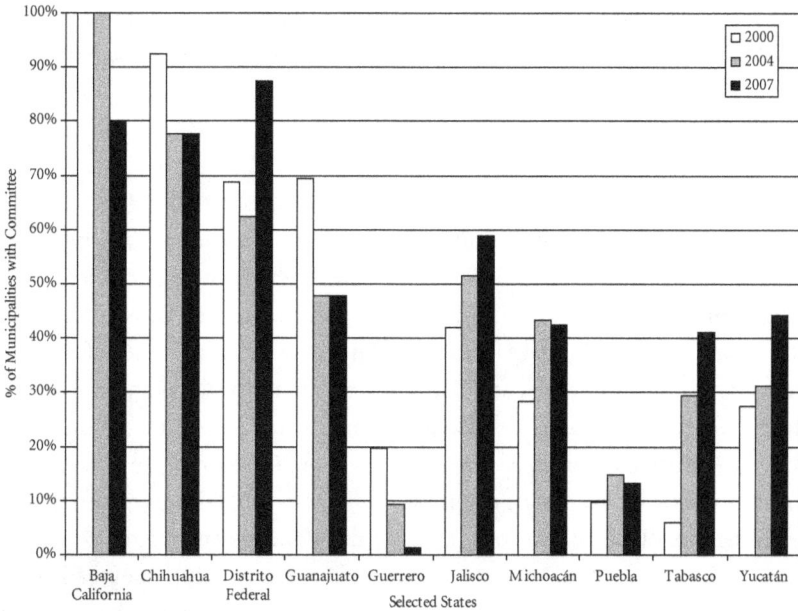

Fig. 14   PAN municipal organization in selected states, 2000–2007. Data provided by the Secretariat of Organization, Partido Acción Nacional.

Disaggregating the data by state reveals the uneven nature of party growth, as does an examination of the sluggish development of party subcommittees, the ostensible base unit of the party. Despite its effort at regional party building, the PAN has had a very inconsistent local presence across Mexico and a surprisingly unstable one over time (fig. 14). Whereas strong PAN states like Baja California and Chihuahua have municipal party committees in three-quarters of their municipalities, the PAN's presence in strong PRD states (like Michoacán and Guerrero) and PRI states (like Puebla) is quite limited. In many states, the party's municipal presence faded after 2000 (see the states on the left-hand side of fig. 14), testament to the power of Fox's candidacy to mobilize his partisans at the local level that year and the volatility of local support.

The party's data on subcommittee foundation are further evidence of the challenges of local party building. Party leaders envisioned the subcommittees as additional spaces for the participation of PAN militants, especially needed in areas where the party committees and councils cannot incorporate all of the party's militants. Unsurprisingly, then, the PAN's most successful efforts were clustered in strong PAN states like Aguascalientes, Chihuahua, and Guanajuato, or in strong PAN cities, like Mérida and Tijuana, where the party had a subcommittee per *colonia*.[44] The distribution of subcommittees also attests to the importance of elite initiative—the number of party subcommittees in Guanajuato, for example, was owed in large part to the efforts of Carlos Medina Plascencia.[45]

Like the PAN, the PRD experienced significant stumbling blocks in the process of building up its presence at the state and municipal levels, resulting in uneven party development. Bruhn (1997) documents the early challenges to party building for the PRD, citing the widespread repression of PRD militants and identifying the Federal District and Michoacán as early poles of institutional development for the party. Zacatecas became a third regional pole, after the gubernatorial victories by Ricardo Monrreal and Amalia García. In other states, the party had only a fleeting presence around elections time, or worse.

In its efforts to create state committees, the party had failed to penetrate the entire national territory by 2002; by 2004, it had a presence in all thirty-two states.[46] These were standard party committees, with the exception of the Puebla office, which was the PRD's analogue to the PAN's state delegation as it was led by a CEN delegate working with a sixteen-member team to rebuild the local party. As often happened in the PAN, the PRD's state party organizations sometimes became zones of conflict as the opportunities for ambitious politicians improved at the local level. Many offices experienced particularly serious divisions during local leadership-selection processes, when the national corrientes inserted themselves into party life by forming conjunctural alliances with local interests.[47] Such conflicts emerged both in states where the party was quite weak (as in Baja California) and where it was stronger (in Guerrero, Tabasco, and Chiapas).[48]

Party leaders acknowledged that in many cases the PRD's presence at the state level was underdeveloped—citing Baja California, Chihuahua, Durango, Jalisco, Nuevo León, and Yucatán as symptomatic of cases in which the party

---

44. The party's data on subcommittees is spotty, since it is provided by municipal and state party officials and not collected at the national level. Like the municipal committees, those structures also appear to be fairly unstable in their presence. For example, according to the PAN's 2004 data, Guanajuato had 827 subcommittees, but by 2007, the party reported only 163. Interview with PAN Secretary of Organizational Development Saíd Mendoza, June 10, 2005.

45. Interview with Dep. Carlos Medina Plascencia (PAN), August 10, 2000,

46. Interview with PRD Secretary of Organization Guadalupe Acosta, June 22, 2004.

47. This was among the primary modes of linkage between state and local party organizations and the national party office throughout the 1990s. See Wuhs (2002).

48. Interview with PRD Coordinator of Institutional Development Alberto López Limón, October 30, 2000.

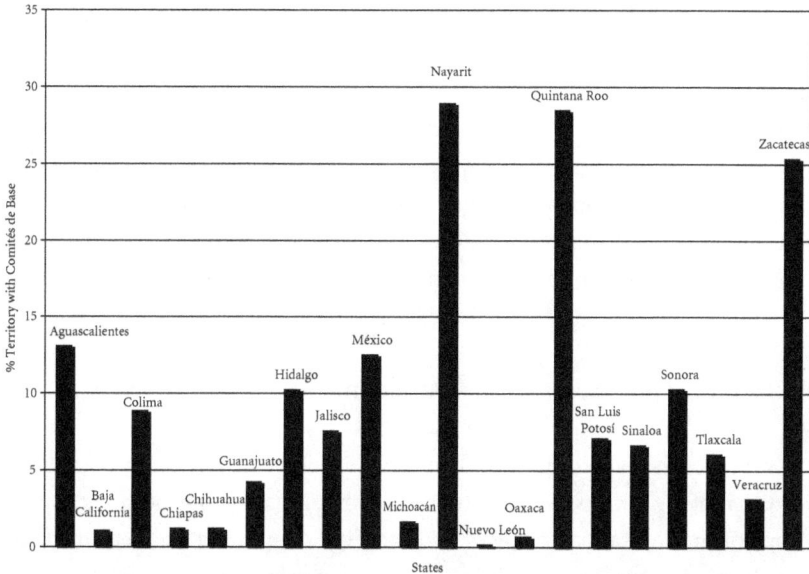

Fig. 15   Construction of PRD comités de base. Data are for 2000. Missing data reflect a failure by state party executives to respond (except for the Federal District party, which does not participate in CEN-directed party building initiatives). Yucatán had no comités de base as of 2000. Data provided by PRD Secretariat of Organization.

had weak municipal structures and virtually no *comités de base*, the base unit of the party.[49] The construction of the comités de base proceeded furthest in Nayarit and Zacatecas, where the PRD has governed—again signaling the importance for party development of strong local leaders—and failed to make significant headway in the north through 2004 (fig. 15).

Although the PRD is missing data on some of its party structures, most notably on the Federal District (Mexico City), it is clear that the party is in

49. Interviews with PRD Secretary of Organization Guadalupe Acosta, June 22, 2004, and Sen. Antonio Soto Sánchez (PRD), November 15, 2000. Often, when PRD leaders discuss the strength of state party organizations, they also address the power of particular corrientes at the state level. For much of the late 1990s and early 2000s, two corrientes dominated much of the subnational apparatus of the party. The clearly dominant group was Nueva Izquierda, followed by the corriente formed around Amalia García. However, the strongest PRD bastions, Michoacán and the Federal District, were strongly influenced by Cárdenas, his son and Michoacán governor (2000–2006) Lázaro Cárdenas Batel, and Federal District-based social movement leaders like René Bejarano and Dolores Padierna. Bejarano's influence over the PRD machine in Mexico City was shaken following a 2004 corruption scandal. Notably, most of the states where PRD leaders recognize their organization as underdeveloped are the strongest PAN states—further testament to Mexico's fractured, regionalized party system.

its organizational infancy. *None* of the reporting states had comités de base in more than 25 percent of their territory. If those structures were the linchpin for long-term party development, as some PRD leaders believed, the party faced serious constraints on its future performance barring radical advances. López Obrador's 2006 presidential campaign presented one opportunity for building local party organizations, although whether such efforts would last depended on the PRD presidential candidate's willingness to work within the party and the desire of his supporters to commit themselves to local party life.

Explaining Party Bureaucratic Development

PAN and PRD leaders guided their organizations through substantial and broad-ranging processes of institutional change, targeting both the operations of the central party offices and their on-the-ground presence throughout Mexico. However, in order to do that they had to reckon with perceived contradictions between being professional bureaucracies and being internally democratic. Both the PAN and PRD featured powerful groups that threatened to derail the reforms based on their strong underlying distrust of "institutions," "bureaucracy," and "professionals."

The changing landscape of competitive politics accounted for much of the shared agenda of the parties. The PRI increasingly recognized opposition victories after 1988, and slowly lost its grasp on electoral administration. Meanwhile, the opposition parties received increasing popular support, improved their access to power through the creation of PR seats in both chambers of the Congress, and, after 1996, gained access to tremendous public funds for party activity. The influence of the IFE funds cannot be understated. By way of example, in 1994, before the reform, $414.8 million pesos were distributed to the parties from public coffers (for campaigns for president, the Senate, and the Chamber), but in 2000, $2.226 *billion* pesos were allocated to the parties (Eisenstadt and Poiré 2005, 22).[50] The incentives offered by the environment encouraged opposition leaders to rethink the nature of their central party offices—particularly after the crucial 1988 election. Electorally oriented contingents within the parties supported national-level organizational development and professionalization, but in both cases, they met with substantial

---

50. Even adjusting for inflation, public financing for political parties increased by almost 70 percent during that period (calculation by author).

opposition. In contrast, no one in either party contested the necessity of building regional party organizations.

Crucial events in 1989 amounted to a turning point in the PAN's development that allowed a virtuous cycle of party development and electoral growth to emerge. During the 1980s, a segment of Mexico's business class worked its way into the PAN, including many of its most prominent leaders of the 1990s and 2000s.[51] This group came to be called the neopanistas. The relatively strong performance of PAN candidate Manuel J. Clouthier in the 1988 presidential election lent support to the growing pragmatic wing in the party's 1989 leadership contest. The pragmatic candidate, Luis H. Álvarez, emerged successful over doctrinaire Gabriel Jiménez Remus. Álvarez was a longtime panista, having been the party's 1958 presidential candidate, but he was also a businessman and pragmatist.

Álvarez's victory was significant in its own right, but it held two particularly important consequences for the PAN's internal life. First, he chose to spend some of his political capital in the divisive decision to accept public funds for the party. Some resources had been available since the 1977 LOPPE reform, but through their preponderant influence in the CEN, doctrinaire leaders had shunned the funding. With the support of Clouthier, Álvarez reversed the policy, which introduced an additional cash flow into the financially strapped party, laying the foundation for its financial takeoff when public financing for parties increased dramatically in 1996.

The second consequence of Álvarez's victory (and, notably, of the acceptance of public funds) was a schism in the party. After years militating in an internal faction (the Foro Democrático y Doctrinario, or Democratic and Doctrinaire Forum), many of the most conservative voices of the PAN left the party in October 1992. Led by Pablo Emilio Madero and Jesús González Schmal, the Foristas objected to the character of Álvarez's leadership (including his unilateral acceptance of public funds) and his willingness to cooperate in Congress with the PRI in the early 1990s.[52] Although many conservative PAN members remained in the party, including Jiménez Remus, the departure of the Foro removed many potential critics of the institutional and organizational developments in the PAN during the 1990s.

---

51. This list includes Francisco Barrio, Vicente Fox, Manuel Clouthier, and others, particularly businesspeople associated with COPARMEX.

52. By most accounts, the PAN cooperation with the PRI facilitated increased recognition of its state- and municipal-level victories. See Eisenstadt (2004). See Loaeza (1999) for further discussion of the Foro.

The PAN leadership grew increasingly electoralist and electorally successful through 2000, picking up major municipal governments and state houses, particularly in northern Mexico. Once the massive funds of the 1996 Código Federal de Instituciones y Procedimientos Electorales (Federal Electoral Institutions and Procedures Code, COFIPE) electoral reform were available to the party, it accessed a positive feedback loop: ample funds enabled the party to build new bureaucracies and even buildings in Mexico City and outlying areas, which in turn facilitated improved electoral performance and thus ensured the receipt of future public funds. The cycle only slowed after Fox was elected, when he failed to bridge divides in the Congress and the party was fined for campaign irregularities in 2000. The party's poor performance in the 2003 midterm elections threatened to end this virtuous cycle, but according to PAN leaders, the organization was astute enough in the 1990s to weather short-term fiscal limitations with some simple administrative belt-tightening, and they would be able to do that again after 2003.[53] The party's strong performance in 2006 promised to reestablish that positive feedback loop.

The PRD began in a very different position. Although many party leaders condemned PRI authoritarianism as least as strongly as PAN leaders did, few if any contemplated refusing public funds; the party was born of an electoral moment in 1988 and remained electoralist after its foundation.[54] But despite a consensus around vote-seeking, the PAN's virtuous cycle eluded the PRD. Two factors placed the PRD on a fundamentally different path. First, the left's success in the 1988 presidential election did not translate into strong initial performances for the PRD. In the 1991 midterm elections, the party's share of the electorate fell significantly from the FDN's 1988 level, to less than 8 percent of the popular vote.[55] The PRD also failed to perform well in the first wave of gubernatorial elections in which it participated. Although the public coffers at the time were relatively small, even the minor positive feedback loop the PAN encountered in the early 1990s was not available to the PRD (table 2). Notably,

53. In congressional elections in 2000, the PAN's vote share was 38.24 percent nationally. In 2003, it garnered 30.73 percent of the vote. Data from the Instituto Federal Electoral, available at www.ife.org.mx, last accessed May 15, 2008. Belt-tightening measures included restructuring the work of the National Executive Committee as well. Interview with García Portillo, June 2, 2004, and with Seldner, June 8, 2004.

54. After debatably winning the 1988 election (though official results had the PRD around 30 percent), the party earned just 25.71 percent of the vote in congressional elections in 1991. Data from the Instituto Federal Electoral, available at www.ife.org.mx, last accessed May 15, 2008.

55. Data from the Instituto Federal Electoral, available at www.ife.org.mx, last accessed May 15, 2008.

Table 2 Total public financing to political parties, 1997–2006 (in millions of current pesos)

	PAN	PRI	PRD
1997	527.2	892.1	391.3
1998	272.5	351.4	247.9
1999	324.0	418.5	297.8
2000	692.7	921.1	656.9
2001	637.5	694.9	279.7
2002	667.1	735.8	294.8
2003	1,308.5	1,445.3	574.2
2004	529.5	567.7	331.3
2005	560.3	603.0	355.5
2006	1,129.3	1,226.9	722.7

Source: Instituto Federal Electoral.

Note: Data for 1997 do not include special funding earmarked for spending in the Federal District, and 2003 data exclude extraordinary disbursements for two particular campaigns.

the gap between the PAN's and the PRD's IFE funding widened dramatically following the PAN's 2000 successes, and even the PRD's partial rebound in 2003 failed to close it. By 2006, the PRD was operating on a significantly tighter budget than were the PAN and the PRI.

Second, the internal divisions within the PRD undermined a consistent approach to party building. Very soon after the party was established, views on party bureaucratic development were embedded in the factional structure of the party. As a result, when the corrientes competed in leadership and candidate-selection processes, rival notions of party bureaucratic development typically featured prominently. Likewise, after the party suffered defeats (as in 2000 and 2006), fundamental organizational issues reappeared on the party agenda. Had the leaders favoring institutionalization (like Amalia García or Jesús Ortega) or the elites advocating the party-front (like Cárdenas and leaders from the social left) regularly been in the minority and deprived of their veto power, the implications of the divisions would have been muted for party affairs. However, from the PRD's foundation, leaders from those two camps nearly alternated in the party presidency, and the party proactively incorporated minority opinions, producing an organization that grew in fits and starts.

The effects of financial constraints and internal divisions played out differently across different party institutional arenas. At both the national and the subnational levels, a paucity of funds hampered institutional change. Even after the 1996 COFIPE reform, the PRD's budget was meager relative to that of the PAN, but had similar funding been available to the PRD, the conflict among the national corrientes would likely have prevented its use for professionalizing the party central office. That is, even when bureaucracy-sympathetic leaders held the party presidency, their best-laid plans were foiled by rival leaders. Pockets of efficiency developed, but the party at large remained unprofessionalized. The PRD remained very weak at the subnational level as well. There, despite the consensus among party leaders of the necessity of local-level presence, budget limitations and the infiltration of national-level corrientes limited the party's growth. The virtuous cycle of institutional development evident in the PAN was mirrored by a vicious cycle in the PRD: internal division undermined consistent efforts at party development, resulting in feeble party institutions and poor electoral performance, yielding paltry funds for party development.

Electoral Imperatives and Institutional Development

In the 1990s, PAN and PRD leaders sought to take advantage of the opportunities offered by the political environment to improve their parties' performance at the ballot box and thus edge toward their ultimate goal of removing the PRI from power. Since 2000, they have aimed to establish their parties' place in Mexico's new competitive system. Many of the leaders of both parties saw the strengthening of party institutions as part and parcel of achieving those goals, and so they set about restructuring the national party office, professionalizing the work of the party, and constructing party offices throughout the Mexican periphery. The PAN met with greater success than the PRD because a higher level of intraparty consensus around party institutional development enabled it to capitalize on a positive feedback mechanism of electoral performance, party finance, and institutional development. In the PRD, by contrast, elites continued to fiercely debate the merits of party bureaucracy and professionalization as late as 2005, contributing to inconsistent institutional development and likely undermining electoral support for the party.

As a process, party bureaucratization prioritizes one element of the democratic imperative (its electoral goals) over all others—of that, there is little dispute. PAN leaders, who act with greater vertical autonomy than do their PRD counterparts, have successfully taken greater steps in that direction. Not coincidentally, they have made greater electoral strides as well. One of the key elements enabling PAN leaders to take those steps was the degree of consensus after 1989 in the party leadership about the need to transform the party organization: Foristas aside, most PAN leaders supported at least some professionalization of party life. The inconsistent approach of the PRD to party development was in fact testament to the extent of internal democracy that endured in the party. Competing sets of elites, holding opposing views, alternated in the party leadership and attempted to advance their respective organizational agendas while holding the reins, all the while ensuring minority voices were represented. No single agenda was demonstrably advanced. Yet if PRD bureaucratic development is a result of its democratic commitments, it is a clear case of savage democracy: party leaders campaigned and clashed around their rival visions of the party, but neglected to consider the impact their competitive zeal was having on the organization's institutional development, on one hand, and on public perceptions of the party, on the other. Something akin might be said of the PAN, where the major dissenting group, the Foro, fled the organization. For a party that associates democracy with order and the rule of law, perhaps there is nothing "savage" there, but the departure of the Foristas did imply a certain tyranny of the majority.

Professionalization of the party as an outcome merits further comment in the context of the democratic imperative. Ultimately, increased use of consultants and experts, the creation of civil services and semi-autonomous bodies, and other indicators of professionalism externalized much of the parties' work. This was precisely the concern of PAN and PRD leaders, who worried about the declining influence of activists in party affairs and the loss of party "mystique." Seen in light of traditional concerns about the emergence of oligarchies in party organizations, professionalization runs the risk of taking oligarchic rule a step further by effectively "outsourcing" partisan work. When tasks traditionally performed by parties are outsourced, activists and rank-and-file members are effectively disempowered. Rival party leaders may be as well. In such an instance, the concerns raised by Michels nearly a century ago become all the more relevant.

6

AFFILIATION VERSUS ALLIANCE VERSUS ABSORPTION

The Mission of Social Linkage: To be the friendly and enthusiastic face that approaches
society, encourages it, and adds society to Acción Nacional's vision for the country.
—Slogan on PAN office wall, 2005

The corporatist system engineered and maintained by the PRI constituted one
of the institutional pillars of PRI rule, especially prior to the 1980s. President
Lázaro Cárdenas first established the national confederations for labor and
peasant representation during his left-leaning government in the late 1930s (see
chapter 2). Under subsequent presidential administrations, corporatism was
transformed from a system of interest representation to a mechanism for con-
trolling organized interests in Mexican society. Although never as hegemonic
as Soviet-styled official organizations, Mexico's "official" trade unions, peasant
associations, and popular associations had unique access to the PRI regime and
benefited from the economic, political, and social goods transferred between
the party and its affiliates. PRI corporatism was thus central to the endurance
of the regime.

The centrality of corporatism to PRI authoritarianism led leaders of the
PAN and PRD to forcefully condemn the very notion of relationships between
parties and organizations from civil society, along with the clientelistic
behavior characteristic of the PRI's relationships.[1] This common position
became ingrained in the very definitions of democracy that guided the PAN
and PRD (see chapter 3). In the cases of candidate selection and bureaucratic

---

1. The strongly negative connotation of corporatism mirrors the strongly negative connotation
that "party" had during and after the transitions from state socialism in Eastern Europe (Linz
and Stepan 1996, 247). The PAN's and PRD's condemnations of PRI corporatism were not simply
partisan debates since these discussions also reached the public sphere. For example, in the
1997–2000 congress, the parties worked together to reform the federal labor law to "get the hands
of government" out of union life and promote union autonomy and democracy. See Martínez
and Velasco (1998).

development, opposition party leaders confronted a trade-off between the two sides of the democratic imperative, in which institutions favoring internal party democracy inhibited the parties' democratizing agendas, or vice versa. PAN and PRD leaders did not face that same dilemma when it came to linking. Linking was perceived as authoritarian, leading those parties to avoid its perception and practice. Following Fox's victory in 2000, though, the PAN and PRD both sought to reposition themselves as interlocutors between civil society and the state. Party leaders believed that doing so was not only critical for effectively competing for power but also for the quality of Mexico's new democracy. They grew increasingly interested in ties with civil society, but recognized that "the challenge is how to approach the pueblo without being corporatist."[2] Overcoming this aversion to linking thus demanded substantial institutional ingenuity. The PRD's identity as a left party further challenged its leaders to take action, since, as one party official noted, "We are a left party, without real representation in unions and in universities, the base of the left."[3]

This chapter analyzes the institutions the parties used to link with civil society before the transition, and it explains the challenges party leaders faced after 2000 as they attempted to build linking institutions and incorporate civil society's interests into political society. It reveals that leaders of the PAN and PRD both sought to forge new relationships with civic organizations after 2000, but that the PAN developed more innovative strategies than did the PRD, which continued to rely on its largely electoralist linking practices. Those differences resulted from the differing internal veto points that linking efforts encountered and the range of institutional alternatives that were politically viable across the two organizations.

Party Leaders and the Logic of Linking

The leaders of political parties manage multiple objectives at any given time. I place particular emphasis on two. First, party leaders want to see their candidates win executive and legislative office. By increasing their parties' presence in elective office, leaders are better able to translate their party's programmatic commitments into public policy while they, themselves, gain more influence.

2. Interview with PAN Director of Administration and Finance Eduardo Seldner Ávila, June 8, 2005.
3. Interview with PRD Secretary of Organization Guadalupe Acosta, June 22, 2004.

Second, party leaders seek to organize and represent the concerns of their activists, members, and voters. The incorporation of civil society into party affairs is central to both those goals. Where parties develop strong ties with segments of civil society (as they did during the postwar era in Europe and in many Latin American countries), they gain stable bases of electoral support, a reliable set of volunteers and activists, and organizational anchors in society, all contributing to higher levels of party and party-system institutionalization (Levitsky and Mainwaring 2006; Mainwaring 1999, 25–39; Mainwaring and Scully 1995; Panebianco 1988).[4] Civil society and its constituent organizations thus represent valuable resources for political parties.

The possible benefits of relationships between political parties and civil society organizations explain why party leaders devote time and energy to building links. Indeed, before, during, and after transitions to democracy party leaders have courted actors from civil society. Yet despite the wide range of organizations and associations that fall under the label of "civil society," empirical studies of parties' efforts to establish links with civil society are surprisingly limited, especially historically. The preponderant emphasis in the literature is on the corporatist alliances pioneered between trade union confederations and labor and social democratic parties in interwar Europe. Trade unions offered those parties the mass base they needed to govern, and in exchange, parties pursued Keynesian policies that led to the construction of welfare states benefiting those constituencies.[5] But although they are crucial for working-class political representation and the establishment of democratic regimes, unions are just one type of organization populating civil society. One of the notable characteristics of the Third Wave democratization cases was the variety of civic organizations that participated alongside class-based actors in those democratic transitions, including human rights organizations, women's

---

4. I adopt the understanding of civil society advanced by Rueschemeyer, Stephens, and Stephens (1992, 49), drawn from Tocqueville (1990) and Gramsci (1971), which defines civil society as "the totality of social institutions and associations, both formal and informal, that are not strictly production-related nor governmental or familial in character." Thus understood, the concept includes authoritarian and pro-democratic organizations, trade unions and bowling leagues, social movement organizations and neighborhood associations.

5. See Huber and Stephens (2001). Because of differences in the evolution of Latin American class structures and party systems, the links between unions and parties were less predictable. In a few cases, unions developed strong ties to socialist, social democratic, and communist parties (as in Chile and Venezuela; see Roberts 1998 and Coppedge 1994). In others they joined populist leaders and their parties (like in Argentina; see Levitsky 2003; Murillo 2003). In still other cases, the ties between left parties and labor were displaced by authoritarian regimes (Peru; see Roberts 1998) or mediated by an interventionist state (Brazil).

collectives, neighborhood associations, environmental movements, and indigenous groups. Unions themselves had lost significant power with the adoption of neoliberal reforms and because of the decimation of unions and their social bases by authoritarian regimes.[6] Even in the post-transition era, linkage with these alternative civil society organizations offers political benefits to parties, while possibly avoiding some of the costs of party-union ties.

Likewise, although historically the most notable type of linking institution was the encapsulating one associated with corporatism, party leaders can draw from a broader array. At the extremes, party leaders can support the complete autonomy of parties and civil society, in effect institutionalizing the *absence* of institutional ties, or parties can absorb civic organizations. Between those extremes, parties and civic organizations can link through overlapping individualized institutions (like memberships, candidacies, and leaderships), through elite-level discussions, through short-term alliances based on momentary political conditions, or through the formation of formal organizational ties (like those characteristic of social democratic parties and trade unions). A final type of linking institution was evident in Mexico—party efforts to support the formation of autonomous civic organizations with partisan sympathies (or *organizaciones afines*).[7]

6. See Collier (1999), Rueschemeyer, Stephens, and Stephens (1992), and Luebbert (1990) on labor movements and democratic development in Europe and Latin America. See Oxhorn (1995) on the diversity of social movement actors in Chile's transition; on women's movements, see Jaquette (1994, 1989); on indigenous movements, see Yashar (1998); and for a discussion of environmental movements and democratization, see Keck (1995). See Roberts (forthcoming; 2002b) on the weakening of labor organizations in Latin America.

7. I draw from Kitschelt's interest in linkages as "direct interactions between party activists and more or less organized external constituencies" (1989, 227). His work on green parties advanced four linking strategies that environmental movements followed vis-à-vis ecological parties in West Germany and Belgium: arms-length relations, selective communication, clientelism, and organizational ties. In later work, Kitschelt and his co-authors (1999, 46–49) identified four "linkage types" that parties deployed in appeals to the electorate: charismatic, clientelist, programmatic, and those associated with proto-parties. Roberts (forthcoming) modifies Kitschelt's typology, identifying three "modes of linkage" with society, substituting personalist linkages (with charismatic and patrimonial subtypes) for Kitschelt's charismatic linkages. Whereas Kitschelt focuses on party strategy as an outcome and Roberts on "modes" of linkage, I am principally concerned with the character of the institutions that structure interactions between parties and civic organizations. Finally, whereas K. Lawson (1980), Kitschelt et al. (1999), and Roberts (forthcoming; 2002b) are interested in party linkages with "society" or "the electorate," and Bruhn (2008) focuses on links between party governments and urban popular movements, I am particularly attentive to links between party organizations and actors in civil society.

Those linking institutions can be (roughly) ordered on the basis of parties' relative penetration of civil society as follows:

Disavowal of linking
Linking via individualized institutions
Linking via elite dialogue
Linking via conjunctural organizational ties
Linking via support for *afín* (sympathetic) organizations
Linking via organizational ties
Linking via organizational absorption/incorporation

Notably, this list is *not* ordered from weak to strong. Although it may be tempting to identify disavowal as a weak institution and formal ties as a strong institution, doing so would be erroneous. Prior to the transition, for example, the PAN's disavowal of institutional linking was likely the most entrenched of the links evident in Mexico between 1991 and 2006. A second problem with gauging the different institutions by strength is that both the PAN and PRD maintained multiple, overlapping linking institutions. Taken together, they *could have* produced stronger overall party-civic organization relationships, but they might also have resulted in institutional schizophrenia were the links not complementary. To add a further layer of complication, it is also important to note that this analysis captures the efforts of PAN and PRD leaders to establish ties with civil society—not necessarily the success they had in doing that (though I do consider their positive and negative outcomes). Through the 2006 election, "autonomous" Mexican civil society and the PRI's corporatist organizations were in a state of flux, assessing the prospects of working with or through political parties and questioning the costs and benefits of continued allegiance to the PRI.

The PAN's Liberal Linking Practices

PAN doctrine and statutes strongly support autonomy of parties from civil society and suggest that civic organizations should isolate themselves from formal politics (which should be the domain of parties). Nevertheless, PAN leaders through the 1990s recognized an important role for civil society in the sowing and cultivating of democratic values. That reality has challenged even long-time party leaders, who acknowledged that "the party has not succeeded in finding organizations and using them to electoral ends without falling into corporatism."[8] The party opened its doors to democratically minded individuals active in civil society, and, in fact, overlapping membership constituted the primary institutional link with civil society during the pre-transition years. However, PAN leaders expected those members to forego their other organizational identity and be "good panistas" once they entered the party office.[9] That did not require renouncing one's membership in the civic organization, although some PAN leaders did just that, but it did mean not working to advance the civic organization's goals through the party.

Two other institutions tied the party to civil society during the pre-transition period. Article 11 of the party's statutes enabled party members to form "homogeneous groups" based on "skills, profession, activity, age, or other rationale" in addition to participating in the municipal life of the party (PAN 1999). Without a defined institutional role, though, the homogeneous groups were low profile, and despite being characterized as *corrientes de pensamiento* (currents of thought), they lacked the presence of the PRD's corrientes. The few that existed were largely informal groups with a common vision and set of objectives, but their individual members acted as part of the larger party.[10] The other institutional tie that the party maintained with civil society was intermittent elite-level dialogue between the party and trade unions, business associations, NGOs, and faith-based groups. Coordinated through the PAN's Secretariat of Relations (later, the Secretariat/Directorate of National Relations), these discussions helped shape the party platform and served as a mechanism for the recruitment of external candidates, upon whom the party often relied to broaden its political appeal.[11]

Despite their party's strong performance in 2000, leaders of the PAN, including President Luis Felipe Bravo Mena, expressed concern in the election's immediate aftermath about the distance between the party and Mexican society: "The PAN doesn't have a social expression in the country. . . . There should be teachers and indigenous people in the party, but the party has not

8. Interview with Sen. María Elena Álvarez de Vicencio (PAN), March 2, 2000. Her comment was seconded by Dep. Juan Miguel Alcántara (PAN), March 8, 2000.

9. Interviews with Alcántara; Álvarez de Vicencio, and PAN-Federal District Secretary of Research Aminadab Pérez Franco, February 29, 2000.

10. Interview with PAN Secretary of Relations Jorge Ocejo Moreno, April 6, 2000.

11. For what panistas often call "citizen candidates," I use the term "external candidates."

worked to cultivate their presence."[12] In response, his CEN forwarded multiple institutional strategies through which the party could fortify its links with civil society.[13] Its initial effort failed: some elites in the PAN sought to adapt the party's article 11 section on homogeneous groups in order to use that institutional space as a means for having a more effective dialogue with civic groups. By generating a *reglamento* (rule) that articulated the process for establishing these groups, reformers aimed to use article 11 to build bridges with organized teachers, *campesinos* (peasants), indigenous Mexicans, and environmentalists, in order to incorporate them into the party's platform and other partisan debates.[14] However, the National Council's more conservative members did not pass the reglamento due to anxieties that the groups would begin demanding candidacies and other resources as corporate entities— likening the party to the PRI and trampling on the PAN's core conception of liberal-individual democracy. Article 11 was acceptable as an institutional space in which individuals with common interests might gather, but converting that space into a mechanism for outreach to organized groups threatened the democratic spirit of the party rank and file, even in the early 2000s.

One of the first successful reforms was the transformation of the PAN's Directorate of National Relations. Before, "we were just a resource, a go-between, not an actor in our own right," according to Director Adriana Hinojosa Céspedes.[15] After 2000, a wave of organizations previously in the PRI's fold approached the PAN seeking corporate affiliation. The PAN rejected those offers, but they helped to invigorate the new work of National Relations. Working with formally constituted organizations (those with statutes and by-laws, like trade unions, chambers of commerce, and teachers' groups[16]) that were both sympathetic to the PAN and politically agnostic, the office aimed to "be a service for the organizations, teach them how to lobby, help them approach the government across all three levels." The new relationships

---

12. Interview with PAN President Luis Felipe Bravo Mena, July 7, 2004.

13. Interviews with PAN Secretary of Organization Alfredo Rivadeneyra Hernández, June 28, 2004, and PAN Secretary of National Relations Adriana Hinojosa Céspedes, June 15, 2004.

14. Interviews with Rivadeneyra Hernández, June 28, 2004, and PAN Secretary of Elections Arturo García Portillo, June 28, 2004.

15. Interview with Hinojosa Céspedes, June 15, 2004.

16. Among the groups that Hinojosa mentioned specifically were two entrepreneurial groups, COPARMEX and the Consejo Coordinador Empresarial (Business Coordinating Council, CCE), from which Ocejo, Gerardo Priego, and Bravo Mena, respectively, originated. She also mentioned the Jewish community and the autonomous trade unions (though those relationships are more transient than are those with COPARMEX and CCE).

with civic groups were documented through biweekly bulletins issued by the Directorate and in regular meetings between organizational leaders and PAN delegates. In 2004, PAN delegates held about thirty meetings per month with organizations, some of which involved on-going work whereas others were exploratory, focused on identifying common political ground. The party's Coordination of Institutional Linkage, a subunit of the National Relations office, maintained a database of the seven hundred organizations with which the PAN had met. Monthly reports chronicling the Directorate's activities were sent to the party president and the direct principal, the Secretary of Social Linkage. The party's legislative delegation sometimes maintained similar linkages: Senator Francisco Fraile (Puebla) maintained regular dialogue with leadership and rank-and-file members of the Unión Nacional de Trabajadores (National Workers' Union, UNT) and other labor groups, and many legislators' local offices focused on constituent-service work with civic groups.[17]

Two other party offices also adopted new linking tasks following 2000, and especially after 2003. Since at least the 1980s, the party had maintained two CEN-level divisions based on identity: Promoción Política de la Mujer (Political Promotion of Women, PPM) and Acción Juvenil (Youth in Action).[18] Prior to Fox's election, the work of both was internal to the party, focused on coordinating relations with the party's female members and its state-level youth leaders.[19] But the impetus that transformed the Directorate of National Relations also redirected the attention of these two offices on outreach, recruitment, and linkage. The field-based work of PPM was indicative of the assertiveness of the PAN's efforts. Its primary focus was turned to the recruitment and training of strong, viable women candidates for the party, both panistas and nonmembers who demonstrated strong dedication to public service. It also sought to increase women's political participation through contact with civic groups of all stripes, but typically working with groups involved in health, education, and welfare issues. Staff in PPM argued their efforts were instrumental to the PAN's high levels of female representation in Congress: in the 2003–2006 Congress, the PAN had forty-seven women deputies, while the

17. Interviews with Sen. Francisco Fraile (PAN), June 16, 2004, and PAN Secretary of Elections Arturo García Portillo, June 2, 2004. Some legislators expressed concerns about losing sight of legislative work through too many constituent service responsibilities. Interview with Sen. Luisa María Calderón Hinojosa (PAN), June 15, 2004.

18. The PAN defines youths as people between 16 and 25 years of age.

19. Interview with PAN General Coordinator of the National Secretary of Youth in Action Carlos Torres Torres, June 1, 2000.

PRI had thirty-seven and the PRD just twenty-six.[20] PPM has focused particular attention on establishing contact with the local organizations of the Sindicato Nacional de Trabajadores de la Educación (National Union of Educational Workers, SNTE). Long a stalwart PRI ally, the mammoth teachers' union had diversified its links with political parties, especially as its longtime leader, Elba Esther Gordillo, repeatedly challenged the authority of the PRI party president, Roberto Madrazo. Youth in Action similarly shifted its labor from training already-dedicated young panistas to drawing more young people into the party and establishing relationships with existing youth organizations.[21]

The creation of a new CEN-level Secretariat of Social Linkage (Secretaría de Vinculación Social) continued the PAN's institutional reform efforts. In early 2004, National Relations, Political Promotion of Women, and Youth in Action were moved under this Secretariat. In one sense Social Linkage served as an umbrella for preexisting institutions in the party, and so might be construed as a bureaucratic reshuffling akin to the Redimesionamiento reforms (chapter 5). However, it represented a far stronger commitment by the party to reclaiming the PAN's tradition of engagement with the community based on core party principles elaborated by founders like Gómez Morin and contemporary leaders like Carlos Castillo Peraza, such as the common good, community action, subsidiarity, and solidarity.[22]

In addition to regrouping National and International Relations, Youth in Action, and PPM under one principal, Social Linkage's Citizen Promotion office designed a host of new linking strategies. The party operated along two logics, according to Secretary of Social Linkage Gerardo Priego Tapia. Consistent with the party's conception of democracy, the PAN aimed, through training, education, and consciousness-raising, to engage and galvanize Mexico's citizenry and support the establishment of autonomous civic organizations. Even after 2000, there were concerns about the construction of an active citizenry in Mexico, because "if you link with dwarves [that is, citizens unaware of their rights and responsibilities], you crush them."[23] Its leaders sought the potential

20. Interview with PAN National Director of Political Promotion of Women Graciela Zertiche, June 13, 2005.

21. Interview with PAN Technical Secretary to the Secretary of Social Linkage Javier Soberano Miranda, June 9, 2004.

22. Interviews with PAN Secretary of Social Linkage Gerardo Priego Tapia, June 15, 2004, and Sen. Luisa María Calderón Hinojosa (PAN), June 15, 2004.

23. Interview with PAN Director of International Relations Rolando García Alonso, June 11, 2004.

electoral benefits of inserting the party into community life as an advocate and a resource. PAN leaders noted that these links, so long as they were not perceived as corporatist, were important for the anchor they could provide the party in the rural sector (where the PRI maintained a dominant position) and the urban areas (where the PRD had significant support).[24] They also hoped that insertion into community life would help rid the PAN of some stereotypical labels (such as a "pavement" party privileging urban interests, a party of the rich, and a radical organization of miniskirt-banning Catholics).

The pilot program and template for the PAN's new Citizen Promotion strategies was PLANTAR (to plant, literally, but also the Spanish acronym for Partido Acción Nacional Rural Action Program). Officially launched on June 13, 2004, PLANTAR was designed to bring the PAN into rural and indigenous Mexican life. A national council of thirty PAN members with rural and indigenous experience and their counterpart state councils coordinated PLANTAR's work, which was structured around seven strategic lines:

- the promotion of rural homogeneous groups in the party;
- the promotion of independent organizations in the rural sector;
- the design of rural development projects;
- the participation of PAN elected officials in rural issues;
- the involvement of PAN local committees in rural issues;
- heightened general presence of the party in rural areas; and
- the training of rural-sector leaders.[25]

In the strategy's founding documents and at the public launch, the PAN took care to specify that "PLANTAR is NOT *an organization nor a confederation, it is a mechanism for the organized participation of Mexicans interested in rural development.*"[26] Even after just a year, staff in Social Linkage judged PLANTAR a success based on increased interest in the party by rural sector, the incorporation

---

24. Interviews with Priego Tapia, June 15, 2004, and with García Portillo, June 15, 2005.

25. By June 2005, the party had set up councils in 23 states and anticipated establishing three more. Strategic lines from "Acción Nacional se PLANTA en el campo MEXICANO," internal document prepared for a July 7, 2004 meeting with the presidents of the PAN's state party committees.

26. From "Acción Nacional se PLANTA en el campo MEXICANO" (see previous note). Emphasis in original.

Fig. 16   Pamphlet for the PAN's PLANTAR (Partido Acción Nacional Rural Action Program) linking strategy. Obtained from the Secretariat of Social Linkage, 2004.

of rural leaders into the party, and the attention it drew from the PRI, which disparagingly referred to it as a "blue CNC."[27]

PLANTAR served as the template for the development of additional sector-based linking strategies in the PAN, three of which were launched in 2005: ComUnidad (CommUnity, targeting urban popular sectors), México Ambientado (Environmental Mexico), and the Consejo Empresarial (Entrepreneurial Council), organizing small and medium-sized businesses.[28] Like PLANTAR, they aimed to address the issues and problems of discrete communities in order to gain credibility in the eyes of citizens and form a lasting tie with voters. ComUnidad, for example, addressed urban problems like drug use, access to education, and public health by offering assistance in filing complaints, disseminating information, and supporting activists.

The PAN had additional linking strategies targeting two other potential constituencies. Through Cautivarte (Captivate Yourself), the party aimed to establish and maintain relations with cultural organizations, and with Maestros en Acción (Teachers in Action), it sought to build a national network of teachers and educators (called ACCIONARED). Teachers in Action, drawing on multiple PAN offices, was a particularly important program because it aimed to capitalize on the power of the PRI-dominated SNTE and its constituency's socializing effect on younger generations. During 2005, about two hundred educators were organized in the network, but the party hoped for seven thousand by the end of that year, and nearly twenty thousand by election day in 2006. Because Teachers in Action engaged with an organized sector of civil society, it followed a different organizational model, which sought to draw individual members of the SNTE into the PAN municipal committees, where they could be incorporated into the party's mission (PAN 2005, 155–58).[29]

In the wake of the 2000 elections, PAN leaders devised a diverse set of institutions to forge links with civic organizations, but those links strongly reflected panista thought and the realities of intraparty politics: the PAN's linking

27. Interviews with PAN National Director of Citizen Promotion Francisco Javier Soberano Mirando, June 15, 2004 and June 15, 2005.

28. The Consejo Empresarial is somewhat different as it draws on already-established relationships between the PAN and the organized business class, most evident in the clear connections between COPARMEX and the PAN—which brought Ramón Corral, Manuel J. Clouthier, and Priego himself to the PAN. Like the PAN, COPARMEX is structured around state and municipal councils, in its case of small-scale entrepreneurs (emprendedores).

29. Interview with Soberano, June 15, 2004. His office coordinated its work with the Political Promotion of Women division.

institutions tended to target individuals, and when the PAN's efforts focused on organizations (as through Citizen Promotion), its goal was to foment the development of autonomous civil society groups (but ones that were afín, or sympathetic) and thus generate electoral support for the party. Its institutions were consistent with the party's commitment to the autonomy of parties and civil society: they were openly and steadfastly anticorporatist. Furthermore, they reflected the party's strong commitments to liberal democracy, through their individualistic character and emphasis on order, evident in National Relations' desire to work with formally constituted organizations rather than social movements or less formalized popular sector groups.

The PRD's Anticorporatist Electoralist Alliances

Article 82 of the PRD's statutes proclaims that the party rejects "all forms of corporatist or other political control that impedes, coerces, or limits the freedom of the members of movements and organizations to freely and democratically decide on issues that affect them" (PRD 1991). The party's dedication to autonomy of party and civil society extended into the legislative arena: among its legislative proposals for the 58th Congress (1997–2000) was the "Autonomy of Social Organizations," aimed at prohibiting unions, confederations, ejidos, cooperatives, producers' organizations, chambers, and colleges from affiliating with political parties.[30] Those examples, however, do not adequately reflect the much murkier relationship that actually exists between the party and civil society, one that has repeatedly left the party open to the corporatist critique, despite the best efforts of party leaders.

The PRD was founded in 1989 as a voice in political society for the social left. Leaders of prominent left and civic associations, like the Asociación Cívica Nacional Revolucionaria (National Revolutionary Civic Association, ACNR), the Asamblea de Barrios (Assembly of Neighborhoods), and COCEI (Coalition of Isthmus Students, Campesinos, and Workers), participated in the establishment of the party and proceeded to occupy important leadership posts in the PRD. However, COCEI and other left organizations voiced concerns about participation in party life—specifically, that their organizations might

30. From an internal document provided by Sen. Leticia Burgos Ochoa (PRD), September 19, 2000.

lose their autonomous political voice through involvement with the party.[31] For that reason, leaders of COCEI and other groups often had to resign their posts while serving partisan functions, which left many of these organizations effectively decapitated.

These organizations also feared that the electoral left was overly reformist and thus not likely to aggressively press for their interests. In order to ensure that the PRD remained the instrument of social struggle that its founders had promised, leaders of six organizations of the social left joined together to form Trisecta, a corriente dedicated to that goal.[32] This corriente remained dominant until the mid-1990s when the adoption of the planilla system for internal elections fractured the coalition.[33] Even after Trisecta dissolved, however, various corrientes continued to advance the interests of the social left, including Movimiento Izquierda Social (Movement of the Social Left, MISOL), which included COCEI, El Barzón, and M27 from Oaxaca; Movimiento Izquierda Libertaria (Free Left Movement, MIL) also called the Cívicos; and the Corriente de Izquierda Democrática (Current of the Democratic Left, CID), which included the powerful Mexico City-based groups led by René Bejarano and Dolores Padierna that was later called the Izquierda Democrática Nacional (National Democratic Left, IDN).

The coalitional foundation of the PRD created a difficult tension for the party and the organizations from the social left, both of which maintained

31. Interview with Dep. Héctor Sánchez López (PRD), September 13, 2000. His concerns were reiterated by many perredistas, including Dep. Eric Eber Villanueva Mukul (PRD). Interview with Villanueva Mukul, November 11, 2000. Although movement leaders were concerned about losing their autonomous voice, Haber (2006) argues that the movement rank-and-file members should have been worrying about losing their leaders. Various PRD members cited those same challenges in author interviews. Bruhn (2008) documents similar effects among urban popular movements in Mexico City.

32. Those organizations (and the leaders originating from them) are the Asociación Cívica Nacional Revolucionaria (including Mario and Francisco Saucedo), Partido Patriótico Revolucionario (Camilo Valenzuela, head of the National Council 2005–2008), the Corriente Izquierda Democrática (René Bejarano, a Mexico City civic leader), the Movimiento Revolucionario del Pueblo, the Unión de la Lucha Revolucionaria, and the Organización de Izquierda Revolucionaria—Línea de Masas (where Rosario Robles and Saúl Escobar Toledo originated). See Sánchez (1999) and Wuhs (2002) for more on the PRD's corrientes. This discussion also draws on interviews with PRD Secretary of Organization J. Humberto Zazueta Aguilar, August 15, 2000; Dep. Felix Salgado Macedonio (PRD), November 9, 2000; and Sánchez López, September 13, 2000.

33. The planilla system was adopted in the party's 1995 Third National Congress and instituted an electoral system for the party presidency and National Council based on proportional representation. The lists that compete in those internal elections (the planillas) typically represent the corrientes of the day.

strong discursive commitments to autonomy despite clear and present ties. As in the PAN, membership was a crucial institution linking the PRD and civil society, but overlapping membership *at foundation* entailed more profound relationships through either the effective absorption of movements and civic groups into the party or the incorporation of civic leaders as party leaders, which fostered informal ties of enduring sympathy between the PRD and the left social organizations.

Once the PRD formed, the party's commitment to represent the interests of civil society was most evident in two types of linking institutions. First, the party used candidacies as mechanisms for forging relationships with organized constituencies. In the party's early years, it relied heavily on external candidates (usually in the PR lists for the Chamber, but also appearing on the Senate PR list after 1997) to develop ties with independent social organizations and hold on to segments of the electorate. Although potentially opening the party to elements of the corporatist critique and clientelistic behavior, some members of the PRD maintained that it was possible for those candidates to represent their groups' interests without demanding side benefits for their constituents.[34] Others disagreed, arguing that the party was unable to avoid the forces of clientelism when the PRD leadership distributed PR candidacies, and that the party weakened civil society through such actions.[35]

Second, the party's links were sustained through the work of bureaucratic agencies within the National Executive Committee. Despite other changes to its organizational structure, the party always maintained a host of identity-based secretariats:

- 1999: Women's Issues; Youth; Social Movements; Labor Issues; Peasants, Rural Development and Credit
- 2003: Equity (Gender); Youth; Social and Labor Movements
- 2006: Equity and Gender; Youth; Social Movements; Labor Issues; Peasant and Indian Affairs; Migrants

Although the secretariats had differentiated tasks, their work involved some key common elements, including establishing contact with existing civic groups in their issue area, fomenting the organization of new groups (especially rivals to

34. Interviews with PRD Secretary of Social Movements Rosendo Marín, June 8, 2005, and PRD Secretary of Indian Communities Saúl Vicente Vásquez, September 8, 2000.
35. Interview with Sen. Demetrio Sodi de la Tijera (PRD), November 6, 2000.

the PRI's sectoral organizations), and representing those interests in debates on the party's platform and through governing institutions.[36] Often, though, the electoral tasks of the party overshadowed those secretariats politically and bureaucratically.[37]

Those modes of institutional linkage existed alongside a plurality of institutions associated with electioneering, before 2000 and after. Within the CEN, the Secretariat of Political Relations and Alliances was charged with forging electoral alliances at the national level and shaping state-level agreements, working closely with the Secretariats of Organization and Electoral Affairs.[38] Beyond constructing the offices and attracting the actors needed to effectively manage the campaign and election (like territorial party headquarters and election observers), the CEN sought a central role in crafting both formal alliances and in elaborating platforms, imagery, and campaign strategies that could fortify party links with civil society and the electorate. It was rarely successful, however, because of the perceived weakness of the party organization by the PRD's presidential candidates and those candidates' own high profiles in Mexican politics. The efforts of campaign teams associated with particular candidates sometimes reinforced, but more often rivaled, the alliance building and linking work of the CEN.[39] Neither fully inside nor outside the party, campaign teams like that of López Obrador in 2005 and 2006 approached civil society from a pragmatic perspective—seeking its support to garner the needed votes in a single election cycle.[40] For example, in 2006, penetrating the PRI's voting blocs in trade unions and the peasantry was crucial to López Obrador's potential victory, and to that end, his core campaign staff included former PRI members who had left the party but retained some ties to its sectoral organizations: Ricardo Monreal (former PRD governor of Zacatecas), Manuel Camacho Solís (former mayor of Mexico City under the PRI), and Leonel Cota Montaño

---

36. Interview with former PRD Secretary of Organization and former Secretary of Political Training Lic. Alejandro Encinas Rodríguez, October 31, 2000.

37. Interview with PRD Secretary of Electoral Affairs Trinidad Morales, June 13, 2005.

38. Interview with PRD Secretary of Political Relations and Alliances Hortensia Aragón Castillo, June 8, 2005.

39. People closer to the campaign team favored a tightly controlled operation outside of party hands. Interview with Secretary of Planning and Institutional Development Agustín Guerrero Castillo, June 9, 2005. The naming of PRD member Jesús Ortega as López Obrador's campaign manager likely allayed some CEN members' concerns (Saldierna 2006).

40. López Obrador's efforts were consistent with Cárdenas's past aims to form broad strategic alliances outside the strict party fray (El Nacional 1998).

(former priísta, former Baja California Sur governor, and PRD party president 2005–2008).

These quasi-partisan linking strategies were deployed outside the PRI's sectors as well. Just as prior PRD candidates had used Brigadas del sol (Sun Brigades, playing on the PRD symbol of the Aztec sun) to raise their profiles, López Obrador's campaigns relied on *redes ciudadanas* (citizens' networks), coordinated by Camacho, Monreal, Socorro Díaz, and others, as its electoral foot-soldiers (Saldierna 2006).[41] Those networks were a mechanism for disseminating the candidate's message, generating support especially in outlying areas, and ensuring that the party had a watchdog presence at all of the *casillas,* or ballot boxes, in the country.[42] One such network in 2006 was Jóvenes por AMLO (Young People for AMLO, as Andrés Manuel López Obrador is widely called)—an Internet-based network dedicated to advancing López Obrador's candidacy. Its website (www.jovenesporamlo.org) featured web links to the PRD's 2006 Alliance for the Good of All, but the text focused exclusively on the López Obrador as an individual and suggested that young people form groups supportive of the candidate in civic associations, clubs, or other interest groups. The use of the networks generated consternation in some quarters since they were explicitly "citizen" and not partisan in nature, suggesting that the links held little in the way of potential staying power for the party. In that case, for example, young people were not directed to the PRD, its website, or the other alliance members. Party leaders were also concerned that such networks amounted to a parallel organization, like Amigos de Fox, and would undermine López Obrador's connection and accountability to the party.[43] Still others suggested that sidelining the party in favor of a handful of political heavy hitters and many political novices underutilized the political expertise that individuals within the CEN had accumulated.[44] Nevertheless, many CEN

41. Notably, both Vicente Fox and Felipe Calderón also built alliances with a broad range of civic organizations during their campaigns. Fox forged those alliances through Amigos de Fox and a series of citizen consultations. Interview with PAN Secretary of Research Salvador Beltrán del Río, February 14, 2000. Calderón's campaign team took care to frame those alliances not as electoral strategy but instead as a means of ensuring the governability of the country, premised on identifying and pursuing common goals central to the country's future. See Núñez (2006).

42. Interview with PRD Secretary of Planning and Institutional Development Agustín Guerrero Castillo, June 9, 2005. Also drawn from press conference by PRD President Leonel Cota, January 4, 2006.

43. Interview with PRD Secretary of International Relations Saúl Escobar Toledo, June 13, 2005.

44. Interview with PRD Secretary of Social Movements Rosendo Marín, June 8, 2005. Marín suggested that López Obrador believed the party was unable to help him achieve his goals, but

members were willing to postpone addressing those concerns until after the 2006 vote, given the apparent likelihood of López Obrador's victory.[45]

Formed from a PRI schism, the PRD was always more vulnerable than the PAN to the corporatist critique. Although it never developed the broad-based organized ties characteristic of many left parties, the party was not without links. The role of the social left in the PRD's foundation imprinted the party with a broad set of links based on absorption and incorporation, whereas the party's narrow base in its early years led party elites to rely quite heavily on external candidates. The party's commitment to participatory democracy encouraged leaders to maintain CEN-based agencies targeted to particular sectors and constituents. The party's presidential candidates introduced yet another layer of linking institutions. Despite those varied efforts, many party leaders, particularly those derived from the social left, remained dissatisfied with the party's linking practices and the shallowness of its participatory democracy.

Explaining the Adaptation of Linking Institutions

Although July 2000 was a watershed moment in Mexican political history, it was clearly not such a moment as far as linking institutions are concerned. Opposition hopes that the PRI's corporatist system would collapse were not met, as evidenced during the stunted efforts to reform Mexico's federal labor law under Fox (Zapata 2006; Mayer 2003). Still, the transition to democracy and the PAN's weak and PRD's strong respective performances in 2003 left party leaders in a predicament similar to the ones they faced with candidate selection and professionalization: they could establish institutional ties with civil society and perhaps gain a stronger foothold in the Mexican electorate, but doing so could generate hostility from the party brass and rank and file. It was clear to leaders of both the PAN and PRD that they could no longer maintain their parties' steadfast commitments to autonomy of parties and civil society. As one PAN leader said, "The elections of 2003 had a clear message: if the PAN

---

that in the seven years that had passed since he was PRD president, the party had undergone a significant process of professionalization.

45. Interviews with PRD Secretary of Youth Issues Cintya Mazas Vásquez June 14, 2005; PRD Secretary of International Relations Saúl Escobar Toledo, June 13, 2005; and PRD Secretary of Planning and Institutional Development Agustín Guerrero Castillo, June 9, 2005.

Table 3 Linking institutions in the PAN and PRD

	PAN	PRD
Disavowal of linking	Official discourse prior to 2000	Official discourse prior to 2000
Linking through individualized institutions	Recruitment of "independent" external candidates; overlapping members; work of Teachers in Action, PPM, and Youth in Action	Recruitment of "independent" external candidates; overlapping members
Linking via inter-organizational elite dialogue	Work of Relations/National Relations, Captivate Yourself	Work of identity-based CEN secretaries (social movements, labor, etc.)
Linking via conjunctural organizational ties	Incorporation of civic leaders as candidates and party members (informal mass link)	Incorporation of civic leaders as candidates and party members; campaign alliances; citizens' networks; campaign organization-based alliances
Linking via support for *aflin* organizations	Citizen promotion programs (PLANTAR et al.)	N/A
Linking via organizational ties	Homogenous groups (aborted)	N/A
Linking via organizational absorption/incorporation	N/A	Incorporation of social left leaders and militants in party at founding, formation of corrientes around social left interests

does not approach the 'pueblo,' it will lose in 2006 and will place in jeopardy its permanence as a political force."[46]

For both parties, the development of new linking institutions presented challenges, even conceptual ones: as one PAN bureaucrat stated, "before, linkage meant offering a *tricolor* [the PRI's emblem] t-shirt."[47] Both parties struggled to not replicate the linking institutions of the PRI: PAN leaders asked themselves how a liberal party could constructively engage with collective actors without becoming clientelistic, whereas PRD leaders struggled to forge ties with their social base without being corporatist, or being *called* corporatist.

In both cases, a plurality of institutional designs resulted (table 3). Most clearly, the PAN and PRD were both resistant to forging formal and enduring organizational ties with civic organizations. Aside from incorporating groups from the social left when PRD was founded, neither party sought to establish any ties that might be construed as corporatist, testament to the opposition both within the parties and in the electorate to such links. Interestingly, it was the PAN, and not the PRD, that broached the possibility of creating such links through the attempt to reform the PAN's reglamentos on the homogeneous groups, defeated precisely because it was seen to approximate the PRI's linking institutions.

A second commonality across the parties was their reliance on candidacies as means of linking party and civil society. Whether external candidates were formal leaders of civic organizations or prominent individuals with informal organizational followings, they were seen as viable mechanisms for bridging the gap between political society and civil society. For example, the PAN incorporated Oaxacan indigenous leader Huberto Aldaz Hernández into its PR list for the 2003–2006 Chamber of Deputies, and the PRD saved one of its few 2006 PR Senate list spots for a member of the Unión Nacional de Trabajadores, a confederation of autonomous unions.[48] The differences

46. Interview with PAN Director of International Relations Rolando García Alonso, June 11, 2004.
47. Interview with PAN Director of International Relations Rolando García Alonso, June 11, 2004.
48. Selection of the PRD's Senate list for the 2006 election was very contentious largely because of the continuing fallout from the 2004 Bejarano scandal (his wife and ally, Dolores Padierna, sought a spot on the list but was denied). The assignment of a spot to the UNT was also bumpy. Initially, Roberto Vega Galina, a leader of the UNT-member Sindicato Nacional de Trabajadores de la Seguridad Social (National Union of Social Security Workers, SNTSS) was chosen, but after allegations that the SNTSS was not truly loyal to the PRD, the decision was made to save the spot for a UNT leader after consulting with UNT members (Saldierna and Becerril 2006). Vega Galina, in fact, had earlier been a deputy for the PRI.

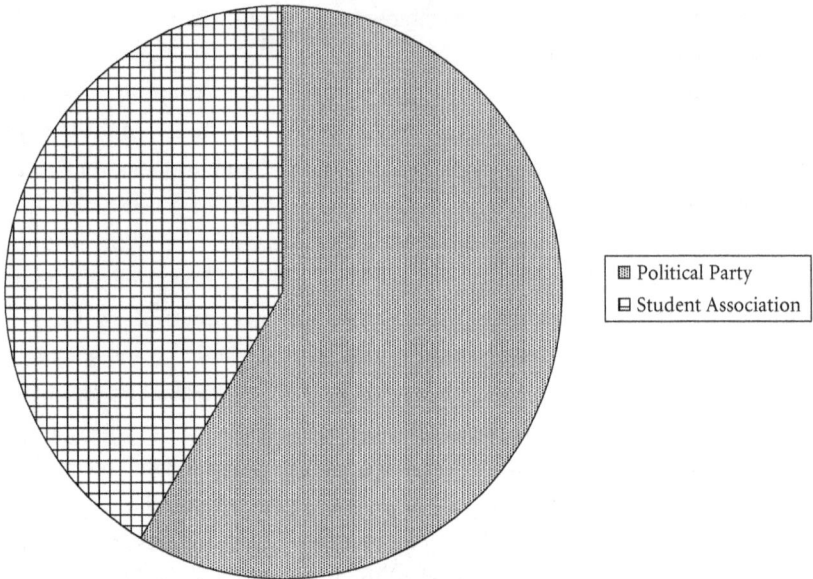

Fig. 17   Prior organizational affiliations of PAN legislators, 1997–2000. Proportion of total survey sample (n = 31). Notably, most deputies acknowledge a partisan history, but the survey does not reveal whether this is their history in their current party or time spent in a different party. Data provided by Manuel Alcántara, director of the Proyecto de Élites Latinoamericanas (Latin American Elites Project, PELA), Universidad de Salamanca (1994–2005).

between the parties' recruitment patterns are evident in data from the Latin America Elites Project. Data from the 1997–2000 and 2000–2003 delegations to the Chamber of Deputies, reveal a stronger partisan history in the PAN than the PRD, and the broader sectoral recruitment of the PRD—especially prior to 2000 (figures 17 through 20). A notable increase between congresses in the number of PRD candidates with union and social movement backgrounds is also apparent.

The parties exhibited marked contrasts in their linking institutions. One was the relative dynamism and originality of their institutional designs. After 2000 and particularly after 2003, PAN leaders enthusiastically pursued multiple avenues to establish ties with civic groups, ranging from individually driven outreach to the aborted homogeneous groups reform, mostly directed by an important new CEN-level agency within the party. In the PRD, party leaders continued to rely on the linking institutions of the past: the CEN secretariats, external candidacies, and campaign-related efforts.

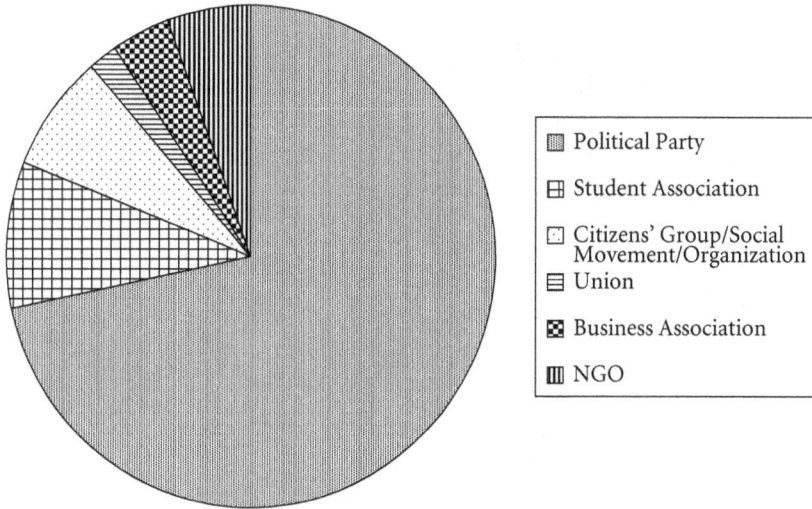

Fig. 18   Prior organizational affiliations of PAN legislators, 2000–2003. Proportion of total survey sample (n = 51). Notably, most deputies acknowledge a partisan history, but the survey does not reveal whether this is their history in their current party or time spent in a different party. Data provided by Manuel Alcántara, director of the Proyecto de Élites Latinoamericanas (Latin American Elites Project, PELA), Universidad de Salamanca (1994–2005).

The developmental prospects of their respective linking efforts offer a second contrast between the PAN and PRD. Because many of the PRD's linking institutions were bound up in campaign efforts (external candidates and the redes ciudadanas, for example), they were certainly conjunctural and likely short-lived. The PAN's efforts were perhaps equally electorally driven, but those strategies aimed to establish the PAN as a political (and not just electoral) presence among new constituencies. Given civic organizations' level of skepticism about parties, the PAN's efforts at presence perhaps held broader, long-term electoral payoffs.

PAN leaders began contemplating institutional change in order to capitalize on the bubble of support the party gained from Fox's candidacy, but when the party's vote share fell in 2003 and it was fined for irregularities associated with Amigos de Fox, institutional change became imperative. The PAN's new linking efforts thus responded to both the party's budgetary pressures and its electoral goals.[49] Those developments led party leaders to reevaluate the party's

49. Interview with PAN Secretary of Social Linkage Gerardo Priego Tapia, June 15, 2004.

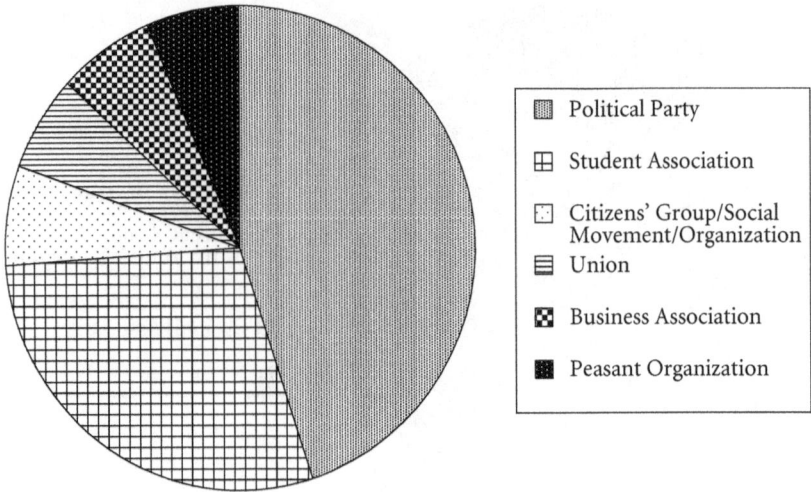

Fig. 19   Prior organizational affiliations of PRD legislators, 1997–2000. Proportion of total survey sample (n = 31). Notably, most deputies acknowledge a partisan history, but the survey does not reveal whether this is their history in their current party or time spent in a different party. Data provided by Manuel Alcántara, director of the Proyecto de Élites Latinoamericanas (Latin American Elites Project, PELA), Universidad de Salamanca (1994–2005).

turn toward professionalization, its linking institutions, and how it used its network of volunteers.[50] The resulting institutions were shaped by leaders' autonomy and by prior linking practices in the party. The failure of the reform of the process for establishing homogeneous groups was significant because it demonstrated the lack of consensus in the party's National Council about new linking efforts. Although the party presidency and CEN were insulated from the rank and file, and so did not need to negotiate with them, their efforts were checked by rival party leaders, who, in this case, were concerned about PAN links approximating those of the PRI.

It was not mere coincidence that the development of subsequent linking institutions in the PAN did not require action on the part of the National Council or revision of the party's fundamental documents. Work in the PAN's central office (including within Political Promotion of Women, Youth in Action, the Directorate of Relations, and Citizen Promotion) was redirected

50. A number of PAN leaders interviewed in 2005 trumpeted the centrality of the PAN's volunteers to the party's electoral success, although some also noted that the party had little choice in relying on that base given its budgetary constraints.

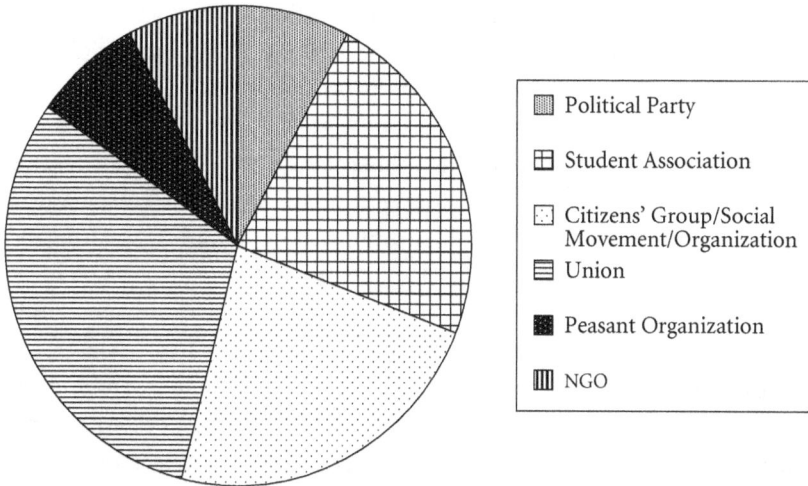

Fig. 20   Prior organizational affiliations of PAN legislators, 2000–2003. Proportion of total survey sample (n = 13). Notably, most deputies acknowledge a partisan history, but the survey does not reveal whether this is their history in their current party or time spent in a different party. Data provided by Manuel Alcántara, director of the Proyecto de Élites Latinoamericanas (Latin American Elites Project, PELA), Universidad de Salamanca (1994–2005).

by presidential initiative. Likewise, the creation of the Secretariat of Social Linkage was extra-statutory. Faced with the possibility of further defeats or setbacks from rival party leaders, the party leadership, under both Bravo Mena and his successor Manuel Espino, worked within its clear and uncontested purview, avoiding possible veto points. Still, the institutional designs that emerged remained consistent with PAN conceptions of democracy and the party's rejection of corporatism. Most of the party's new linking efforts were individualized (Teachers in Action, Youth in Action, PPM, and external candidacies, though external candidates may have been accompanied by "corporate sympathies"). The most ambitious new institutions, those administered by Citizen Promotion, still rejected corporatism and reflected the PAN's belief that civic organizations and political parties should be autonomous by relying, again, on creating elective affinities between the two types of organizations, not formal ties (PAN 2005).

The poor performance of Cárdenas and the PRD in 2000, when the party received just 17 percent of the vote, led PRD leaders to contemplate the party's failure to attract the support of the popular classes who would benefit, in their

mind, from its election. In the wake of that election, conflict among the corrientes reached a fever pitch, as competing groups assigned responsibility for
the party's showing, and many in the party began to speak of "refounding" it.
But although 2000 was discouraging for the PRD, and 2003 was for the PAN,
the PRD's improved performance at midterm inspired party leaders to unite
around its 2006 prospects, spurred on by the tremendous popular support for
López Obrador that came amid an effort to remove him from Mexico City's
mayoral office in 2003 and 2004. Despite concerns in many corners of the
party about its weak articulation with civil society, this newfound party unity
did not build consensus around establishing new links with civic groups.
Instead, the PRD continued to rely on its preexisting linking institutions: the
incorporation of civic leaders or refugees from other parties as external candidates, the work of its CEN secretariats, and the conjunctural electoral alliances
forged through the Secretariat of Relations and Alliances, by campaign teams,
or through subnational party offices.

The stability of the PRD's linking institutions did *not* reflect consensus that
they were effective. Indeed, party leaders of opposing camps either regarded
them as electorally ineffective or as merely electoralist. The PRD's inability
to make significant efforts toward building new linking institutions reflects
the realities of intraparty political life. Although the party leadership united
around propelling López Obrador to the presidency in 2006 and riding his
coattails, linking institutions treaded on the most divisive issue in PRD politics
(and the basis for the party's lasting corrientes): whether the party ought to
adopt the form of an institutionalized left party or a party-movement. On one
side of that issue were advocates of regularized relationships with civic actors
along the lines of the social-democratic model, tied more closely to the factions
of Amalia García and Jesús Ortega and disparagingly called "bureaucratic"
and "electoralist" by their party opponents.[51] The other camp (tied to the
social-movement-based corrientes) more often expressed concern about the
decapitation of social movements and the maintenance of movement autonomy. For example, in discussing the 2006 election, one CEN member argued
that further institutional development and organization was the key to success,
while a PRD senator believed it was best to return to the party-front model of

51. Interview with PRD Secretary of Electoral Affairs José Antonio Rueda Márquez, July 6,
2004.

the 1988 FDN coalition.[52] The same conflict reared its head in debates about campaign "ownership," when party leaders disagreed about whether campaigns should operate out of the party office with CEN support or through candidates' campaign teams, as well as in debates about the citizen networks. The problems resulting from those strategic differences were compounded by the relationships that individual corrientes formed with civic organizations—ties that did not extend across factions to benefit the party as a whole.[53] The PRD's linking institutions were locked into the realities of national party politics.

An examination of the PRD's linking practices within Mexico City supports this claim.[54] Since the moment when Cárdenas was elected mayor in 1997, the local party had maintained strong ties with *movimientos urbanos populares* (urban popular movements), especially those associated with local leader René Bejarano. Movement members were strongly represented in the PRD's delegation to the Asamblea Legislativa del Distrito Federal (Legislative Assembly of the Federal District, ALDF, the local legislature), and the movements themselves served important campaign functions, and in return, those legislators worked to provide the benefits that movement activists sought (such as housing, infrastructure, or other tasks delegated to state and local governments). Those ties, especially relative to other links the PRD maintained, were fairly regularized and stable, quite different from those managed by the CEN. Why? They were built in a context of party dominance, which assured the PRD in the Distrito Federal of reliable access to the government resources it used to maintain those patronage-based links. The centrality of the use of government resources to those relationships highlights a very important distinction between ties among party *organizations* and social movements (the focus in this chapter) and those among party *governments* and social movements (as examined in Bruhn 2008). In this case, the PRD derived much of its support from urban constituents because of the particularistic benefits PRD governments conferred based on legislative action. Those links also developed in a rarefied partisan environment within the PRD. While the CEN and National

---

52. Interviews with PRD Secretary of Political Relations and Alliances Hortensia Aragón Castillo, June 8, 2005, and Sen. Demetrio Sodi de la Tijera (PRD), July 5, 2004. These differences were likely compounded by the different time horizons that PRD actors had for the benefits of their linking efforts. Candidates like López Obrador may have operated on a shorter horizon than did party bureaucrats and activists interested in the longer-term development of the organization. See Pierson (2004).

53. Interview with PRD Secretary of Political Training Fernando Belauzarán, June 13, 2005.

54. This discussion is drawn from Bruhn (2008; 2005).

Council featured often-bitter divisions among competing factions, the capital was consistently governed by PRD mayors favorably disposed to the party-front model (Cárdenas, Robles, and López Obrador) and the party itself was clearly dominated by social-movement-based actors. The veto players that plagued the national party organization were by and large absent, enabling party and government leaders to fortify those relationships over time.

Lastly, the PRD faced an additional strategic obstacle in the formation of new types of links with civic organizations. In corporatist or post-corporatist Mexico, both the PAN and PRD judged certain types of linking institutions to be politically unviable—especially those Kenneth Roberts (2002) calls encapsulating linkages. This type of link is historically the mainstay of mass, left, indigenous, and even green parties in Latin America, Europe, and elsewhere (Van Cott 2005, 13–15). But in Mexico, the continuing associations between corporatism and PRI authoritarianism made such ties "undemocratic." In that environment, PAN leaders drew from the party's core conception of democracy as the realm of free and autonomous individuals to create new linking institutions that they hoped would generate individual sympathies (a lot of individual sympathies) for the party. Notably, apart from the aborted reform of the homogeneous groups, they steered clear of "the collective," which is central to encapsulating links. The PRD's emphasis on collective rights and participatory democracy seemed to prioritize linkage with civil society, but the delegitimation of the formal institutional ties typical of left parties presented institutional designers in the PRD with a very constrained set of institutional alternatives. That limited range, compounded by the restrictions imposed by national party politics, made institutional innovation particularly challenging.

Institutional Innovation and Democratic Representation

In a dynamic political environment in which parties faced volatile electoral support, leaders of the PAN and PRD sought to take advantage of the weakening of the PRI's corporatist hold on "official" Mexican civic groups while tapping into autonomous civil society as well. Doing so, party leaders reasoned, would bolster turnout in favor of their party and help their organizations develop a stronger and more durable foothold in the Mexican electorate. In both the PAN and PRD, leaders recognized that it was not just the political future of their party that was at stake, but also the longevity of the Mexican party system. Both parties steadfastly avoided developing linking institutions that

Table 4 Benefits and costs of linking institutions

	Benefits	Costs
Disavowal of linking	Avoid corporatist critique	
Linking through individualized institutions	Recruit popular leaders as external candidates	Minimal growth of members and popular support
Linking via elite dialogue	Incorporate civic organizations' position issues into party platform	
Linking via conjunctural organizational ties	Recruit external candidates and organized voters	Undermine civil society confidence in parties through short-term alliances
Linking via support for afín organizations	May build long-term party support in electorate	Potential for corporatist critique (e.g., blue CNC)
Linking via organizational ties	Establish mass base for party	Undermine core democratic commitments of party; expose party to corporatist critique
Linking via organizational absorption/incorporation	Establish mass base for party	Undermine core democratic commitments of party; expose party to corporatist critique

might be considered corporatist. The PAN crafted a new set of institutions and re-engineered existing institutions to target potential organized constituents and engender new political sympathies for the party. In the PRD, leaders relied on the vestiges of the party's foundation to represent civil society in the party, established CEN-driven efforts to develop organized constituencies, used campaign-centered electoral links, and, like the PAN, used external candidacies to draw in civic organizations and their members.

The long-term payoffs of these new linking institutions are not yet clear. Each of the types of linking institutions contemplated here has distinct benefits and costs to parties and their leaders (table 4).

Disavowal, the most visible type of linking institution prior to 2000, offered the PAN and PRD the ability to both sidestep the corporatist critique and continue to politically attack the PRI for its monopolistic links. Given the Mexican public's opposition to corporatism, this shared position held a certain logic, at least for a time. However, it did not help either of the parties build strong roots in Mexican society. Nor did the parties' reliance on overlapping memberships, particularly when both civic groups and the parties themselves asked individuals to leave one organization's identity at the other's door. The use of external candidates held greater potential payoffs for the parties, though at greater cost and with some uncertainty. For example, distributing candidacies to civic leaders deprived party members of candidacies and exposed parties to clientelistic demands, and there was no guarantee that external candidates would act as loyal partisans once in government. Some former external candidates left the party fold, like Senator Layda Sansores (Campeche), who left the PRI to be a candidate for the PRD, only to endorse Fox in the 2000 election. Still, where external candidates were leaders of civic organizations or maintained organized followings, they served as mechanisms to draw organized groups to the parties, at least during the election season. If and when those strategic and conjunctural ties showed parties to be simply electoralist, civil society's confidence in parties and the party system were likely further weakened, but such ties at least had developmental possibilities.

Two of the other types of linking institutions offered more likely long-term payoffs for the parties. Elite dialogue among civic groups and parties facilitated the incorporation of salient issues into party platforms and thus fostered informal ties of sympathy between the two types of organizations. In some cases, those informal ties were quite enduring—the PAN maintained a strong but loose connection to the Confederación Patronal de la República Mexicana (Mexican Employers Confederation, COPARMEX) from at least the 1980s through 2006 based on similar programmatic commitments and resulting in the recruitment of external candidates and the entrance of COPARMEX members into the party. The PAN's efforts through Citizen Promotion had similar potential to generate enduring sympathies, though the time horizon for payoff was unclear, and through them, the party risked exposing itself to the corporatist critique. Finally, the two types of institutions that promised a lasting party base, organizational ties and incorporation, were not pursued by either party after the PRD's foundation. Those institutions invited allegations of corporatism, and they contravened how both parties conceived of democracy as it related to the representation of civil society. Stated simply, that institutional design was fraught with problems, and leaders of both parties recognized that fact, though its avoidance was likely more damaging to the PRD than to the PAN.

The receipt of those payoffs was contingent on civil society responding to party overtures, and reciprocity could not, in fact, be taken for granted. Civic organizations of varied stripes in Mexico remained suspicious of formal institutions and especially political parties—another legacy of PRI rule.[55] When organizations from civil society did overcome their skepticism and establish relationships with parties, they often surprised parties with their strategic actions. Rather than develop singular ties with either the PAN or the PRD, three organizations, COPARMEX, the SNTE, and the Asociación Nacional de Actores, pursued links with multiple political parties—either because they were angling for political power in their own right or because they had particular political interests they sought to protect.[56] Their experience was not unique. As the PAN's Director of National Relations said, "Now, unions have to lobby with everyone" to advance their agendas.[57] Interviews with prominent civic groups confirmed that logic. Although the Frente Auténtico del Trabajo (Authentic Workers' Front, FAT) expressed greatest sympathies for the PRD's program, its leaders chose to maintain contact with multiple parties, in part because of questions about the PRD's "sinful" tendencies toward corporatism. Even COPARMEX, generally perceived as an ally of the PAN, met regularly with the PRD leadership and acknowledged a long-term political relationship with PRD leader Dolores Padierna.[58] Although those examples were not generalizable, they spoke to the challenges the parties faced in the post-2006 context of weak political loyalties and electoral volatility as they sought to stabilize their links with civil society and broaden their bases of political support.

The response from civil society was not the only limitation on the likelihood of parties' successful linking. Rather than representing coherent strategies for bringing political society into dialogue with civil society, the parties pursued multiple avenues simultaneously as they attempted to establish their long-term roots, on

55. Interview with PRD Secretary of Peasant Issues and Indian Communities Juan Mezhua Campos, June 8, 2005.

56. Interview with PAN Secretary of Elections Arturo García Portillo, June 15, 2005. He argued that the SNTE, increasingly autonomous from the PRI, was seeking to maximize its own independent power base in the 2006 elections. The National Actors' Association, meanwhile, was diversifying its party ties because it foresaw review of copyright legislation that would hold important implications for its members.

57. Interview with Hinojosa Céspedes, June 15, 2004.

58. Interviews with Erick Quesnel Galván, Coordinator of the National Office of the FAT, June 15, 2004, and Gabriel Aguirre, Director of Legislative Relations, COPARMEX, July 7, 2004. Aguirre also noted that COPARMEX had contact with 323 of the five hundred members of the 2003–2006 Chamber of Deputies, including 153 PRI members.

one hand, and continue performing well electorally, on the other. It was likely that those multiple strategies and the parties' different partners sometimes worked at cross-purposes. The typical origin of linking strategies at the level of the CEN or National Council of the parties presented two related problems. Civil society likely perceived party overtures for what they were: largely electoralist efforts by national party leaders. Despite all their maladies, were local parties to become the engines of new linking efforts, the response from civil society might be improved. The PRD's experience in Mexico City certainly supports that suggestion, though that case is in many ways exceptional. Designing and directing linking efforts from the central party office also subjected those efforts to turnovers in the party leadership and shifts in the dominant coalition of the party, and threw them into the world of factional politics. Again, linking at the local level might have mitigated some of these potential conflicts (though surely introducing others).

In many ways, the linking efforts of the PAN and PRD after 2000 were outliers in Latin America. As those parties courted the PRI's former allies, autonomous civic groups and their members in Latin America were moving instead toward individualized modes of linkage and indeed embracing more contingent patterns of political support (Roberts 2002, 21). Although it is true that some of the PAN's and PRD's new linking strategies targeted individuals, the PAN and PRD also focused on collective ties and long-term sympathies. At a time when "membership parties" were waning internationally, it bears asking what the likely payoffs are for pursuing these strategies. (see Dalton and Wattenberg 2000, especially the chapter by Scarrow, Webb, and Farrell). Likewise, the parties' linking efforts raise important questions about what alliances between civil society and political parties mean about party identity. When asked in 2004 what "type" of party the PAN was, PAN President Luis Felipe Bravo Mena replied, "That's a good question."[59] What are the implications for interest representation when a historically center-right, Christian Democratic party courts urban popular classes, teachers, and environmentalists, and when a left party disarticulated from the organized working classes becomes the voice of dissident business activists (Shadlen 2004, 96)?

59. Interview with PAN President Luis Felipe Bravo Mena, July 7, 2004.

7

THE END OF SAVAGE DEMOCRACY?

We've taken *democratismo* to the highest level, and it has battered us.
—PRD Deputy, 2000

Democracy has many meanings and many consequences, some expected and others unexpected. Calls for popular sovereignty and participatory democracy facilitated the rise of Hugo Chávez in Venezuela and the decline of the quality of democracy in that country.[1] Democracy promised stability in postwar Bosnia-Herzegovina but gave rise to ethno-nationalist parties and the international community's entrenched presence (Coles 2007). Mexicans and Mexican political parties also believed in the promises of democracy. Leaders of the PAN and PRD built their parties around democratic ideals, embedding notions of the rule of law, contestation, participation, and equality into their institutions. Even the PRI now champions democracy through its vision of a "social democratic" order (PRI 2006). This book analyzes the power of those democratic ideals and their institutional manifestations, arguing that parties' commitments to democracy not only limited the possibilities for institutional development and party change but also had unexpected outcomes akin to what has been seen in Venezuela and Bosnia-Herzegovina. Considered by many to be a panacea, democracy can in fact be savage. In the PAN and PRD, those savage consequences arose from processes of institutional change across three realms of party life.

The Logics and Choices of Party Leaders

Across different arenas of party life, party leaders faced difficult trade-offs between advancing their electoral goals, and thus hastening regime

---

1. According to Freedom House, Venezuela has experienced a reduction in political rights and civil liberties since the election of Chávez. Data available at www.freedomhouse.org.

democratization, and safeguarding their parties' democratic credentials. Open selection rules, professionalized and bureaucratic national party offices, and stable bases of support from civil society promised better election-day outcomes, but each carried significant political costs including the alienation of activists, volunteers, and rank-and-file members. The trade-offs that party leaders faced, and thus the possibilities for savage democracy's development, were historically and institutionally contingent. The regime's limited opening of the 1980s, itself a result of the PRI's loss of legitimacy, reconfigured the political landscape for opposition voices. Two effects of that reconfiguration were particularly important to the origin of the dilemmas that party leaders faced. First, the regime's political liberalization contributed to shifting the bases of electoral competition in Mexico from its historic left-right axis toward a democratic-authoritarian one. Second, the new structure of political opportunities both enabled opposition political actors to mobilize more openly and with greater success, and it facilitated the entry of new actors into politics.[2] Taken together, those circumstances shaped the institutional-social environment that opposition party leaders confronted from the early 1990s until after 2000, one characterized by: (1) a party-systemic emphasis on issues of democratic development; (2) a political space in which competition among parties increasingly determined access to power; and (3) a growing community of ambitious politicians, but one divided among long-time party activists, recently arrived social activists, and newly engaged politicos, all with competing political visions.

That diverse group of political actors met in two organizations, the PAN and (after 1989) the PRD, which both held fervently prodemocratic commitments for their internal party lives and strongly prodemocratic objectives for Mexican politics, though the PAN's vision of democracy centered on institutions and the rule of law whereas the PRD's focused on broad-based participation and social justice. Those democratic visions infused parties' internal institutions, constraining some actions, privileging particular types of voices, and influencing the strategic behavior of both individual actors and the parties. Although party leaders often sought to adapt the institutions of party life, they never had "free rein." One particularly enduring and important constraint on party leaders' actions was the strongly democratic character of existing party institutions.

---

2. By structure of political opportunities, I am referring to both Tarrow's (1994) conceptualization and Schlesinger (1994), who focuses more on opportunities for ambitious politicians to win office.

Democracy was imprinted on the parties at their founding moments, shaped how subsequent institutional decisions were made, and made some institutional outcomes more favorable and likely than others. The outcomes of those processes sometimes fortified party democracy and sometimes improved the quality of regime democracy. They also sometimes led to the perverse outcome I call savage democracy.

When party leaders attempted to adapt institutions, they typically did so in response to a shift in parties' political environments. For the PAN and PRD, the effects of electoral volatility frequently triggered institutional debates. Loss or underperformance figured prominently in the PRD's decision to shift to closed primaries after its poor showing in 1991 and again after the PAN's victory in 2000. The PAN's rules for presidential and gubernatorial selection were also opened after tepid performances in the hopes of selecting more viable candidates in the future. The PAN's vibrant linking efforts grew from concerns raised by the party's performance in 2003, though party leaders had expressed worries earlier about the party's shallow roots in civil society and weak ties to the electorate. And finally, both parties' efforts to professionalize and fortify their local organizations reflected leaders' desires to improve their individual performances relative to the PRI.

The relationship between environmental shifts (like electoral results) and party institutional change was not mechanistic. For example, during the 1990s, the PRD experienced tremendous peaks and valleys in terms of its appeal to the populace, and yet, many of its institutions exhibited stability. Meanwhile, in races for seats in the Chamber of Deputies, the PAN retained very closed rules for picking its SMD candidates, despite their typically embarrassing performance. Environmental changes do not *cause* institutional adaptations. Their effects are mediated by the institutional context in which party leaders operate, causing or drawing attention to institutional failures and so presenting leaders with the opportunity to make decisions about institutional change. Whether leaders make decisions and what their decisions are is, in turn, shaped by their relative autonomy from other party actors and the character of preexisting institutions. Although mechanisms of accountability (like leadership-selection rules) shaped their actions, often their choices appeared more closely tied to the realities of party politics, especially the power of veto players. Despite the indirect nature of party-president election within the PAN, for example, party leaders failed in their efforts to open legislative candidate selection; that statutory change required support from the party's more conservative National Assembly, which the leaders were unable to muster. Likewise, even when bureaucracy-sympathetic leaders like Amalia García headed the PRD, opposing *corrientes* that favored a party-front model of organization could derail bureaucratizing and professionalizing efforts.

Leaders' actions were also profoundly constrained by existing institutions, in several related ways. The forces associated with institutional resilience limited the likelihood of adapting institutions. When institutions were already in place, actors had often habituated themselves to them, while the institutions themselves were subject to the self-perpetuating force of path dependency. Those forces, compounded by coordination problems, reduced the likelihood that actors would attempt to adapt institutions. Even when they did, existing institutions, infused by the democratic imperative, continued to hold them back. For example, by legitimizing some alternatives and stigmatizing others, these democratic institutions influenced what leaders imagined in terms of possible change. Stigmatization was most clearly visible in the case of the linking institutions that followed a model of encapsulation. And the profoundly democratic institutions of the PAN and, particularly, the PRD increased the number of potential veto players, positioned to stymie efforts at institutional change.

Picking Paths: Explaining Modes of Institutional Change

Given those opportunities and constraints, it is not surprising that reformers are very strategic as they consider paths of institutional change. Still, it is not yet clear why they pick the paths they do (Pierson 2004, 160; Thelen 2003, 231–32). The range of institutional changes in candidate selection, bureaucratic development, and linking examined here offers a chance to contemplate the determinants of party leaders' choices. Sometimes leaders sought to overcome the obstacles associated with institutional resilience to engineer adaptations to institutions. When they elected to avoid those obstacles, they turned to other strategies to meet their objectives: institutional layering, institutional conversion, and even the pursuit of change through indirect methods. In some cases, they built new institutions from scratch, and finally, leaders sometimes left institutions as they were—because of the power of institutional momentum, because of opposing political coalitions, or because there were few viable alternatives.

Formal Adaptation. Relatively few of the institutions considered here were changed the "hard way," through formal processes of adaptation. That path was followed principally in the cases of candidate-selection rules, institutions that hold delimited and exclusive jurisdiction over particular zones of party activity. When party leaders faced decisions about adapting those rules to respond to shifts in the political environment, their set of choices was significantly limited: they could navigate the world of party politics to adapt the rules through statutory reform, they could leave the rules as they found them, or they could work around them. Decisions to open selection processes ended successfully when party leaders faced few internal obstacles, as in the PRD's shift to primaries in the early 1990s and the PAN's change to closed primaries for executive contests. Leaders often tried to formally adapt those institutions despite objections within the party, signaling their perceived centrality to electoral performance, but as the PAN's experience with its SMD Chamber of Deputies candidates demonstrates, reformist leaders sometimes could not sidestep those objections.

Adding Institutional Layers. In many cases, party leaders pursued alternative paths, rather than adapting institutions through formal, statutory processes. In cases of institutional layering, new institutions are grafted on top of stable existing ones, resulting in the proliferation of, and perhaps contradictions among, them (Schickler 2001, 15–16; Orren and Skowronek 1994; Thelen 2003, 226). By adding new layers, institution builders can avoid confrontations with constituencies supporting existing institutions and circumvent other reproductive forces while still crafting new rules and practices to advance their interests. The PAN and PRD both offer cases of institutional layering—unsurprising given that both parties contained powerful potential veto players (pragmatist and doctrinaire tendencies in the PAN; strong corrientes in the PRD).[3]

The PAN's strongly liberal-individualist orientation favored overlapping memberships and external citizen-candidates as mechanisms for bridging the party-society gap. However, as politics grew increasingly competitive, and as the PRI's hold over organized constituencies weakened, reformers in the party sought to develop new institutions that would add greater structure and support to that bridge. The first effort, the reform of the PAN's homogeneous groups, was abandoned because of internal opposition to statutory change.

---

3. Although Schickler demonstrates that formal institutions can be layered (as in budget committee structures in the U.S. congress), the primary formal institutions examined here were not. Candidate-selection rules are unique institutions in the sense that each particular rule is discrete (not affecting other rules) and complete (delimiting the entire process). Thus, layering such rules was not an option. When party leaders could not adapt those rules, they tended to use their centralized faculties (including veto powers).

Reformers learned from that experience, and worked within the CEN (where they encountered fewer veto points) to insert a new layer, the Secretariat of Social Linkage, and redirect (or convert, see below) the activities of a number of existing offices. Even that new layer, though, was still shaped by the PAN's discourse of democracy and individualism, emphasizing the role of the individual in his or her community. Although the political payoffs of those initiatives were not clear in 2006, the logic and process of the institutional changes involved certainly were.

Something akin to layering occurred repeatedly in the PRD's linking efforts as well. The party always maintained CEN-level secretariats intended to represent organized constituents (like social movements, women, and organized workers) in party debates and to fortify the relationships with those constituencies. Despite the party's bureaucratic transformations, those constituent offices were static, and no new stratum was inserted above or below them. However, outside the formal party organization, institutional layering was a regular occurrence, to the chagrin of some actors inside the PRD. Campaign-based linking efforts, like the citizen networks of the López Obrador 2006 campaign, aimed to circumvent what campaigners judged to be ineffective linking institutions by establishing loosely partisan, vote-getting ties in lieu of building enduring political relationships.

Redirecting Existing Institutions. Kathleen Thelen (2003, 228) defines converted institutions as those designed to serve one set of objectives but that are turned to other purposes. That definition implies that institutions have an identifiable singular objective. In reality, though, institutions often serve multiple, or different, purposes for different constituents, even at moments of institutional design. This complexity may make institutional conversion less enduring than layering processes, since the circumstances that led to a particular institution's conversion may be more likely to disappear than are new institutional layers. For example, at face value, it appears that candidate-selection rules are poor targets for institutional conversion, since they are such discrete institutions. Yet party leaders repeatedly converted them. Without sacrificing their core institutional purpose (candidate selection), PRD and PAN leaders also deployed the rules as linking institutions, by using them to select as external or citizen candidates the leaders of prominent civic groups that it was hoped would gravitate toward the parties. Once an external candidate was selected, they remained "selected," but the converted institution's function faded if an organized constituency failed to follow the selected leader or candidate, or if that individual failed to perform as a partisan bridge to civil society (for example, in cases where the person abandoned the party or his or her social base). Converted institutions may not retain their secondary functions because they lack asset specificity in their new capacity, something common to most new institutions. Until converted institutions are embedded in organizational life, they face substantial uncertainty.[4]

After the creation of Social Linkage, many of the PAN's citizen promotion programs were converted from a focus on the development and training of existing PAN members to the cultivation of new members and the establishment of ties with civil society. Party leaders redirected the offices of National Relations, Political Promotion of Women, and Youth in Action after the party's tepid performance in the 2003 elections. Those cases attest that conversion does not necessarily imply institutional discontinuity. Indeed, many of the staff members working in those areas post-conversion were the same longtime panistas that had occupied similar posts prior to their redirection. Although conversion and layering might be used to avoid political conflict or obstacles to change, they may not be contentious in their own right.

Changing Second-Order Institutions. A third, innovative strategy of institutional development pursued by party leaders was indirect, via adaptations in secondary or second-order institutions in order to facilitate first-order institutional change. This was a smart strategic tactic for leaders who held objectives that were unpalatable to any of the potential veto players in the party, as it enabled them to remove opposing leaders from their institutional position, increase their own clout, or change the balance of power in intraparty affairs. Four examples, three of which relate to changes in candidate selection, illustrate how these indirect paths operated and their potential effects on first-order institutions.

In 1996, the PAN adapted its membership rules to capitalize on support it received after its candidate's performance in the 1994 presidential contest. Under party president Felipe Calderón, the adherente layer was created and endowed with limited rights to participate in internal party affairs (including

---

4. The PAN's aborted Homogenous Groups reform offers a telling, though inverse, example. Article 11 of the PAN's statutes was, according to many panistas, designed to enable dedicated and like-minded PAN members to have a forum to deliberate and propose sector-based policy alternatives. It was not intended as a basis for political organization or faction development inside party life. PAN members opposed to using article 11 as a linking institution feared that the converted institution would develop interests around it, and the statute would be the basis for organized groups (gremios) making demands of the party. Ultimately, the conversion effort failed because of those concerns.

the 2000 and 2006 presidential candidate-selection processes). The lax requirements for adherente status effectively opened those nominations to much of
the electorate, creating a capacity to fundamentally alter future selection outcomes (even though the adherente presence was moot in 1999 and the more
conservative candidate triumphed in 2005). The increasingly strict delegate-
selection rules the PAN used for its convention-based selection processes had
the opposite effect—often privileging conservative activists who had strong
local bases of support. The nomination of the SMD deputies was effectively
closed through the adoption of those second-tier delegate-selection institutions. The PRD, after its disappointing 2000 performance, placed additional
conditions on its membership in the hopes of changing how its selection
process unfolded by protecting party selection processes from infiltration,
demagoguery, and the other maladies they occasionally faced, although the
party moved to open primaries shortly afterward, abrogating any effect of
membership rule changes.

A further example demonstrates the powerful effect that even informal
indirect institutional changes can have on first-order institutions. When
Manuel Espino was named president of the PAN in 2005, he altered the logic
for nominating his quota of the members of the CEN by moving from the
inclusion of prominent leaders (informally organized into teams) to regionalized representation (by state, though still including many prominent leaders).[5]
No statutory or regulatory changes were required for Espino to make such
a change, despite the potentially profound nature of its impact in terms of
introducing new agendas to national party politics. The PAN's CEN formulates
the party program, negotiates with other political actors, has substantial veto
powers (as in the case of state delegations), and has final authority over candidate-selection decisions, especially the party's PR candidates; changing the
cast of characters involved in those deliberations may substantially alter the
decisions that organ reaches in the future.

New Institutional Designs. In a handful of cases, institutions were built
from the bottom up—representing efforts by PAN and PRD leaders to design
fresh ways of doing their work. One clear instance of this was the construction of state and municipal party committees by both organizations. The
PAN's efforts began in force after 1986, when its leaders sought to move the
locus of local party organization from the legislative districts (three hundred

---

5. See Wuhs (2002, 92–96) on the procedures used by the parties to select their leaders.

throughout the country) to the municipalities (about 2,500). That effort was accompanied by a strengthening of the PAN's state level offices, which in turn became engendered such factional conflict that state delegations were imposed in almost half of them between 1986 and 2005. The PRD also aimed to establish local party branches in this period. Progress was difficult there as well, hampered by the PRI's opposition, budgetary constraints, and strong national leadership paired with weak local leadership. The building of PAN subcommittees and PRD comités de base has been even slower. Both parties experienced these challenges in the absence of major coordination problems or veto threats within the parties, which suggests how powerfully environmental factors shape the possibilities for institutional development. The PRI's targeted repression of the PRD contributed to its inability to capitalize on a virtuous cycle of electoral success, party finance, and organizational growth. Despite having encountered that virtuous cycle, the PAN's growth was sluggish. Therein lies an important and ironic implication for democratic development in Mexico: despite political opening and widespread support for democratic change, Mexico from the 1990s on did not offer a hospitable environment for party development because after decades of PRI rule, voters' and citizens' tremendous skepticism of parties itself exerted a veto.

The other clear case of new design was the crafting of linking institutions by the PAN after the establishment of the Secretariat of Social Linkage. Those strategies (including PLANTAR, ComUnidad, and Maestros en Acción) also show the varied effects that political environments have on processes of institution building. They shape the political imagination of institutional designers, as the source of ideas and in identifying institutional goals. Volatile electoral support paired with a financial crunch in the party awakened PAN leaders to the party's need for roots in civil society and a broader array of activists and campaigners. The weakening of the PRI's corporatist network likely influenced which sectors of society were targeted by the PAN's efforts. Maestros attempted to make inroads into the SNTE, a one-time stalwart PRI supporter turned unruly and undependable, while PLANTAR sought to establish a panista anchor in rural areas where the PRI's ability to maintain its historical clientelist network faltered. The precise character of the strategies reflected the institutional time in which they were developed: they were explicitly anti-PRI and anticorporatist in nature, pairing the construction of individual sympathies for the party with support for the proliferation of autonomous but sympathetic civic organizations.

Resilient Institutions. Despite a wide array of successful processes of institutional change, it should be noted that there were countless cases of failure and institutional stability (some examined here, but many not). In addition to path-dependent forces, institutional change is checked by coordination problems among institutional designers, the use of veto powers, and actors' adaptations to existing arrangements that privilege stability and inhibit the design of alternatives (asset specificity, to use Paul Pierson's [2004] terminology). The experiences of the PAN and PRD highlight how some of those factors operated in practice. Multiple PAN adaptation efforts encountered vetoes at the hands of either rival leaders or the party base, like the failed opening of the SMD candidacies for the Chamber of Deputies and the aborted adaptation of the homogeneous groups article. The static nature of the parties' PR candidate-selection rules the lasting presence of the PRD's corrientes and speak to the effect of asset specificity. In the former case, leaders recognized that those closed rules were their most direct influence over nomination processes, influence they sought to use to their own or the party's best interest. The likelihood of those rules changing was minimal, barring an uprising among party members. After the disappointing 2000 election for the PRD, factional leaders agreed at a national meeting to abolish the corrientes and refound the party. Despite the recognition that doing so could bring greater unity, those commitments disappeared shortly thereafter because the factions perform valuable political functions (like organizing leadership competitions, structuring debate about congressional leaders, and picking PR candidates), and their institutional foundation, the planilla system, had not been removed.

These accounts suggest that two factors combine to influence the path of institutional change (table 5). The first is the level of institutional specificity. Specific institutions, like candidate-selection rules, have delimited and exclusive jurisdiction over certain zones of activity, which requires that reformers use formal processes of institutional adaptation. Institutions that are less specific, like linking strategies, have less fixed and more easily duplicable functions, and thus they are more easily layered, converted, or built from scratch. The second determinant of institutional paths is the degree of organized opposition to change in party affairs (associated with the likelihood of coordination problems and of veto efforts).

When opposition to change is low for specific institutions, party leaders pursue the straightforward path of formal adaptation. For example, when the PRD shifted to closed primaries for its candidate selection in the early 1990s,

Table 5 Paths of institutional change

Strength of Opposition	Institutional Specificity	
	High	Low
High	Indirect paths use of institutional prerogatives Extra-institutionalism	Layering Conversion
Low	Formal adaptation New institutions	Formal adaptation Layering Conversion Indirect paths

Cárdenas was able to build sufficient support to amend the party statutes and regulations. His rival Muñoz Ledo was not able to muster a significant veto threat. When opposition is high, however, formal adaptation processes are less successful (like the failed opening of the PAN's SMD deputies rule). In such cases, party leaders may pursue indirect but equally formal adaptation processes (like amending membership rules) to achieve their goals. They may also turn to any institutional prerogatives they retain related to that institution's function. The CEN of the PAN, for example, retains the right to veto candidates, and both parties' executives have great input on the naming of alliance candidates. Where opposition is high and party leaders have no institutional prerogatives to draw on, they can either tolerate institutional stability or act outside existing institutions—both of which hold potentially dire consequences for party performance and the electorate's perception of the party.

When institutions are less specific, party leaders have a broader array of options. Both parties, for example, evidenced multiple ways of generating links with civic organizations. Still, the extent of organized opposition to institutional changes shaped the path party leaders chose. Considering again the PAN's linking institutions, party leaders centralized their efforts in the executive committee where they were less subject to pressures from their intraparty opposition. In that case, the strength of the opposition also limited institutional development by keeping linking institutions less specific. Had an organized opposition not been present in the PAN, the homogeneous groups reform (a more specific, statutory institution) might have been enacted.

In many cases, institutions were not adapted even when they performed poorly. This was particularly true in the PRD, where linking institutions were stable but weak and the central party office remained underdeveloped despite its apparent role in the party's underwhelming electoral performance. What makes the PRD especially interesting is that the party's institutions (specific and less so, formal and informal) often did not work satisfactorily and lacked strong internal support, yet leaders did not change them except through the proliferation of new institutional layers.

The explanation for PRD institutional stability lies in a preexisting institution that strongly conditions leaders' capacity to set agendas and act to achieve them: the planilla system that is used to elect the party's president and National Council members. This institution is a quintessential case of savage democracy. The planilla system, adopted in 1995, was designed to democratize party life by improving the representation of minority voices by guaranteeing them a voice in party affairs through proportional-representation contests to elect the party leadership. It also served as a basis for the development of corrientes, initially conceived as informal institutions to facilitate the ideological representation of the varied interests that came together at PRD's foundation in 1989. But the democratic hopes for the planilla system were supplanted by a series of unexpected outcomes. Despite repeated efforts to institutionalize the corrientes and increase their ideological content, they were primarily a means of achieving spaces of power within the party and securing candidacies. The corrientes, with all their pathologies, penetrated state and local party organizations as well.[6] To the extent that the corrientes had programmatic content, they represented the entrenched differences of opinion among PRD leaders regarding several overlapping issues of party development. Key among those differences were whether the PRD should be an institutionalized left party or a party-movement and the types of links that the party should maintain with civil society. The institutionalized representation of these extremely important distinctions through the planilla system, paired with the ideological turnover of that came with sequential PRD presidents, explains why the PRD by and large failed to adapt its institutions. The planilla system's proportional representation institutionalizes the presence of veto players and effectively constrains the prospects for institutional change.

6. See Wuhs (2002, chapter 5).

The planilla system's adoption in 1995 constituted a critical juncture in the development of the PRD because of the way in which party forces organized around it via the corrientes.[7] Although it was no model party beforehand, the adoption of this system placed the party on a path marked by intense internal conflict and institutional weakness. Its presence explains the continued battles among party corrientes and the failed efforts at their abolition, which in turn explain many of the maladies the party suffers across institutional arenas. Unfortunately for the PRD, there is no clear second critical juncture on the political horizon. Even the election of López Obrador to the Mexican presidency was unlikely to resolve the PRD's internal conflicts. Instead, it might have exacerbated them by introducing a new dimension of conflict around governance practices.

In 1989, the PAN experienced its own transformative shift, when President Luis H. Álvarez decided to accept public funds and to selectively collaborate with the PRI in the Chamber of Deputies. That decision enabled the party to access the virtuous cycle of party development and electoral performance (chapter 5), particularly after the departure of the Foristas. Some within the PAN credit Álvarez's personal leadership for that fundamental change in the party's direction. However, his victory in the party's presidential contest in 1989 was owed to Clouthier's strong performance as the 1988 presidential candidate and the increasing clout of the neopanistas in the party. In terms of its effects on competitive politics, these developments in the PAN may rival the PRD's adoption of the planilla system, but it would be difficult to call the PAN's transformation a critical juncture in party institutional life since it resulted from several independent decisions taken over a decade rather than a single moment, and because it did not create structures around which internal forces could organize and institutional design and change could revolve.

---

7. Historical institutionalists frequently make reference to a core set of theoretical constructs: reproduction and reproductive cycles, developmental paths or trajectories, path dependency, and critical junctures. This last idea refers to events or outcomes at particular historical moments that induce path-dependent processes (Pierson 2004, 195). Collier and Collier (1991), for example, argued that the mode of labor incorporation in South America and Mexico was a critical juncture that profoundly influenced future regime dynamics, while Mahoney (2001) demonstrated how differing nineteenth-century conceptions of liberalism shaped later patterns of political development in Central America.

Table 6 Institutional changes in the PAN and PRD, 1991–2006

	PAN	PRD
Candidate selection	Selective opening, esp. in executive contests; continued use of conventions and centralized PR nomination	Aggressive opening of all rules except very centralized PR nominations
Bureaucratic development	Aggressive professionalization; weak state and local development	Weak professionalization; very weak state and local development
Linking	Aggressive and multi-directional linking change: new layers, converted agencies, continued reliance on external candidates	Few changes: continued reliance on external candidates and CEN agencies, significant campaign-centered efforts

Adding Up to Oligarchy? The Consequences of Institutional Change

The changes the PAN and PRD experienced in their selection rules, bureaucracies, and linking strategies add up to pronounced transformations in the nature of each party's organization (table 6). Although there are countless dimensions along which the parties might be compared to their former selves, one particularly salient question for the PAN and PRD is whether their leaders accumulated more power through those changes. After all, the concentration of influence among leaders was the key component of Michels's (1962) iron law. When leaders gain more power, he argued, their interests depart from those of the rank-and-file members, leading to autocracy. In the introduction to this book, I suggested that rather than blame leaders, as individuals, for the pathologies of this iron law, it ought to be embedded in the world of institutions, since leaders usually come and go, but institutions tend to stick. The operative question is: Did those institutions create oligarchies?

Leaders of the PAN certainly amassed more power during the period examined here. The party's professionalization effort strengthened the administrative capacities of the central party office, a process facilitated by financial support from the IFE based on the party's electoral performance. Although substantial development occurred in the PAN's state-level party offices as well, they were so plagued by difficulties that it had the backhanded effect of further empowering the national party through its control of the state delegations. The PAN's linking institutions were also reconfigured at the national level, through the efforts of the new Secretariat of Social Linkage. Much of the work of this secretariat was performed "on the ground," but the vision and direction of these changes were crafted in the CEN. Likewise, to the extent that external candidacies were mechanisms for linking, they too were subject to approval by the national leadership.

Some PAN candidate-selection rules were opened (like those for executive contests), while others were stable (the PR rules) and some were even closed at the margins (the SMD deputies). Party leaders did not formally accumulate significantly more power through any of those changes. However, the shift from conventions to primaries, despite increasing the scope of the selectorate, endows leaders with more authority by disempowering local party organizations and their activists (Katz 2001, 291–92). From that point of view, only in its SMD Chamber of Deputies processes is the PAN's national leadership reined in. Those rules privilege the most conservative members of the party and according to party leaders regularly produce candidates with little possibility of performing well, a fact borne out by the PAN's poor record of winning SMD deputy seats.[8] Of course, those rules were also the subject of a failed exchange—recall that PAN leaders offered members more voice in naming party leaders in exchange for reducing their influence over precisely these nominations.

The PRD is reputedly more centralized than the PAN, and until very recently was often referred to as one man's party—a machine built around Cuauhtémoc Cárdenas. After the 2000 presidential election, Cárdenas's profile in the party diminished, but the assumptions about how internal party life operated in the PRD remained. The party's institutions suggest something quite different, though. The central party office of the PRD was sorely underdeveloped as a result of frequent turnover, repeated fiscal crises and corruption problems, and disagreements about whether party development would be a benefit or a liability. Its weak development extended to state and municipal party offices as well. At face value, the national leadership seemed poorly positioned to be oligarchic. The party's linking institutions were similarly feeble, often overshadowed by the efforts of the party's candidates to mobilize both party members and nonmembers during the campaign season. The PRD's selection

---

8. Opening this selection process was discussed at the party's National Assembly in June 2007.

rules clearly offered leaders significant influence; given Richard Katz's (2001) argument about primaries and elite power, the PRD's processes were universally beholden to leaders' desires.

PAN and PRD leaders, by 2006, were more powerful than their predecessors, at least across the three areas of institutional life examined here. Of course, it is also tempting to draw comparisons across the two organizations about the relative strength of their leaders, though doing so is risky business. Based on the data presented here, it seems that PAN leaders are significantly stronger than their counterparts in the PRD, primarily due to differences in party bureaucratic development but also the nature of linking institutions. That assessment flies in the face of conventional wisdom, which holds the PAN up as a decentralized organization and the PRD as a caudillo-driven, elitist party. But effectively discussing the strength of party leaders requires shifting the focus from exclusive attention to formal institutions to a mix of formal and informal institutions. One explanation for the counterintuitive finding is that institutions matter more in daily PAN life than they do in the PRD. As an organization, the PAN has long trumpeted its institutional fortitude, and PAN members repeatedly distinguished their party from the PRD on those grounds. Implicit in their statements was an emphasis on rational-legal authority structures and formal institutions. In the PRD, however, traditional and charismatic authority structures played and continue to play a central role—whether the figurehead was Cárdenas, Rosario Robles, or Andrés Manuel López Obrador. Power in the PRD operated through institutions, but also outside of them. Indeed, the weak institutions of the PRD and the strength of its charismatic leaders may constitute yet another vicious cycle in which the party is caught: weak parties depend on strong leaders to ensure their survival, and strong leaders are loathe to build institutions that may hem in their influence in the future.

The same institutional changes that empowered party leaders have fundamentally altered the role of party members in electoral affairs. Where both parties once prioritized naming candidates that had the support of the party rank and file, by 2006 they had turned (at least potentially) to the electorate, resulting in the selection of less partisan candidates and altering the behavior of elected officials by changing the actors to whom they were accountable. Opening also undermined the importance of party membership and alienated activists and volunteers from the party organization. Parties' linking institutions similarly sought to branch out beyond party members. The PAN's efforts targeted rural people, indigenous populations, and urban popular sectors, while PRD-affiliated campaign efforts courted the median voter through nonpartisan appeals. Party activists were not excluded and lost no statutory power as they did in candidate selection, but their voices and interests were surrounded by a cacophony of other, sometimes louder and often opposing, voices. The parties' efforts at bureaucratic development aimed to strengthen centralized administration and supplant volunteers with political professionals. The PAN largely succeeded in its efforts, whereas the PRD's attempts stalled because of internal disagreements. Longtime PAN leaders cited professionalization as one of the factors alienating both party activists and many fellow leaders, while repeated and vociferous debates on the theme in the PRD revealed to party members and the electorate at large the extent of discord in the organization.

Savage Democracy and the Development of Mexican Democracy

> There is no doubt: Democracy is being born. The question for each person is what does democracy do for me? The answer is that democracy does nothing for me. And this is tremendously dangerous.
>
> —Enrique Semo, Mexican intellectual, 2000

Although democratization has had many unintended consequences in Mexico, perhaps the most savage and most problematic one is the shifting nature of political representation resulting from transformations in party organization. As political leaders favored their electoralist goals, party members' capacity to influence decisions declined, as did the likelihood that their parties would advance their interests in governing bodies.

Political parties are the main link between citizens and their governments. They are the primary means through which citizen preferences are aggregated, channeled toward the state, and transformed into policy ("substantive" or "mandate" representation). It is also through parties that elected officials are held responsible for their actions, in what is known as "accountability" representation (Fiorina 1980, 26; Manin et al. 1999; Powell 2004; Stokes 2001). Although parties have other responsibilities in democratic settings, without effective parties, representation suffers. Party members used to figure prominently in discussions of representation, especially during the era of mass parties. That type of party, with its large and formally enrolled membership, opened representative channels for newly enfranchised voters in exchange for their electoral support, and, especially in Europe and North America, "enhanced the democratic legitimacy and stability of political systems" (Scarrow 1996, 1). Since the 1970s, mass parties from those regions witnessed declining memberships and strengthened central party offices (detailed in Aldrich 1995, 15; Dalton and Wattenberg 2000; and Schlesinger 1994, 2). Confronting new electoral realities, many former mass parties sought voters outside their traditional bases, a change associated with the development of catch-all parties and the contagion from the right (Epstein 1980, 257–60; Kirchheimer 1966).

The institutional changes evident in the PAN and PRD during Mexico's protracted transition to democracy in many ways resemble those experienced by parties in the advanced industrialized countries since the 1970s, leading some authors to argue that Mexican party politics have been "Americanized" and that the PAN, PRD, and the PRI are moving toward catch-all status (Klesner 2005; Mizrahi 2003, 5; Shirk 2005). But if the institutional changes in the PAN and PRD indeed constitute such a turn, it has occurred under vastly different circumstances and, importantly, "out of sequence."[9] The American and European shift away from mass membership parties occurred at least a generation after the consolidation of democratic regimes and in political systems marked by broad-based participation. Furthermore, the move at least coincided with and arguably resulted from the de-alignment of the electorate. Voters spurned parties, not the other way around (Dalton 2000, 36). Parties responded by broadening their electoral appeals—all in the context of democratic institutions that were widely perceived as legitimate.

Mexico followed a very different sequence. The PAN and PRD turned from their members before the country had even experienced a transition to democracy: Mexicans in the late 1980s and early 1990s (when the parties began to turn) were only beginning to see the possibility of meaningful competition for power and the potential value of party membership, regularized participation, and institutional representation. Likewise, these institutional changes in the PAN and PRD occurred during a period of increasing, not declining, partisanship. Despite Mexicans' skepticism about parties, significant and identifiable cadres shifted their loyalties to the PAN and PRD during the transition years. But whereas in Europe, the affiliation of new cadres of voters to particular parties was "crystallized" for decades after World War II, growing affiliation in Mexico coincided with reduced roles for members in party affairs. It occurred

---

9. Pierson (2004, chapter 2) offers an insightful discussion of sequencing and temporality in rational choice and historical institutionalism.

before parties were entrenched in the electorate and prior to the formation of lasting attachments to particular parties.

The demands of political competition, the dominant face of the democratic imperative, led party leaders to shift their efforts from fortifying their links to activists and members to courting the broader electorate. Paired with modern modes of political organization and campaigning, this logic of institutional change within parties, by party leaders, made political sense and resonated with the experiences of many parties in the advanced industrial countries. But although the same signs of a catch-all turn were arguably present in Mexico, the country and its parties were in a very distinct institutional time and space. At the precise moment when the PAN and PRD could have forged meaningful relationships with distinct segments of the electorate, they turned to "the electorate." Although the PAN and PRD were unlikely to develop into true mass parties, they might have established stable roots for themselves in civil society and among Mexico's citizens.[10] Instead, they adopted electoralist modes of political organization.

The turn away from membership at the moment of political opening will have long-lasting consequences. Indeed, it may constitute a critical juncture in the development of Mexican politics. Those "Americanizing" developments placed Mexico on a less fortuitous path than the one often imagined for it, which would run parallel to that of the United States, toward party institutionalization and democratic consolidation. Although parties continue to monopolize the channels of representation between citizens and the state, they are only weakly legitimate in the eyes of those citizens. Mexicans, on average, have "not very much" confidence in their political parties, according to data from the World Values Survey; in only three Latin American countries (Argentina, the Dominican Republic, and Peru) do parties score lower.[11] The institutions that once guaranteed influence for party activists and members have largely been dismantled, weakening the one foothold the parties once

10. Indeed, during the Fox sexenio, their combined memberships totaled between five and six million people, about five percent of the Mexican population Data provided by the PAN's Secretariat of Organization, and by PRD Secretary of Organization Guadalupe Acosta in interview with author, June 22, 2004.

11. Norris (2002) presents data from the World Values Survey (1995–2001) on Mexicans' confidence in their political institutions. Mexico scores in the lower half of her sample of 13 countries on the mean value of confidence in political parties. Mexicans have less confidence than do Americans, Canadians, Salvadorans, and Brazilians, and about the same as Venezuelans and Colombians. During the survey period, Venezuela's party system was undergoing a dramatic process of collapse.

had in the electorate. Although retaining their powerful place in the political system, party leaders have limited the incentives voters have to form lasting attachments to particular parties. The result, especially when paired with the centrist drift of the parties, will likely be increased electoral volatility and a truncation of the range of views represented in the political system.

The sequence followed in Mexico may threaten the longevity of Mexico's democratic experiment by undervaluing party membership, undercutting representation, and undermining the institutionalization of the party system. Prior to Mexico's democratic transition, analysts were cautiously optimistic about the country's democratization process, as long as the PRI could be removed power. In the PAN and PRD, they saw parties that were reasonably developed and not overly personalistic, and, based on election returns, that seemed to have fairly identifiable bases of support. Furthermore, prior to 2000, the Mexican party system featured parties that were ideologically distinct, offering voters a meaningful choice at the ballot box. No one idealized the PAN and PRD, but relative to other new democracies in Latin America and Eastern Europe, where the construction of an effective political society seriously impeded democratic development, Mexico seemed well-positioned. As Mexico experiences the second post-authoritarian sexenio, caution may be outweighing optimism. PAN and PRD leaders together ousted the PRI from power, but in doing so, they weakened their own democratic lives and closed many of their representative channels. Increasingly isolated from their activists, members, and the Mexican voter, the parties themselves may be future victims of savage democracy.

This story of institutional change and party development holds important insights for future studies in politics. When I began this project in the mid-1990s, analysts dedicated a lot of time and energy to understanding the conditions under which the new democracies of the Third Wave would "consolidate." One of the primary concerns they raised was the relative strength of the party system or of political society (Mainwaring and Scully 1995; Linz and Stepan 1996). Notably absent from many studies of party systems and democratic development was in-depth analysis of the world of party politics. As is quite clear from this book, excising party politics from studies of democratic development is a grave error. Parties are the on-the-ground face of formal, electoral, democratic politics. Warts and all, they continue to represent the primary link between citizens and the state, making their capacity to effectively perform their varied duties important, especially in new democracies that are weakly legitimate.

The way that parties' internal institutions develop and operate is crucial to understanding transformations in the patterns of participation and representation that are so critical to democratic development. The experiences of the PAN and PRD demonstrate how relatively minor and discrete institutional adaptations have profound cumulative effects on party organization and for party systems and regimes. In particular, Michels's concerns about divisions between the leaders and the led remain very salient today: in Mexico, even the most prodemocratic parties are growing away from their rank-and-file members. This is a particularly inauspicious development because, as in Venezuela prior to the collapse of the party system, Mexican parties hold tremendous institutional power but not the trust of the citizens.

Party leaders are central actors in processes of institutional change. They are simultaneously empowered and constrained by party institutions to adapt to shifts in the opportunity structures of their organizations. That is, leaders should be understood as institutional figures—not directing institutions from above, but acting among those institutions. Their capacity to act is determined by their institutional surroundings, their own power, and the institutional "punishing power" of others. Even in contexts where informal institutions are very important, like the PRD, leaders' actions are constrained institutionally. Beyond the more obvious limits on leaders (such as no-reelection), two particular and interrelated ones featured prominently in this book.

The first is the context of institutional change. Institutions are not designed in a vacuum nor does the evolution of existing institutions occur in one. Rather, they are strongly conditioned by the contextual elements of "institutional time" and "institutional space."[12] The brand of authoritarianism built by the PRI shaped the foundation and developmental possibilities of the opposition parties. Even when opposition party leaders ostensibly had the capacity to make decisions autonomously, they were not autonomous. They operated in spatial and temporal contexts that influenced the institutional adaptations they imagined and that structured their decision making, resulting in some striking similarities in the PAN and PRD despite their divergent histories and opposing

---

12. Ekiert and Hanson (2003b, 20) define institutional time as "regularized patterns of social action enforced by institutional characteristics of particular regimes" and institutional space as the "political construction of formal national and international boundaries and jurisdictions." Because space is a constant in this analysis, I devote less attention to it here.

programs. Even after 2000, PRI rule continued to influence how the parties restructured their internal institutions.[13]

The second limitation on leader's institutional decisions emphasized here was the power of ideas. Ideas occupy an awkward place in institutional studies—although attention to ideas in institutional analyses is growing, they remain inadequately incorporated into explanatory efforts outside international relations (Lieberman 2002). Margaret Weir (1992, esp. 207–9) sought to address the interaction of ideas and institutions in U.S. employment policy, and she found that existing political institutions prevented Keynesian ideas from establishing a firm foothold in the United States.[14] Her account privileges institutions over ideas, which is perhaps accurate in that case but a potentially problematic assumption, especially at moments of institutional design. At those crucial times, ideas are powerful forces in their own right. Reproductive forces like path dependency may make institutions less penetrable by "new" ideas (as Weir suggests), but the effects of "founding" ideas often endure, codified as they are in political institutions. There can be little doubt that institutions shape the preferences of political actors and the strategies they pursue. What the PAN and PRD convincingly show is the profound way that ideas condition the structure of institutions. Ideas about democracy were embedded in PAN and PRD institutions at the parties' foundations, and those visions guided processes of institutional design, influenced the paths of institutional change that leaders pursued, and limited the range of institutional alternatives available to them.[15]

13. Institutional time has been reframed in studies of democratization as the effect of prior regime types on democratic trajectories. See the insightful review essay by Snyder and Mahoney (1999). Similar legacies of institutional design appear significant in other polities that experienced transitions from one-party rule during this period. In Senegal, Taiwan, and South Korea, the imprint of this variant authoritarian rule conditioned not just internal party organization but also the nature of presidentialism, legislative composition, and the bases for competition in the party system (Wuhs 2007).

14. Weir (1992, 207) argues that those institutions severed potential connections between public philosophies ("broad concepts that are tied to values . . . and that can be represented in political debate") from expert-driven programmatic ideas ("statements about cause-and-effect relationships attached to a method for influencing those relationships"). She later notes that Reagan's ability to conjoin the two around supply-side economics (despite its dubious reputation among economists) was the key to his success.

15. In lieu of "democracy" as a rallying cry, Senegal's pro-democratic opposition organized around the idea of "change" (*sopi*, in Wolof). Drawing from Deegan-Krause's (2006; 2003) work in Eastern Europe, I argue elsewhere (Wuhs 2007) that these transitional "issues" predispose party systems to unstable and unanchored patterns of party competition since the issues themselves disappear with alternation, leaving behind actors still structured around them and an electorate divided by them.

The influence of time, space, and ideas on institutional design and development evident in the Mexican parties suggests that studies of institutions need to conjoin two concurrent strands of research. Following divides among types of institutionalisms, scholars tend to examine either the politics of institutional design or the processes involved in institutional development and resilience. Although important distinctions exist among schools of institutionalists, our analyses suffer from the stark divisions among them. Though it is now widely recognized that design is more than the outcome of strategic bargains among self-interested individuals, too often those interactions are extracted from their surroundings. Scholars need to deploy the tools of historical institutionalism to embed those moments within their temporal, spatial, and ideational contexts. Likewise, decisions made by designers undoubtedly affect not just the initial construction of institutions but also the prospects of long-term institutional development and future efforts at institutional change. In light of the staying power of institutions, it is essential that we effectively examine the interplay of actors, contexts, ideas, and interests. Only then will we improve our understanding of how institutions evolve.

EPILOGUE: THE LEGACY OF THE DEMOCRATIC IMPERATIVE

On July 2, 2006, Mexico experienced a tremendously contentious and ultimately divisive presidential election. PAN candidate Felipe Calderón and PRD/Alliance for the Good of All candidate Andrés Manuel López Obrador both soundly defeated PRI candidate Roberto Madrazo, but a razor-thin margin separated the top two candidates. After prolonged deliberation by the Tribunal Federal Electoral (Federal Electoral Tribunal, TRIFE) and months of protest by López Obrador's supporters, Calderón was designated president-elect of Mexico. He assumed office in a chaotic inauguration ceremony on December 1, 2006. The campaign and election taught us many things about the future of Mexican politics, including the challenges facing the PRI, the regionalization of party competition, and the nature of Mexico's emerging programmatic politics.

It also held important lessons about institutional development in Mexico and its implications for democratic consolidation there. The post-electoral upheaval revealed the power of the past to influence contemporary politics. Calderón and López Obrador campaigned, protested, and waited in an anachronistic institutional time: although the transition was in the past and the PRI was a non-opponent in 2006, the leading candidates' pronouncements drew on the ideational and institutional frameworks that constituted the democratic imperative. It should come as little surprise that the candidates and their parties had adapted to the institutional context of transitional politics. However, the post-electoral period also demonstrated that other political institutions had been habituated to the exigencies of the democratic imperative. Although the election itself is now past, it leaves two questions behind: when will the democratic imperative's lock on Mexican politics be opened, and what are the prospects for democratic deepening until it does?

The Setting and Staging the Post-Electoral "Democratic" Battle

The showdown that occurred between López Obrador and Calderón and their parties after the 2006 election had its origins in developments over the course of the Fox sexenio. Two preconditions were particularly crucial. First, without PRD participation, the Congress named a new cohort of Citizen Councillors to the Instituto Federal Electoral in 2003, setting the stage for the PRD's condemnation of future IFE actions. Second, the PAN and PRI launched an attempt at *desafuero* (lifting of immunity from prosecution) in an effort to remove López Obrador from the office of mayor of Mexico City, based on allegations that he violated an injunction by opening a hospital access road on expropriated land. The desafuero not only ultimately failed, but it also aggravated existing tensions among the parties and gave López Obrador a significant bump in his approval ratings and overall political profile.

The PRD candidate's high profile enabled him to pull significantly ahead in the polls. Then, during the final months of the campaign, Calderón's campaign team became increasingly aggressive in its negative attacks on López Obrador, in particular raising concerns about similarities between López Obrador and Venezuelan President Hugo Chávez.[1] Although the PAN attacks also denounced his redistributive proposals and his critiques of neoliberalism, those spots most importantly questioned whether López Obrador would abide by democratic institutions if elected. The advertisements, along with comments from President Fox and López Obrador's absence from the first presidential debate in late April, contributed to Calderón's surge in the polls in early May. The two candidates were in a statistical tie during the final weeks of the campaign, setting up a tremendous test for the country's electoral institutions.

About forty-two million Mexicans cast ballots on July 2, nearly 59 percent of the eligible pool of voters. Although the IFE used a highly reputable preliminary reporting system (called the PREP), the margin between Calderón and López Obrador was so slim that the IFE declined to call the election that night. The candidates themselves were less reticent, with both announcing their victories before the press. By the end of the next day, not only had the IFE declared Calderón the victor (pending district tallies), but López Obrador had demanded a full recount of the vote. When the final tallies were completed on July 5, they revealed a very narrow margin of victory for Calderón: 35.89 percent to 35.31 percent, a difference of about 243,000 votes.

López Obrador challenged the results both through formal institutions and in the streets. He quickly filed an eight-hundred-page legal brief with the TRIFE

---

1. By this time, it was clear that PRI candidate Madrazo would be an also-ran. See Langston (2007).

documenting various irregularities in the IFE's management of the electoral process. His chief complaints included disparate levels of party financing, Fox's inappropriate campaigning for Calderón, the use of social spending to sway voters, and some procedural issues, including the late replacement of poll workers and possible manipulation of the PREP. All told, he alleged that irregularities had occurred at more than 52,000 polling stations. Once he had registered his objections with the TRIFE, López Obrador called on his supporters to march in defense of democracy. A massive protest in mid-July was followed by the successful blockade of Paseo de la Reforma and several other major streets in downtown Mexico City, and the occupation its main square, the Zócalo. All of this caused a severe disruption of the city's social, commercial, and political life. With the support of the Mexico City government (then governed by PRD member Alejandro Encinas), López Obrador sustained the occupation for nearly two months, until just before Independence Day (September 16).

Amid López Obrador's campaign of civil disobedience, the TRIFE's deliberations about his complaints continued. In early August, the tribunal announced it would recount the votes at only 11,839 polling stations, just 9 percent of the total, earning the country's electoral institutions further harsh criticism from López Obrador. On September 5, the TRIFE finally announced that there was insufficient evidence of fraud for a general annulment, which effectively anointed Calderón as president and provoked new tactics by López Obrador.[2] Despite shrinking public support, defections from some of the Alliance partners, and silence from prominent PRD leaders (notably, Governors Lázaro Cárdenas Batel of Michoacán and Amalia García of Zacatecas), López Obrador continued to fill the Zócalo with protestors throughout the fall. It would be the site of both of his self-declaration as the *Presidente legítimo de México* (Legitimate President of Mexico) at his National Democratic Convention marking Independence Day and of his taking the oath of office on the anniversary of the Mexican Revolution (November 20).[3] Although he did not follow through with his initial plans to shut down the legislative palace of San Lázaro, his supporters almost prevented Calderón from being sworn in on December 1. Only after a scuffle between PAN and PRD legislators was Calderón able to climb to the podium and don the presidential sash.

2. Statistical studies examining López Obrador's allegations have suggested that even if his allegations did hold, they would not have changed the election outcome (Aparicio 2006).

3. Some PRD leaders still referred to him as the presidente legítimo as late as April 2007. Interview with PRD Secretary of Political Relations and Alliances Hortensia Aragón Castillo, April 24, 2007.

The Candidates' "Democratic" Pronouncements

Calderón and López Obrador both wanted to win the presidency—indeed, each declared that he had. The way that the two candidates defended their postures after the election revealed the extent to which they and their parties had been shaped by transitional politics. Although some analysts argue that López Obrador's actions reflect a messianic disposition (Grayson 2007), his actions and those of Calderón drew very clearly from the conceptions of democracy that their parties espoused, highlighting one legacy of the democratic imperative for contemporary Mexican politics.

During and after the campaign, Calderón proposed continuity with Fox's moves toward liberal democracy. Calderón's actions throughout the postelectoral deliberations revealed his disposition toward this model of democracy. In the weeks following the election, Calderón argued that the contest was "absolutely legitimate. The legitimacy comes from the law, and the democratic way in which the election was carried out" (McKinley 2006b). In his testimony before the TRIFE, he noted: "It is here and not in the street that the election should be graded. We will not allow the votes of millions and millions of Mexicans to be canceled out by demagoguery and senselessness" (Murray and Barrera 2006). He insisted on following the formal rules of vote-counting and recounting, and promised to respect the institution's findings. Of course, circumstances also favored a strongly institutionalist approach for Calderón, since precedent seemed to mitigate against a general recount.

In contrast, López Obrador avowedly advocated a vision of democracy premised on legitimacy over legality and the will of the masses (the *pueblo*) over the rights of individuals. The "defense of democracy" required civil disobedience and mass rallies—that is, politicking in the court of public opinion rather than the electoral court (Stevenson 2006).[4] Even after the TRIFE's final ruling, he impugned Calderón's legitimacy as the president of Mexico: "I will not recognize anyone who parades himself as the head of the federal government without legitimate credentials" (Economist 2006). After again questioning the objectivity of the country's electoral authorities, he further remarked, "to hell with the institutions" (Economist 2006). Like Calderón's comments, the PRD candidate's logic for calling and sustaining the protests centered on

---

4. Eisenstadt (2007) argues that these tactics (termed *contracesiones*) worked well for López Obrador in the 1990s, during the waning years of PRI legitimacy, but were misplaced in the context of Mexico's new democratic regime.

democracy: it was only through mass mobilization that he and his supporters could ensure that democracy survived in Mexico.

Although Calderón's posture during the tribunal's deliberations was consistent with that of his party, López Obrador's actions constituted a noteworthy departure from the democratic commitments of his party, even if many PRD leaders went along with him. PRD ideals strongly support mass mobilization in defense of the interests of the popular classes and of democracy, especially since protest is often one of the few tools left for the party's class base. It is also the case that PRD leaders trust institutions less than their PAN counterparts; they often regard them as insufficient guarantors of the public good because they privilege individual rights over the collective will that remains at the heart of PRD ideals. To a point, then, the post-electoral protests that López Obrador organized were consistent with the PRD's modus operandi. However, his sustained effort to undermine the country's electoral institutions, the denial of the institutional basis for democracy, and his manipulation of an undefined "popular will" as a claim to democratic legitimacy differs radically from his party's past posture. If the PRD continues to hew to López Obrador's political rhetoric, 2006 might be looked back on as a critical juncture in Mexican politics, when the left turned anti-institutional.

Mexico's "Democratic" Institutions

With López Obrador's protests in the past and Calderón widely recognized as Mexico's legitimate president, we can turn our attention to the lasting political questions raised by the post-electoral debacle.[5] Many hot-button issues swirled in the air during the campaign, including entrenched class inequalities, enduring corruption, and renegotiation of NAFTA. During the protests, these issues also became rallying cries. Amid those protests, though, an even more profound set of political debates framed the comments and actions of ordinary Mexicans, the candidates, political experts, and even the electoral authorities of the IFE and TRIFE. This election called attention to fundamental disagreements about the kind of democracy Mexico has and the kind of democracy Mexicans want. Mexico is not alone in facing these debates. Much of Latin America's recent left turn is owing to dissatisfaction with the quality of demo-

5. That said, López Obrador was still able to assemble thousands of protestors in the Zócalo on the one-year anniversary of the election.

cratic governance since the transitions from authoritarian rule. Although there are exceptions (like Brazil and Chile), Latin American left leaders like Hugo Chávez of Venezuela and Evo Morales of Bolivia campaigned and governed on the notions of participatory democracy, including increasing popular control and extending the idea of democracy beyond elections.[6]

This idea of democratic deepening, and the implied idea of shallow democracy, can help us understand the behavior of the IFE and TRIFE in the wake of López Obrador's allegations of improprieties. According to most press accounts, it seemed that many of López Obrador's complaints were without merit. As Calderón himself stated, "There is no legal evidence to support the possibility of a complaint. In this election, the votes have already been counted, vote by vote, at the time they should have been counted, at the closing of the polls, as happens in all the world" (McKinley and Thompson 2006b). Still, there were significant errors revealed in the initial review of district tallies in the week after the election. One reporter noted that the ballots, "bore the fingerprints of Mexico's burgeoning, if messy, democracy. The voters had made their marks with black crayons in any variety of ways—huge smeared crosses, neat checks, circles, smudges" (Thompson and McKinley 2006). The same polling site in Guadalajara revealed errors on tally sheets serious enough to double the votes for Calderón and bump up Madrazo's tally by one hundred votes (Thompson and McKinley 2006). Although many similar irregularities were found in checking the tally sheets, the IFE regarded the vast majority as arithmetic in nature, rather than systematic evidence of fraud. Indeed, IFE President Luis Carlos Ugalde reported that international observers had declared the July 2 vote to be the most transparent in Mexico's history, free of evidence that could "cloud the transparency of the counting process or affect the results" (McKinley and Thompson 2006c).

López Obrador's demands for a recount obviously resonated with his mass supporters, who, following the candidate's cues, argued that if there had been no fraud, then all parties would have agreed to a vote-by-vote recount. And his position also found support among some members of the political class. For many observers, it was simply the best way to resolve doubts about the victor. A *New York Times* editorial on July 7 advocated a total recount on the grounds there were sufficient ambiguities raised in the district tallies (New York Times Editorial Desk 2006). And while Ugalde maintained that IFE could not call for

6. Roberts (1998, esp. chapter 2) refers to these as democratic deepening.

a general recount, one electoral law expert, John M. Ackerman of the UNAM, saw no specific prohibitions against one, arguing that the TRIFE had significant latitude in its decision since "many of Mexico's electoral laws are so new and therefore untested" (McKinley and Thompson 2006a).

Ultimately, of course, the TRIFE ordered recounts at only 11,839 polling stations. The report from one of those recounts raised further concerns about the integrity of the process:

> In one polling place, one hundred fewer ballots were accounted for than were delivered to the poll workers. "I'm missing a lot of ballots," the judge told the lawyers. At another polling place, two null ballots, on which more than one candidate had been marked, were included in the stack for Mr. Calderón, a point the lawyer for Mr. López Obrador quickly pointed out. What was more, the envelope that was supposed to hold null ballots was missing from the packet. It was found in the envelope containing ballots from an adjoining polling place. (McKinley 2006a)

As was the case with the district tallies, the TRIFE concluded that despite the episodes like the ones recounted above, there was insufficient evidence to support claims of *systematic* fraud that would lead to annulment. Although the attitudes of Calderón and López Obrador toward recount and annulment could be predicted by their partisan origins and their political ambitions, the logic of actors within the IFE and TRIFE merits further examination. Instead of dispelling doubts through a more extensive recount, election officials followed the letter of the electoral law. Why did the IFE so avowedly defend its process and the tribunal rule as it did, despite the extent of irregularities noted, the degree of social unrest following the election, and the relative freedom they had to interpret Mexican electoral law?

Although López Obrador's camp argued that the electoral authorities were just another tool of the elite class, a more likely explanation centers on the role of those institutions during the transition and the challenges of moving beyond it in democratic Mexico.[7] Like the candidates and their parties, Mexico's electoral authorities adopted particular positions during the PRI's waning years.

7. Of course, elections are always imperfect mechanisms for filtering citizen preferences, plagued by subjectivities (Coles 2007). It may well be that in addition to the institutional argument I advance, Mexico's electoral authorities were reticent to call a new election because it could unleash a broader set of critiques about Mexican democracy.

The context in which those authorities were constructed demanded that they be impervious to the pernicious influence of the PRI, something they achieved with notable success after 1996. The evidence of the success of that institution building was in the intense autonomy with which the IFE and TRIFE took action and handed down rulings, a technocratic style that disregarded social conditions in the interest of finding fair solutions to complicated political problems. During the transition years, such a position was clearly called for since the legality of elections was so often in dispute. In post-2006 Mexico, the legality of electoral processes is on surer footing. It may now be time for the electoral authorities to consider how to weigh legitimacy alongside legality as they contemplate future actions.

A Savage Future?

Mexican candidates and parties spent the better part of two decades locked into a space dominated by democracy. Unsurprisingly, Calderón, López Obrador, and other political leaders took their cues from that environment in their post-electoral pronouncements. The protests following the July 2 election highlight several challenges facing Mexico's new democratic regime. First and foremost, López Obrador's successful mobilization of thousands of people attests to the profound frustration that many Mexicans feel about their daily lives. Part of that is due to the shallow nature of democracy in Mexico, where individuals may have political rights but lack meaningful social and economic ones, though it also reflects their deep dissatisfaction with parties and other political institutions. It also warns of the potential for serious, entrenched conflicts between the PAN and PRD, and even the PRI, about the form and content of democratic rule, as well as processes and actions associated with being democratic. Should those conflicts be waged within formal political institutions, they promise further tests for, and likely future attacks on, the country's electoral institutions. If those conflicts move into the streets, a different but equally savage set of developments could well follow.

APPENDIX 1: SELECTED CHANGES IN MEXICAN ELECTORAL LAW, 1946-2000

Electoral Law of 1946 (Ley Electoral de 1946)

- Required that parties be national organizations
- Established that federal government institutions (including most importantly the Comisión Federal de Vigilancia Electoral and the Secretaría de Gobernación) were responsible for electoral oversight; effectively transferred responsibility of election oversight to the PRI

Amendments of 1963

- Established the Party Deputies system, a form of proportional representation (PR), in the Chamber of Deputies, offering seats to opposition parties that could win 2.5 percent or more of the national vote; opposition party representation in the two-hundred-or-so seat Chamber was limited to twenty seats per party
- Required all elected party candidates to take office; boycotts would result in the loss of party registration

Electoral Law of 1977 (Ley Federal de Organizaciones Políticas y Procesos Electorales—LOPPE)

- Altered the rules for party registration, allowing for definitive and conditional (probationary) registration and legalizing parties to the political left of the PRI
- Restructured the Chamber of Deputies, increasing the number of SMD seats to three hundred, abolishing the party deputies system, and establishing one hundred PR seats for opposition parties elected from four PR districts

Electoral Law of 1986 (Código Federal Electoral—CFE)

- Increased the total number of seats in the Chamber of Deputies to five hundred by adding one hundred PR seats (for a total of three hundred SMD and two hundred PR seats); all PR seats in the Chamber of Deputies were also opened to all parties (not just the opposition parties)
- Established a governability clause that assured the winning party in congressional elections (that is, the PRI) a simple majority of seats in the Chamber even in the event it did not gain a majority of votes in the election

Electoral Law of 1990 (Código Federal de Instituciones y Procedimientos Electorales—COFIPE)

- Created the Instituto Federal Electoral as an autonomous public organism, representing a crucial step in the development of independent and professionalized electoral supervision in Mexico
- Strengthened the governability clause by assuring that the party that receives the plurality of SMD seats in the Chamber of Deputies will be assigned enough PR seats to establish a simple majority
- Restructured the public financing of party organizations by establishing four types of public funding: (1) for electoral activities, based strictly on the parties' vote shares in the previous federal congressional election; (2) for general activities (normal party activity), amounting to 10 percent of the electoral activity sum; (3) for specific activities, meaning the state reimbursed parties for up to 50 percent of the expenses they accrued in research and civic education; and (4) matching funds, amounting to 50 percent of the annual amount that each party's legislators were required to donate to party coffers

Electoral Law of 1993 (COFIPE) (regulated the 1994 federal elections)

- Altered the composition of the Senate, increasing the number of senators to four per state and creating the "first minority senator" seat—assigned to the top opposition party senate candidate in order to increase pluralism in the upper house
- Limited the dominance of a single party in the Chamber, disallowing control of more than 60 percent of the seats by a single party

- Strengthened the autonomy of the IFE at the district and local levels by increasing citizen control and reducing executive and party influence in the IFE councils at all levels
- Revised the rules for party finance by (1) prohibiting government, international, enterprise, and ecclesiastical support of party organizations; (2) limiting anonymous donations to 10 percent of the party budget and single individual donations to 1 percent of the budget and total individual donations to 5 percent of the budget; and (3) tightening the auditing procedures for parties

Electoral Law of 1994 (COFIPE)

- Further reduced the role of parties in IFE councils; parties maintained their representation, but lost their voting power except via the two delegates from each legislative chamber. In 1994, the IFE's General Council included the Federal Secretary of the Interior (Secretario de Gobernación), the General Director of the IFE, the Secretary of the IFE General Council, the four legislative representatives, six citizen councillors, and representatives from all registered parties

Electoral Law of 1996 (COFIPE)

- Affirmed and strengthened the autonomy of the IFE from the executive branch by reducing the voting members of the General Council to its president and eight electoral councillors, elected to seven-year terms by two-thirds vote of the Chamber of Deputies
- Transformed the structure of the Senate, retaining the same number of seats (128) but electing three from each state (two majority senators and one first-minority senator) and thirty-two by proportional representation from single, national lists.
- Restructured and modified the rules for public financing of party activity, establishing three modes of support: (1) for ordinary activities (normal party activities), 70 percent of which is distributed according to the prior federal congressional election's vote shares and 30 percent of which is distributed equally among all parties with congressional representation; (2) for campaign activities in federal election years, a sum equal to the parties' support for ordinary activities in the same year (and so dependent on prior electoral successes); (3) for specific activities, meaning the General Council

reimburses the parties for up to 75 percent of expenses accrued performing activities in the public interest, such as civic education and research

- Increased the total amount of public support for parties fivefold, in order to limit the influence of private resources, which can be no more than 10 percent of the sum of public support for ordinary activities
- Tightened oversight and sanctioning for violations of campaign finance rules.

APPENDIX 2: MEXICAN ELECTION RESULTS, 1970–2006

Year	Party	Presidential vote share (in percentages)	Chamber of Deputies vote share (in percentages)
1970	PRI	87.8	83.53
	PAN	11.04	14.21
1976	PRI	92.75	85.17
	PAN	0	8.99
1982	PRI	71.63	69.29
	PAN	16.42	17.54
	LEFT	3.65	4.37
1988	PRI	51.22	50.37
	PAN	16.96	17.96
	FDN/LEFT	30.89	4.45
1991	PRI		58.47
	PAN		16.82
	PRD		7.91
1994	PRI	48.69	48.58
	PAN	25.92	24.98
	PRD	16.59	16.12
1997	PRI		39.11
	PAN		26.61
	PRD		25.71
2000	PRI	36.11	36.92
	PAN	42.52	38.24
	PRD	16.64	18.68
2003	PRI		23.14
	PAN		30.73
	PRD		17.61

(continued)

Year	Party	Presidential vote share (in percentages)	Chamber of Deputies vote share (in percentages)
2006	PRI	22.26	28.21
	PAN	35.89	33.39
	PRD	35.31	28.99

Source: Prepared by the author based on data from Klesner (1997) and the Instituto Federal Electoral.

APPENDIX 3: NATIONAL PARTY ORGANS OF THE PAN AND PRD

Both the PAN and the PRD vest supreme authority in a national assembly. The PAN's Asamblea Nacional (National Assembly) meets once every three years and is responsible for naming the members of the Consejo Nacional (National Council). It also analyzes the reports of the National Council and the Comité Ejecutivo Nacional (National Executive Committee, CEN). The assembly may be called into special session in order to modify party statutes or debate other transformative decisions for the party. The PAN's Comités Directivos Estatales (state executive committees), and the CEN select the assembly members. Like its PAN counterpart, the PRD Congreso Nacional (National Congress) meets at least once every three years to approve and modify the party's principles, statutes, program, and strategy. The overwhelming majority of delegates to the National Congress are elected in municipal-level assemblies, the remainder being delegates from state party councils, presidents of the Comités Ejecutivos Estatales (state executive committees), members of the PRD's CEN, and delegates from the PRD's National Council.

Day-to-day running of both organizations is left to their national councils and national executive committees. The PAN's National Council consists of more than 250 members, including the president and secretary-general of the party, former presidents of the party, all state party presidents, its legislative leaders, the national coordinator for local deputies, and 250 delegates selected by the state delegations at the PAN National Assembly. This body has the responsibility of electing the president of the party, the members of the CEN, and a number of other party posts, in addition to approving budgetary decisions and party regulations, resolving conflicts in the party organization, and developing the party platform. The National Council meets at least once each year (often, three to four times). The National Council, on the president's proposal, elects the twenty to forty members of the CEN for three-year terms; the National Council itself suggests two-thirds of the members and the president proposes the rest. The CEN is charged with executing the party's statutes and regulations, formulating party program, maintaining the electoral rolls for the party, and forming subunits as necessary to ensure adequate functioning of the party. It is also responsible for negotiating with other political actors, has a number of veto powers over other party organs, and may convoke the National Assembly and the National Council as it sees necessary. The president of the PAN is president of the Assembly, National Council, and CEN. This single individual represents the party and is responsible for the adequate enforcement of the party's rules and regulations.

Between meetings of its National Congress, the PRD's National Council is the supreme organ of the party, responsible for formulating party program in accordance with the decisions of the National Congress. The National Council structures the relationships the party maintains with other political institutions, and it appoints all CEN members except for the president and secretary-general of the party. The National Council must approve all party regulations and budget decisions, and it appoints delegates to a number of committees. It has over two hundred members, including the state party presidents, former presidents of the PRD, and representatives for Mexicans living outside of Mexico. Members are also drawn from the party's state councils, the national legislature, and the PRD National Congress. The twenty or so members of the CEN are charged with executing the resolutions of the National Council and proposing new policy and organizational initiatives. In so doing, the CEN may create secretariats as necessary and move personnel within the party apparatus. The party president, elected by direct, secret, and universal vote by PRD members through an internal proportional-representation system, called the planilla system, is the legal representative of the party and head of the CEN and National Council.

REFERENCES

Aldrich, John H. 1995. *Why Parties? The Origin and Transformation of Political Parties in America.* Chicago: University of Chicago Press.

Aparicio, Javier. 2006. Fraud or Human Error in Mexico's Presidential Election? *Voices of Mexico* 77 (October–December). Available at http://www.cide.edu/investigadores/aparicio/elecciones/fraudorerror.pdf (last accessed on March 4, 2008).

Appleton, Andrew M., and Daniel S. Ward. 1997. Party Response to Environmental Change: A Model of Organizational Innovation. *Party Politics* 3 (3): 341–62.

Bille, Lars. 2001. Democratizing a Democratic Procedure: Candidate Selection in Western European Parties, 1960–1990. *Party Politics* 7 (3): 363–80.

Borjas Benavente, Adriana. 2003. *Partido de la Revolución Democrática: Estructura, organización interna y desempeóo público, 1989–2003.* 2 vols. Mexico City: Gernika.

Bratton, Michael, and Nicholas Van de Walle. 1997. *Democratic Experiments in Africa: Regime Transitions in Comparative Perspective.* New York: Cambridge University Press.

Bruhn, Kathleen. 1997. *Taking on Goliath: The Emergence of a New Left Party and the Struggle for Democracy in Mexico.* University Park: The Pennsylvania State University Press.

———. 2005. With Friends like These: Protest Strategies and the Left in Brazil and Mexico. Working Paper no. 321. Notre Dame: Helen Kellogg Institute for International Studies, University of Notre Dame.

———. 2008. *Urban Protest in Mexico and Brazil.* New York: Cambridge University Press.

Burgess, Katrina. 2004. *Parties and Unions in the New Global Economy.* Pittsburgh: University of Pittsburgh Press.

Camp, Roderic Ai. 2002. *Mexico's Mandarins: Crafting a Power Elite for the Twenty-first Century.* Berkeley and Los Angeles: University of California Press.

Carr, Barry. 1992. *Marxism and Communism in Twentieth-Century Mexico.* Lincoln: University of Nebraska Press.

Centeno, Miguel Angel. 1994. *Democracy Within Reason: Technocratic Revolution in Mexico.* University Park: The Pennsylvania State University Press.

Cleary, Matthew R. 2007. Electoral Competition, Participation, and Government Responsiveness in Mexico. *American Journal of Political Science* 51 (2): 283–99.

Clemens, Elisabeth, and James Cook. 1999. Politics and Institutionalism, Explaining Durability and Change. *Annual Review of Sociology* 25:441–66.

Coles, Kimberley. 2007. *Democratic Designs: International Interventions and Electoral Practices in Postwar Bosnia-Herzegovina*. Ann Arbor: University of Michigan Press.

Collier, Ruth Berins. 1999. *Paths Toward Democracy: The Working Class and Elites in Western Europe and South America*. New York: Cambridge University Press.

Collier, Ruth Berins, and David Collier. 1991. *Shaping the Political Arena: Critical Junctures and Regime Dynamics in Latin America*. Princeton: Princeton University Press.

Coppedge, Michael. 1994. *Strong Parties and Lame Ducks: Presidential Partyarchy and Factionalism in Venezuela*. Stanford: Stanford University Press.

Cornelius, Wayne A., Ann L. Craig, and Jonathan Fox, eds. 1994. *Transforming State-Society Relations in Mexico: The National Solidarity Strategy*. La Jolla: Center for U.S.-Mexican Studies, University of California, San Diego.

Craig, Ann L., and Wayne Cornelius. 1995. Houses Divided: Parties and Political Reform in Mexico. In *Building Democratic Institutions: Party Systems in Latin America*, ed. Scott Mainwaring and Timothy Scully. Stanford: Stanford University Press.

Crotty, William J., ed. 1968. *Approaches to the Study of Party Organization*. Boston: Allyn and Bacon.

Dalton, Russell J. 2000. The Decline of Party Identification. In *Parties Without Partisans: Political Change in Advanced Industrial Democracies*, ed. Russell J. Dalton and Martin P. Wattenberg. New York: Oxford University Press.

Dalton, Russell J., Scott Flanagan, and Paul Beck, eds. 1984. *Electoral Change in Advanced Industrial Democracies*. Princeton: Princeton University Press.

Dalton, Russell J., and Martin P. Wattenberg, eds. 2000. *Parties Without Partisans: Political Change in Advanced Industrial Democracies*. New York: Oxford University Press.

Deegan-Krause, Kevin. 2003. Slovakia's Second Transition. *Journal of Democracy* 14 (2): 65–79.

———. 2006. *Elected Affinities: Democracy and Party Competition in Slovakia and the Czech Republic*. Stanford: Stanford University Press.

De Janvry, Alain, Gustavo Gordillo, and Elisabeth Sadoulet, eds. 1997. *Mexico's Second Agrarian Reform: Household and Community Responses*. La Jolla: Center for U.S.-Mexican Studies, University of California, San Diego.

Dion, Michelle. 2000. La economía política del gasto social: El Programa Nacional de Solidaridad, 1988–94. *Estudios Sociológicos* 18 (53): 329–362.

———. 2005. The Political Origins of Social Security in Mexico During the Cárdenas and Ávila Camacho Administrations. *Mexican Studies/Estudios Mexicanos* 21 (1): 59–95.

———. n.d. Workers and Welfare in Latin America: Mexico in Historical and Comparative Perspective. Manuscript under review.

Domínguez, Jorge I., and Chappell Lawson, eds. 2005. *Mexico's Pivotal Democratic Election: Candidates, Voters, and the Presidential Campaign of 2000*. Stanford: Stanford University Press.

Domínguez, Jorge I., and James A. McCann. 1996. *Democratizing Mexico: Public Opinion and Electoral Choice*. Baltimore: Johns Hopkins University Press.

Downs, Anthony. 1957. *An Economic Theory of Democracy*. New York: Harper and Row.

Duverger, Maurice. 1964. *Political Parties: Their Organization and Activity in the Modern State*. London: Lowe and Brydone.

ECLAC (Economic Commission for Latin America and the Caribbean). 1995. *Panorama Social de América Latina*. Santiago, Chile: ECLAC.

Economist. 2006. Game, Set, and Matches. September 9.

Eisenstadt, Todd. 2004. Courting Democracy in Mexico: Party Strategies and Electoral Institutions. New York: Cambridge University Press.

———. 2007. The Origins and Rationality of the "Legal Versus Legitimate" Dichotomy Invoked in Mexico's 2006 Post-Electoral Conflict. *PS: Political Science and Politics* 40 (1): 39–44.

Eisenstadt, Todd, and Alejandro Poire. 2005. Campaign Finance and Playing Field "Levelness" Issues in the Run-up to Mexico's July 2006 Presidential Elections. Working Paper, Center for US-Mexican Studies, University of California, San Diego.

Ekiert, Grzegorz, and Stephen E. Hanson, eds. 2003a. *Capitalism and Democracy in Central and Eastern Europe: Assessing the Legacy of Communist Rule*. New York: Cambridge University Press.

———. 2003b. Time, Space, and Institutional Change in Central and Eastern Europe. In *Capitalism and Democracy in Central and Eastern Europe: Assessing the Legacy of Communist Rule*, ed. Grzegorz Ekiert and Stephen E. Hanson. New York: Cambridge University Press.

El Nacional. 1998. Pretenden PAN y PRD dividir al sindicato de ferrocarrilleros: Flores. January 15.

Epstein, Leon D. 1980. *Political Parties in Western Democracies*. New York: Praeger.

Farrell, David M., and Paul Webb. 2000. Political Parties as Campaign Organizations. In *Parties Without Partisans: Political Change in Advanced Industrial Democracies*, ed. Russell J. Dalton and Martin P. Wattenberg. New York: Oxford University Press.

Fiorina, Morris. 1980. The Decline of Collective Responsibility in American Politics. Working Paper no. 320, California Institute of Technology, Division of the Humanities and Social Sciences.

Flanagan, Scott C., and Russell J. Dalton. 1990. Models of Change. In *The West European Party System*, ed. Peter Mair. Oxford: Oxford University Press.

Fox, Jonathan. 1994. Political Change in Mexico's New Peasant Economy. In *The Politics of Economic Restructuring: State-Society Relations and Regime Change in Mexico*, ed. Maria Lorena Cook, Kevin Middlebrook, and Juan Molinar Horcasitas. La Jolla: Center for U.S.-Mexican Studies, University of California, San Diego.

Gallagher, Michael, and Michael Marsh, eds. 1988. *Candidate Selection in Comparative Perspective: The Secret Garden of Politics*. Thousand Oaks, Calif.: Sage.

Galvan, Dennis. 2001. Political Turnover and Social Change in Senegal. *Journal of Democracy* 12 (3): 51–62.

Garrido, Luis Javier. 1982. *El partido de la revolución institucionalizada: La formación del nuevo estado en México (1928–1945)*. Mexico City: Siglo XXI.

———. 1993. La ruptura: La Corriente Democrática del PRI. Mexico City: Grijalbo.

George, Alexander L., and Timothy J. McKeown. 1985. Case Studies and Theories of Organizational Decision Making. *Advances in Information Processing in Organizations* 2:21–58.

Gramsci, Antonio. 1971. *Prison Notebooks: Selections*. Ed. and trans. Quintin Hoare and Geoffrey Nowell Smith. New York: International Publishers.

Grayson, George W. 2007. *Mexican Messiah: Andrés Manuel López Obrador.* University Park: The Pennsylvania State University Press.

Greene, Kenneth F. 2002. Opposition Party Strategy and Spatial Competition in Dominant Party Regimes: A Theory and the Case of Mexico. *Comparative Political Studies* 35 (7): 755–83.

———. 2007. *Why Dominant Parties Lose: Mexico's Democratization in Comparative Perspective.* New York: Cambridge University Press.

Grindle, Merilee S. 1977. *Bureaucrats, Politicians, and Peasants in Mexico: A Case Study in Public Policy.* Berkeley and Los Angeles: University of California Press.

———. 2007. *Going Local: Decentralization, Democratization, and the Promise of Good Governance.* Princeton: Princeton University Press.

Grzymala-Busse, Anna M. 2002. *Redeeming the Communist Past: The Regeneration of Communist Successor Parties in East Central Europe.* New York: Cambridge University Press.

Gunther, Richard, José Ramón Montero, and Juan J. Linz, eds. 2000. *Political Parties: Old Concepts and New Challenges.* New York: Oxford University Press.

Haber, Paul Lawrence. 1994. The Art and Implications of Political Restructuring in Mexico: The Case of Urban Popular Movements. In *The Politics of Economic Restructuring: State-Society Relations and Regime Change in Mexico,* ed. Maria Lorena Cook, Kevin Middlebrook, and Juan Molinar Horcasitas. La Jolla: Center for U.S.-Mexican Studies, University of California, San Diego.

———. 2005. *Power from Experience: Urban Popular Movements in Late Twentieth-Century Mexico.* University Park: The Pennsylvania State University Press.

Hansen, Roger D. 1971. *The Politics of Mexican Development.* Baltimore: Johns Hopkins University Press.

Harmel, Robert, and Kenneth Janda. 1982. *Parties and Their Environments: Limits to Reform?* New York: Longman Press.

Hartlyn, Jonathan. 1998. *The Struggle for Democratic Politics in the Dominican Republic.* Chapel Hill: University of North Carolina Press.

Harvey, Neil. 1998. *The Chiapas Rebellion: The Struggle for Land and Democracy.* Durham: Duke University Press.

Huber, Evelyne, Dietrich Rueschemeyer, and John D. Stephens. 1997. The Paradoxes of Contemporary Democracy: Formal, Participatory, and Social Dimensions. *Comparative Politics* 29 (3): 323–42.

Huber, Evelyne, and John D. Stephens. 2001. *Development and Crisis of the Welfare States: Parties and Policies in Global Markets.* Chicago: University of Chicago Press.

Inglehart, Ronald. 1977. *The Silent Revolution: Changing Values and Political Styles Among Western Publics.* Princeton: Princeton University Press.

Inglot, Tomasz. 2003. Historical Legacies, Institutions, and the Politics of Social Policy in Hungary and Poland, 1989–1999. In *Capitalism and Democracy in Central and Eastern Europe: Assessing the Legacy of Communist Rule,* ed. Grzegorz Ekiert and Stephen E. Hanson. New York: Cambridge University Press.

Jaquette, Jane S., ed. 1989. *The Women's Movement in Latin America: Feminism and the Transition to Democracy.* Boston: Unwin Hyman.

———. 1994. *The Women's Movement and Latin America: Participation and Democracy.* Boulder, Colo.: Westview Press.

Jacquez, Antonio. 1997. Las diversas corrientes fundadoras, diluídas por la hegemonía del expriísmo, han perdido su rostro. Inmerso en la crisis ideológica de fin de siglo, y en busca del sufragio, el PRD rehuye su identificación con la izquierda tradicional. *Proceso,* August 17.

Kanthak, Kristin, and Rebecca B. Morton. 2003. Primaries and Turnout. Working Paper. Available at http://www.nyu.edu/gsas/dept/politics/faculty/morton/KanthakMort.pdf (last accessed on March 6, 2008).

Katz, Richard S. 2001. The Problem of Candidate Selection and Models of Party Democracy. *Party Politics* 7 (3): 277–96.

Keck, Margaret E. 1995. Social Equity and Environmental Politics in Brazil: Lessons from the Rubber Tappers of Acre. *Comparative Politics* 27:409–24.

Kiavelo, M. A. 2005. "M. A. Kiavelo" (column). *El Norte* (Monterrey), October 20.

Kirchheimer, Otto. 1966. The Transformation of the Western European Party Systems. In *Political Parties and Political Development,* ed. Joseph La Palombara and Myron Weiner. Princeton: Princeton University Press.

Kitschelt, Herbert. 1989. *The Logics of Party Formation: Ecological Politics in Belgium and West Germany.* Ithaca: Cornell University Press.

———. 1994. *The Transformation of European Social Democracy.* New York: Cambridge University Press.

Kitschelt, Herbert, Zdenka Mansfeldova, Radoslaw Markowski, and Gabor Toka. 1999. *Post-Communist Party Systems: Competition, Representation, and Inter-Party Cooperation.* New York: Cambridge University Press.

Klesner, Joseph L. 1997. Dissolving Hegemony: Electoral Competition and the Decline of Mexico's One-Party-Dominant Regime. Paper presented at the annual meeting of the American Political Science Association, Washington, D.C.

———. 2005. Electoral Competition and the New Party System in Mexico. *Latin American Politics and Society* 47 (2): 103–42.

Langston, Joy. 2001. Why Rules Matter: Changes in Candidate Selection in Mexico's PRI. *Journal of Latin American Studies* 33 (3): 485–511.

———. 2002. Breaking Out Is Hard to Do: Exit, Voice, and Loyalty in Mexico's One-Party Hegemonic Regime. *Latin American Politics and Society* 44 (3): 61–88.

———. 2003. Rising from the Ashes? Reorganizing and Unifying the PRI's State Party Organizations After Electoral Defeat. *Comparative Political Studies* 36 (3): 293–318.

———. 2006a. The Birth and Transformation of the Dedazo in Mexico. In *Informal Institutions and Democracy in Latin America,* ed. Gretchen Helmke and Steven Levitsky. Baltimore: Johns Hopkins University Press.

———. 2006b. The Changing PRI: Decentralization and Legislative Recruitment. *Party Politics* 12 (2): 395–413.

———. 2007. The PRI's 2006 Electoral Debacle. *PS: Political Science and Politics* 40 (1): 21–26.

Lawson, Chappell H. 1997. Mexico's New Politics: The Elections of 1997. *Journal of Democracy* 8 (4): 13–27.

———. 2000. Mexico's Unfinished Transition: Democratization and Authoritarian Enclaves in Mexico. *Estudios Mexicanos/Mexican Studies* 16 (2): 267–87.

———. 2002. *Building the Fourth Estate: Democratization and the Rise of a Free Press in Mexico.* Berkeley and Los Angeles: University of California Press.

Lawson, Kay, ed. 1980. *Political Parties and Linkage: A Comparative Perspective.* New Haven: Yale University Press.

Levi, Margaret. 1997. *Consent, Dissent, and Patriotism.* New York: Cambridge University Press.

Levitsky, Steven. 2003. *Transforming Labor-Based Parties in Latin America: Argentine Peronism in Comparative Perspective.* New York: Cambridge University Press.

Levitsky, Steven, and Scott Mainwaring. 2006. Organized Labor and Democracy in Latin America. *Comparative Politics* 39 (1): 21–42.

Levy, Daniel C., and Kathleen Bruhn. 2006. *Mexico: The Struggle for Democratic Development.* 2nd ed. Berkeley and Los Angeles: University of California Press.

Lieberman, Robert C. 2002. Ideas, Institutions, and Political Order: Explaining Political Change. *American Political Science Review* 96 (4): 697–712.

Linz, Juan, and Alfred Stepan. 1996. *Problems of Democratic Transition and Consolidation: Southern Europe, South America, and Post-Communist Europe.* Baltimore: Johns Hopkins University Press.

Lipset, Seymour Martin, and Stein Rokkan. 1967. Cleavage Structures, Party Systems, and Voter Alignments: An Introduction. In *Party Systems and Voter Alignments: Cross-National Perspectives,* ed. Seymour Martin Lipset and Stein Rokkan. New York: Free Press.

Loaeza, Soledad. 1999. *El Partido Acción Nacional: La larga marcha, 1939–1994: Oposición leal y partido de protesta.* Mexico City: Fondo de Cultura Económica.

Luebbert, Gregory. 1991. *Liberalism, Fascism, or Social Democracy: Social Classes and the Political Origins of Regimes in Interwar Europe.* New York: Oxford University Press.

Lujambio, Alonso. 2001. Democratization Through Federalism? The National Action Party Strategy, 1939–2000. In *Party Politics and the Struggle for Democracy in Mexico,* ed. Kevin J. Middlebrook. La Jolla: Center for U.S.-Mexican Studies, University of California, San Diego.

Lundell, Krister. 2004. Determinants of Candidate Selection: The Degree of Centralization in Comparative Perspective. *Party Politics* 10 (1): 25–47.

Lustig, Nora. 1998. *Mexico: The Remaking of an Economy.* 2nd ed. Washington, D.C.: Brookings Institution.

Mabry, Donald J. 1973. *Mexico's Acción Nacional: A Catholic Alternative to Revolution.* New York: Syracuse University Press.

Magaloni, Beatriz. 1997. The Dynamics of Dominant Party Decline: The Mexican Transition to Multipartysm. Ph.D. diss., Duke University.

———. 2006. *Voting for Autocracy: Hegemonic Party Survival and its Demise in Mexico.* New York: Cambridge University Press.

Mahoney, James. 2001. *The Legacies of Liberalism: Path Dependence and Political Regimes in Central America.* Baltimore: Johns Hopkins University Press.

Mahoney, James, and Dietrich Rueschemeyer, eds. 2002. *Comparative Historical Analysis in the Social Sciences.* New York: Cambridge University Press.

Mainwaring, Scott. 1999. *Rethinking Party Systems in the Third Wave of Democratization: The Case of Brazil.* Stanford: Stanford University Press.

Mainwaring, Scott, and Timothy R. Scully. 1995. Introduction: Party Systems in Latin America. In *Building Democratic Institutions: Party Systems in Latin America.* ed. Scott Mainwaring and Timothy R. Scully. Stanford: Stanford University Press.

Mainwaring, Scott, and Matthew Soberg Shugart, eds. 1997. *Presidentialism and Democracy in Latin America.* New York: Cambridge University Press.

Mair, Peter, ed. 1990. *The West European Party System.* New York: Oxford University Press.

Manin, Bernard, Adam Przeworski, and Susan C. Stokes. 1999. Elections and Representation. In *Democracy, Accountability, and Representation,* ed. Adam Przeworski, Susan C. Stokes, and Bernard Manin. New York: Cambridge University Press.

Martínez, Fabiola, and Elizabeth Velasco. 1998. Iniciativas de PAN y PRD buscan romper el corporativismo sindical. *La Jornada* (Mexico City), August 11.

Mayer, Jean. 2003. The Mexican Federal Labour Law Reform Process, 2001–2003. *LABOUR, Capital and Society* 36 (1): 72–102.

Mayer, William G. 1996. Caucuses: How They Work, What Difference They Make. In *In Pursuit of the White House: How We Choose Our Presidential Nominees,* ed. William G Mayer. New York: Chatham House Publishers.

McCann, James A. 1996. Presidential Nomination Activists and Political Representation: A View from the Active Minority Studies. In *In Pursuit of the White House: How We Choose Our Presidential Nominees,* ed. William G. Mayer. New York: Chatham House Publishers.

McKinley, James C. 2006a. In a Presidential Tone, Calderón Rejects Recount. *The New York Times,* July 14, section A.

———. 2006b. Mexico Recount Begins and Protests Go On. *The New York Times,* August 10, section A.

McKinley, James C., and Ginger Thompson. 2006a. Leftist Candidate of Mexican Elections Claims Fraud. *The New York Times,* July 8, Web Edition.

———. 2006b. Leftist Predicts Unrest Without Complete Recount of Mexican Election. *The New York Times,* July 9, section A.

———. 2006c. Conservative Wins in Mexico in Final Tally. *The New York Times,* July 7, section A.

Meinke, Scott, Jeffrey K. Staton, and Steven T. Wuhs. 2006. State Delegate Selection Rules for Presidential Nominations, 1972–2000. *Journal of Politics* 68 (1): 181–93.

Meyer, Michael C., and William H. Beezley. 2000. *The Oxford History of Mexico.* Oxford: Oxford University Press.

Michels, Robert. 1962. *Political Parties: A Sociological Study of the Oligarchical Tendencies of Modern Democracy.* New York: Collier Books.

Middlebrook, Kevin J. 1995. *The Paradox of Revolution: Labor, the State, and Authoritarianism in Mexico.* Baltimore: Johns Hopkins University Press.

Mizrahi, Yemile. 1994. Rebels Without a Cause: The Politics of Entrepreneurs in Chihuahua. *Journal of Latin American Studies* 6:137–58.

———. 2003. *From Martyrdom to Power: The PAN in Mexico.* Notre Dame: University of Notre Dame Press.

Molinar Horcasitas, Juan. 1991. *El tiempo de la legitimidad.* Mexico City: Cal y Arena.

Moreno, Alejandro. 1998. Party Competition and the Issue of Democracy: Ideological Space in Mexican Elections. In *Governing Mexico: Political Parties and Elections,* ed. Mónica Serrano. London: Institute of Latin American Studies, University of London.

Murillo, María Victoria. 2003. *Labor Unions, Partisan Coalitions, and Market Reforms in Latin America.* New York: Cambridge University Press.

Murray, Kieran, and Cynthia Barrera. 2006. Thousands Join Mexican Protest. *The Toronto Star,* July 31, News.

New York Times. 2006. A Recount in Mexico. July 7, section A.

Norris, Pippa. 2002. Civic Engagement: Mexico in Comparative Perspective. Working Paper, John F. Kennedy School of Government, Harvard University.

North, Douglass C. 1990. *Institutions, Institutional Change, and Economic Performance.* New York: Cambridge University Press.

Nuñez, Ernesto. 2006. Firma Calderón alianza ciudadana. *Reforma* (Mexico City), National Section, February 1.

O'Donnell, Guillermo. 1973. *Modernization and Bureaucratic Authoritarianism.* Berkeley: Institute of International Studies, University of California.

Omaña del Castillo, Ricardo. 2005. Paga Creel caro su error. *El Norte* (Monterrey), local section, October 9.

Orren, Karen, and Stephen Skowronek. 1994. Beyond the Iconography of Order: Notes for a "New Institutionalism." In *The Dynamics of American Politics: Approaches and Interpretations,* ed. Lawrence C. Dodd and Calvin Jillson. Boulder, Colo.: Westview Press.

Ostrom, Elinor. 1995. New Horizons in Institutional Analysis. *American Political Science Review* 89:174–78.

Oxhorn, Philip. 1995. *Organizing Civil Society: The Popular Sectors and the Struggle for Democracy in Chile.* University Park: The Pennsylvania State University Press.

PAN (Partido Acción Nacional). 1939. *Principios de doctrina.* Revised in 1965 and 2002. Mexico City: Partido Acción Nacional.

———. 1999. *Estatutos generales.* Comité Ejecutivo Nacional. Revised in 2002 and 2004. Mexico City: Partido Acción Nacional.

———. 2000. *Reglamentos.* Comité Ejecutivo Nacional. Revised in 2002 and 2004. Mexico City: Partido Acción Nacional.

———. 2002. *Reglamento de los órganos estatales y municipios.* Comité Ejecutivo Nacional. Mexico City: Partido Acción Nacional.

———. 2005. *Manual de la vinculación con la sociedad.* Mexico City: Partido Acción Nacional.

Panebianco, Angelo. 1988. *Political Parties: Organization and Power.* New York: Cambridge University Press.

Pennings, Paul, and Reuven Y. Hazan. 2001. Democratizing Candidate Selection: Causes and Consequences. *Party Politics* 7 (3): 267–76.

Pérez, Matilde, and Georgina Saldierna. 1999. Disparejo, el avance del PRD; le sobra "burocratización." *La Jornada* (Mexico City), February 23.

Pierson, Paul. 2000. Increasing Returns, Path Dependence, and the Study of Politics. *American Political Science Review* 94 (2): 251–67.

———. 2004. *Politics in Time: History, Institutions, and Social Analysis.* Princeton: Princeton University Press.

Pierson, Paul, and Theda Skocpol. 2002. Historical Institutionalism in Contemporary Political Science. In *Political Science: The State of the Discipline,* ed. Ira Katznelson and Helen V. Milner. New York: W.W. Norton.

Powell Jr., G. Bingham. 2004. Political Representation in Comparative Politics. *Annual Review of Political Science* 7: 273–96.

PRD (Partido de la Revolución Democrática). 1991. *Declaración de principios y estatutos.* Comité Ejecutivo Nacional. Revised in 2000 and 2001. Mexico City: Partido de la Revolución Democrática.

———. 2002. *Reglamento general de elecciones internas/Reglamento de afiliación.* Comité Ejecutivo Nacional. Mexico City: Partido de la Revolución Democrática.

PRI (Partido Revolucionario Institucional). 2006. *Declaración de principios.* Mexico City: Partido Revolucionario Institucional.

Rahat, Gideon, and Reuven Y. Hazan. 2001. Candidate Selection Methods: An Analytical Framework. *Party Politics* 7 (3): 297–322.

Reveles Vázquez, Francisco. 1993. Sistema Organizativo y Fracciones Internas del Partido Acción Nacional 1939–1990. Master's thesis, Universidad Autónoma Nacional de México, Mexico City.

Roberts, Kenneth M. 1998. *Deepening Democracy? The Modern Left and Social Movements in Chile and Peru.* Stanford: Stanford University Press.

———. 2002a. Party-Society Linkages and Democratic Representation in Latin America. *Canadian Journal of Latin American and Caribbean Studies* 27 (53): 9–34.

———. 2002b. Social Inequalities without Class Cleavages in Latin America's Neoliberal Era. *Studies in Comparative International Development* 36 (4): 3–33.

———. Forthcoming. *Changing Course: Party System Change in Latin America's Neoliberal Era.* Cambridge: Cambridge University Press.

Rodriguez, Victoria. 1997. *Decentralization in Mexico: From Reforma Municipal to Solidaridad to Nuevo Federalismo.* Boulder, Colo.: Westview Press.

Rodríguez, Victoria E., and Peter M. Ward, eds. 1995. *Opposition Government in Mexico.* Albuquerque: University of New Mexico Press.

Rueschemeyer, Dietrich, Evelyne Huber Stephens, and John D. Stephens. 1992. *Capitalist Development and Democracy.* Chicago: University of Chicago Press.

Rustow, Dankwart A. 1967. *A World of Nations: Problems of Political Modernization.* Washington, D.C.: Brookings Institution.

Saldierna, Georgina. 2006. Jesús Ortega coordinará la campaña de Lúpez Obrador. *La Jornada* (Mexico City), January 13.

Saldierna, Georgina, and Andrea Becerril. 2006. Entre pugnas y jalones el PRD define sus candidatos al Senado. *La Jornada* (Mexico City), January 15.

Samuels, David. 2004. From Socialism to Social Democracy: Party Organization and the Transformation of the Workers' Party in Brazil. *Comparative Political Studies* 20 (1): 1–26.

Sánchez, Marco Aurelio. 1999. *La elite en crisis: Problemas organizativos, indeterminación ideológicas y deficiencias programáticas.* Mexico City: Plaza y Valdés.

Sartori, Giovanni. 1976. *Parties and Party Systems: A Framework for Analysis.* New York: Cambridge University Press.

Scarrow, Susan E. 1996. *Parties and their Members: Organizing for Victory in Britain and Germany.* New York: Oxford University Press.

Schickler, Eric. 2001. *Disjointed Pluralism: Institutional Innovation and the Development of the U.S. Congress.* Princeton: Princeton University Press.

Schlesinger, Joseph A. 1994. *Political Parties and the Winning of Office.* Ann Arbor: University of Michigan Press.

Schmitter, Philippe C. 1974. Still the Century of Corporatism? In *The New Corporatism,* ed. Thomas Stritch and Fredrick Braun Pike. Notre Dame: University of Notre Dame Press.

Scott, Robert E. 1965. *Mexican Government in Transition.* Urbana: University of Illinois Press.

Shadlen, Kenneth C. 2004. *Democratization Without Representation: The Politics of Small Industry in Mexico.* University Park: The Pennsylvania State University Press.

Shirk, David A. 2005. *Mexico's New Politics: The PAN and Democratic Change.* Boulder, Colo.: Lynne Rienner.

Smith, Peter. 1979. *Labyrinths of Power: Political Recruitment in Twentieth-Century Mexico.* Princeton: Princeton University Press.

Snyder, Richard, and James Mahoney. 1999. The Missing Variable: Institutions and the Study of Regime Change. *Comparative Politics* 32 (1): 103–22.

Solinger, Dorothy J. 2001. Ending One-Party Dominance: Korea, Taiwan, Mexico. *Journal of Democracy* 12 (1): 30–42.

Solt, Frederick. 2003. Explaining the Quality of New Democracies: Actors, Institutions, and Socioeconomic Structure in Mexico's States. Ph.D. diss., University of North Carolina.

Spalding, Rose. 1981. State Power and Its Limits: Corporatism in Mexico. *Comparative Political Studies* 14 (2): 139–61.

Stanger, Allison. 2003. Leninist Legacies and Legacies of State Socialism in Postcommunist Central Europe's Constitutional Development. In *Capitalism and Democracy in Central and Eastern Europe: Assessing the Legacy of Communist Rule,* ed. Grzegorz Ekiert and Stephen E. Hanson. New York: Cambridge University Press.

Steinmo, Sven, Kathleen Thelen, and Frank Longstreth, eds. 1992. *Structuring Politics: Historical Institutionalism in Comparative Analysis.* New York: Cambridge University Press.

Stevenson, Mark. 2006. Mass Protest March Demands Recount in Mexican Presidential Race. *Associated Press Worldstream,* International News, July 16.

Stokes, Susan C. 2001. *Mandates and Democracy: Neoliberalism by Surprise in Latin America.* New York: Cambridge University Press.

Tarrow, Sidney. 1994. *Power in Movement: Social Movements, Collective Action, and Politics.* New York: Cambridge University Press.

———. 1996. States and Opportunities: The Political Structuring of Social Movements. In *Comparative Perspectives on Social Movements: Political Opportunities, Mobilizing Structures, and Cultural Framings,* ed. Douglas McAdam, John D. McCarthy, and Mayer N. Zald. New York: Cambridge University Press.

Thelen, Kathleen. 1999. Historical Institutionalism in Comparative Politics. *Annual Review of Political Science* 2. Palo Alto, Calif.: Annual Reviews.

———. 2003. How Institutions Evolve. In *Comparative Historical Analysis in the Social Sciences,* ed. James Mahoney and Dietrich Rueschemeyer. New York: Cambridge University Press.

Thelen, Kathleen, and Sven Steinmo. 1992. Historical Institutionalism in Comparative Politics. In *Structuring Politics: Historical Institutionalism in Comparative Analysis,* ed. Sven Steinmo, Kathleen Thelen, and Frank Longstreth. New York: Cambridge University Press.

Thompson, Ginger, and James C. McKinley. 2006. Suspense Grows as Vote Count in Mexico Race Wraps Up. *The New York Times,* July 6, section A.

Tocqueville, Alexis de. 1990. *Democracy in America.* New York: Vintage Books.

Van Cott, Donna Lee. 2005. *From Movements to Parties in Latin America: The Evolution of Ethnic Politics.* New York: Cambridge University Press.

Vargas Llosa, Mario. 1991. Mexico: The Perfect Dictatorship. *New Perspectives Quarterly* 8:23–24.

Ware, Alan. 1996. *Political Parties and Party Systems.* Oxford: Oxford University Press.

Wattenberg, Martin. 1986. *The Decline of American Political Parties,* 1952–1984. Cambridge: Harvard University Press.

Weber, Max. 1978. *Economy and Society: An Outline of Interpretative Sociology,* ed. Guenther Roth and Claus Wittich. Berkeley and Los Angeles: University of California Press.

Weir, Margaret. 1992. Ideas and the Politics of Bounded Innovation. In *Structuring Politics: Historical Institutionalism in Comparative Analysis,* ed. Sven Steinmo, Kathleen Thelen, and Frank Longstreth. New York: Cambridge University Press.

Weldon, Jeffrey. 1997. The Political Sources of Presidentialism in Mexico. In *Presidentialism and Democracy in Latin America,* ed. Scott Mainwaring and Matthew Soberg Shugart. New York: Cambridge University Press.

Wuhs, Steven T. 2001. Barbarians, Bureaucrats, and Bluebloods: Fractional Change in Mexico's National Action Party. In *Party Politics in Mexico: National and State-level Analyses of the National Action Party,* ed. Kevin J. Middlebrook. La Jolla: Center for U.S.-Mexican Studies, University of California, San Diego.

———. 2002. Opposing Oligarchy? Mexican Democratization and Political Party Transformation. PhD diss., Department of Political Science, University of North Carolina, Chapel Hill.

———. 2004. Selecting Candidates: What Mexico Should (and Shouldn't) Learn from the United States. *Election Law Journal* 3 (3): 521–29.

———. 2006. Democratization and the Dynamics of Candidate Selection Rule Change in Mexico, 1991–2003. *Estudios Mexicanos/Mexican Studies* 22 (1): 33–56.

———. 2007. The Savage Implications of Democratic Transition: Mexico's Move from One-Party Rule in Comparative Perspective. *International Studies Review* 9 (2): 348–56.

Yashar, Deborah. 1998. Contesting Citizenship: Indigenous Movements and Democracy in Latin America. *Comparative Politics* 31 (1): 23–42.

Zapata, Francisco. 2006. Mexican Labor in a Context of Political, Social, and Economic Change, 1982–2002. In *Changing Structure of Mexico: Political, Social, and Economic Prospects,* ed. Laura Randall. Armonk, N.Y.: M. E. Sharpe.

INDEX

Promoción Política de la Mujer (Political
    Promotion of Women, PPM), 95–96,
    111–14, 125–26
proportional representation seats, selection
    rule changes for, 53–60
pro-regime/anti-regime axis, opposition
    parties and, 39–40
public financing of political parties, trends in,
    82–86
public opinion polling, PRD use of, 52–53

Quadregessimo Anno, 23n.3

rational choice institutionalism, 3–6, 4n.3,
    5n.4, 139–41
recto ejercicio (just exercise) of authority,
    panista ideology, 28
redes ciudadanas (citizens' networks), 104–5
Redimensionamiento (redesigning) program,
    66–67; civil society linkages and, 96
regime decision making, PRI transformation
    in, 18
regional party development, opposition party
    strategies for, 75–82. See also municipal
    party organizations; state party
    organizations
Rerum Novarum, 23n.3
research methodology, 7–9
resilient institutions, development of, 128
Revolutionary Family, 38
Rincón Gallardo, Gilberto, 27n.9
Roberts, Kenneth, 114
Robles Berlanga, Rosario, 52, 72–74, 101n.32,
    114, 134
Ruíz Massieu, José Francisco, 19
Rustow, Dankwart, 10

Salinas de Gortari, Carlos, 1, 17–18, 21, 27
Sansores, Layda, 116
Saucedo, Mario and Francisco, 101n.32
savage democracy: limitations of, 119–41;
    Mexican democracy and, 135–41; origins
    of, 1–6
Second-order institutions, changes in, 125–26
Secretariat of Social Linkage (Secretaría de
    Vinculación Social) (PAN), 96, 111, 124–25,
    127, 133–35
Secretariats of Organization and Electoral
    Affairs (PRD), 103
Secretariat of Political Relations and Alliances
    (PRD), 103, 112
Semo, Enrique, 135

Senegal: authoritarianism and, 11n.3; political
    change in, 140n.13; 197
sexenio: of Fox, 143–44; of López Portillo, 17
short-term appointments (puestos de término),
    in PAN, 67–70
Sindicato Nacional de Trabajadores de
    la Educación (National Union of
    Educational Workers, SNTE), 96, 99–100,
    117–18
Sindicato Nacional de Trabajadores de la
    Seguridad Social (National Union of
    Social Security Workers, SNTSS), 107n.48
single-member-district (SMD) seats, 45;
    candidate-selection rules and, 48–53,
    133–35; PAN selection rules for, 54–55,
    58–61, 121–22, 126, 128; PRD selection rules
    for, 51–52, 55–61, 121–22
Sistema Integral de Desarrollo de Personal
    (Integrated System for Personnel
    Development, SIDEP), 68–70
social democracy: Mexican parties' vision
    of, 119; PRD democratic imperative and,
    31n.15
state corporatism, Mexican authoritarianism
    and, 11n.3
state-led industrialization, PRI
    authoritarianism and, 15
state-level conventions, PAN rules selection
    and, 48–51
state party organizations: legacy of, 132–35;
    opposition parties' development of, 75–82;
    PAN development of, 75–80, 126–27;
    PRD development of, 74n.34, 80–82
state socialism, institutional change and, 37
strongman rule, Mexican heritage of, 72

Taiwan, authoritarianism and, 11n.3, 140n.13
teachers, PAN linkages to, 96, 99–100
technocrats, emergence of, 18
technology access, party professionalization
    and, 64
tercera vía (third way) ideology, 23
Thelen, Kathleen, 5, 124–25
Tlatelolco Square demonstration (1968), 1, 18
totalitarianism: cross-regional comparative
    research on, 11n.3; institutional change
    and, 37
training programs (capacitación), in PAN,
    68–69
Tribunal Federal Electoral (Federal Electoral
    Tribunal, TRIFE), 143–50
Trisecta (PRD corriente), 101

www.ingramcontent.com/pod-product-compliance
Lightning Source LLC
Chambersburg PA
CBHW021906020426
42334CB00013B/502